# Trade and Culture



Governments that seek to liberalize trade can find that doing so is often in tension with their desire to achieve the objectives of cultural policy. This is because measures like local content requirements can seem like discriminatory practices when viewed through the lens of trade liberalization. This tension has prompted a long-standing debate, with great variation in how countries have approached it.

*Trade and Culture: The Ongoing Debate* explores this variation across geographic space. It also seeks to explain the evolution in these various policies over time. Policies are not static, largely due to domestic politics, shifts in the international trading system and technological developments. The chapters in this volume explore the different approaches to the trade and culture debate and provide an up-to-date look at current versions of these policies in Canada, the European Union, South Africa, Latin America, South Korea, the United States and China.

This book will be of great value to scholars and researchers interested in cultural policies and the politics of international trade.

This book was originally published as a special issue of the *International Journal of Cultural Policy*.

**Patricia M. Goff** is Associate Professor of Political Science at Wilfrid Laurier University in Waterloo, Canada. Her research interests include the politics of trade and the complex governance challenges of reconciling rival policy objectives. She has held visiting positions at the University of Southern California, USA, and the Graduate Institute in Geneva, Switzerland.

# Trade and Culture

## The Ongoing Debate

*Edited by*
**Patricia M. Goff**

Routledge
Taylor & Francis Group
LONDON AND NEW YORK

First published 2021
by Routledge
2 Park Square, Milton Park, Abingdon, Oxon OX14 4RN

and by Routledge
52 Vanderbilt Avenue, New York, NY 10017

*Routledge is an imprint of the Taylor & Francis Group, an informa business*



*British Library Cataloguing in Publication Data*
A catalogue record for this book is available from the British Library

ISBN 13: 978-0-367-63998-3

Typeset in Myriad
by Newgen Publishing UK

**Publisher's Note**
The publisher accepts responsibility for any inconsistencies that may have arisen during the conversion of this book from journal articles to book chapters, namely the inclusion of journal terminology.

**Disclaimer**
Every effort has been made to contact copyright holders for their permission to reprint material in this book. The publishers would be grateful to hear from any copyright holder who is not here acknowledged and will undertake to rectify any errors or omissions in future editions of this book.

# Contents

# Citation Information

The chapters in this book were originally published in the *International Journal of Cultural Policy*. When citing this material, please use the original page numbering for each article, as follows:

**Introduction**

*Trade and culture: the ongoing debate*
Patricia M. Goff
*International Journal of Cultural Policy*, volume 25, issue 5 (2019), pp. 547–551

**Chapter 1**

*Canada's cultural exemption*
Patricia M. Goff
*International Journal of Cultural Policy*, volume 25, issue 5 (2019), pp. 552–567

**Chapter 2**

*Trade, culture and the European Union cultural exception*
Lilian Richieri Hanania
*International Journal of Cultural Policy*, volume 25, issue 5 (2019), pp. 568–581

**Chapter 3**

*South Africa's trade in cultural goods and services with a focus on cultural trade with BRICS partners*
Nicolette Cattaneo and Jen Snowball
*International Journal of Cultural Policy*, volume 25, issue 5 (2019), pp. 582–601

**Chapter 4**

*Latin America: trade and culture at a crossroads*
Grace Jaramillo
*International Journal of Cultural Policy*, volume 25, issue 5 (2019), pp. 602–614

**Chapter 5**

*Cultural politics in the South Korean cultural industries: confrontations between state-developmentalism and neoliberalism*
Woongjae Ryoo and Dal Yong Jin
*International Journal of Cultural Policy*, volume 26, issue 1 (2020), pp. 31–45

## Chapter 6

*Trade and culture: the United States*
Gilbert Gagné
*International Journal of Cultural Policy,* volume 25, issue 5 (2019), pp. 615–628

## Chapter 7

*China and the "culture and trade" debate: a holistic approach*
Rostam J. Neuwirth
*International Journal of Cultural Policy,* volume 25, issue 5 (2019), pp. 629–647

## Chapter 8

*The end of cultural policy?*
Per Mangset
*International Journal of Cultural Policy,* volume 26, issue 3 (2020), pp. 398–411

# Notes on Contributors

**Nicolette Cattaneo**, Department of Economics and Economic History, Rhodes University, Makhanda-Grahamstown, South Africa.

**Gilbert Gagné**, Department of Politics and International Studies, Bishop's University, Sherbrooke, Québec, Canada.

**Patricia M. Goff**, Department of Political Science, Wilfrid Laurier University, Waterloo, Ontario, Canada.

**Grace Jaramillo**, Department of Political Science, University of British Columbia, Vancouver, Canada.

**Per Mangset**, Telemark Research Institute, Bø, Norway.

**Rostam J. Neuwirth**, Faculty of Law, University of Macau, Taipa, Macau, China.

**Lilian Richieri Hanania**, Sciences Po Law School, Paris, France.

**Woongjae Ryoo**, Department of Media and Communication, Hanyang University, Seoul, Korea.

**Jen Snowball**, South African Cultural Observatory, Port Elizabeth, South Africa, and Department of Economics and Economic History, Rhodes University, Makhanda-Grahamstown, South Africa.

**Dal Yong Jin**, School of Communication, Simon Fraser University, Vancouver, Canada.

# Introduction

# Trade and culture: the ongoing debate

Patricia M. Goff

**ABSTRACT**

The debate over how to reconcile trade liberalization with cultural policy is a long-standing one. There is great variation in how countries have navigated this debate. Furthermore, evolving individual policy approaches show noteworthy dynamism, largely in response to domestic politics, shifts in the international trading system and technological developments. This volume explores different approaches to the trade and culture debate across geographic space, as well as the evolution across time through analysis of seven cases – Canada, the European Union, South Africa, Latin America, South Korea, the United States and China.

In November 2017, Asia-Pacific Economic Cooperation (APEC)[1] met in Da Nang, Vietnam for what was billed as a momentous gathering. Despite Donald Trump's decision to withdraw the United States, the eleven remaining signatories of the Trans-Pacific Partnership (TPP) were expected to ratify the agreement. A high-profile leaders' meeting was to be the site of the final announcement. However, at the last minute, Canadian Prime Minister Justin Trudeau was a no-show, postponing agreement and setting off a media frenzy about his apparent snub. One prominent explanation for his actions was that the parties had not reached agreement on the promotion and protection of culture.

For those who are new to trade, this might have been perplexing. But, those who had followed Uruguay Round General Agreement on Tariffs and Trade (GATT) or North American Free Trade Agreement (NAFTA) negotiations, among others, recognized a long standing issue, namely how to reconcile trade liberalization objectives with those of cultural policy. In Da Nang, Canada was revisiting an issue that it had raised in 1988 while negotiating the Canada–US Free Trade Agreement (CUSFTA). Canada is not the only government to pursue this track. France pushed hard for audiovisual industry protections in late 1980s-early 1990s GATT talks. The European Union later pursued this strategy too. Korea has also sought cultural protections, notably in its free trade agreement with the United States. In fact, concerns about culture have come up repeatedly in trade negotiations over the last several decades. Following the Da Nang meeting, trade-watchers might have felt compelled to say, 'here we go again.'

Despite the prevalence of this issue across time and space, there is great variation in the aspects of culture that governments seek to protect, as well as the strategies that they employ to do so. For example, Canada has long focused on cultural industries, generally understood to include books, magazines, periodicals, newspapers, film and video, audio and video music recordings, and radio, cable and television broadcasting. By contrast, France (and, by extension, the EU) has emphasized the narrower category of audiovisual industries, primarily television and film.

Interestingly, at least thirty trade agreements in the last ten years have included provisions to protect traditional knowledge (TK). Latin American governments, led by Peru, as well as the government of New Zealand, have been key parties to this phenomenon, often with the encouragement of their respective Indigenous communities. This suggests a variety of understandings about which aspects of culture might be threatened by trade liberalization or, alternatively, can benefit from inclusion in trade agreements.

Of course, culture encompasses many aspects of our lives and not all of them are part of the trade and culture debate. Nonetheless, things like film and music have a 'dual nature' (Garcia Leiva 2017, 767). They are lucrative economic products, but also 'vectors of identity.' Certain countries have pretty consistently been associated with one or another side of this divide. The US has perennially opposed exceptions for cultural industries. On the other hand, France and Canada have maintained that cultural industries make a socio-cultural and political contribution beyond their commercial value. The United States has staked out its position in large part due to the enormous export revenue that its industry generates. As Sands (2001) puts it, 'In the United States, what Canadians call culture is part of an entertainment industrial complex that combines publishing with broadcasting, cable and satellite system, filmmaking, video and television production, theatre, music performance, recording and distribution' (Sands 2001, 484).

The central challenge in navigating the trade and culture debate arises when the principles of the trading system are applied to the goals and strategies of cultural policy. Cultural policy can serve a variety of objectives, ranging from support for local artists to funding public broadcasting. These policy choices are idiosyncratic, reflecting often complex national (and sometimes sub-national or supra-national) values, preferences, philosophical predispositions, historical legacies and domestic politics. Regardless of the objectives, tried-and-true regulatory approaches that have long served cultural policy goals in a particular place can come under fire, not because they are controversial or ineffective cultural policy tools. Instead, they are assessed by trade policy criteria in the context of trade negotiations. As a result, trading partners can characterize legitimate, favoured cultural policies as protectionist trade strategies and sometimes target them for dismantlement. In response, governments may seek to carve out space to continue seemingly discriminatory local cultural policies because they are thought to achieve an important socio-cultural or political objective.

This phenomenon springs, in part, from the fact that over 160 countries have committed to the principles of the multilateral trading system through their membership in the WTO. Non-discrimination is a key principle underpinning the trading system (VandenBossche 2008, 321). Its two components are the most-favoured nation (MFN) and national treatment obligations. 'In simple terms, the MFN treatment obligation prohibits a country from discriminating between other countries; the national treatment obligation prohibits a country from discriminating against other countries' (Van Den Bossche 2008, 321).

There are exceptions, some built into the international trading system. For example, developing countries benefit from the Generalized System of Preferences, which imposes less stringent liberalization requirements on them, like longer implementation timelines. In addition, Article 20 of the GATT Agreement sets out circumstances under which governments can discriminate for reasons such as national security or a public health concern. However, cultural policy only benefits from *negotiated* exceptions. More commonly, cultural measures can be framed as discriminatory trade practices. From a cultural policy standpoint, a domestic content requirement for radio or television can be easily justified in terms of a desire to ensure that local voices are heard. However, from a trade policy standpoint, such a measure appears to grant an advantage to local television and radio programming producers that is not afforded to foreign ones. Opponents of these measures argue that they fly in the face of the national treatment principle.

To be sure, many aspects of domestic cultural policy do not overlap with trade policy. In addition, ample room exists to criticize or support the merits of specific cultural policies regardless of their compatibility with trade policy. These dimensions of cultural policy are not the main focus of this volume. Instead, contributors assess the unique challenges across a variety of geographical contexts in simultaneously achieving the trade and cultural policy goals that governments have identified as desirable. They shine a light on the different ways that a sampling of governments across the world have addressed the nexus between trade and culture. Their different strategies are driven by economic, cultural, and/or socio-political concerns and they can be significant sticking points in trade agreement negotiations.

Indeed, these various concerns are such that efforts to reconcile trade and culture do not only differ across geographical space, with individual governments adopting idiosyncratic policies or perspectives. They can also vary across time within a particular country. Shifts in national approach are driven by a range of factors, as contributors to this volume show. These factors can be grouped into three broad categories – domestic factors, developments in the world of trade, and developments in culture. In terms of domestic factors, political and economic developments are critical. For example, Cattaneo and Snowball show how South Africa's relationship to the trade and culture debate is a function partly of political efforts to move beyond the apartheid era and also to promote economic development. Similarly, Jaramillo describes how shifts in partisan leadership in Latin America had consequences for how the trade and culture debate was navigated, as did efforts to make neo-liberal economic reforms. Furthermore, Ryoo and Jin show that South Korea's oscillation between state-led economic policies and International Monetary Fund (IMF)-imposed neoliberal reforms link trends in Korean cultural policy, also, to strategies of economic development.

Developments in the world of trade have also had an impact on how various governments relate to trade and culture. The current trading system dates to the post-WWII period when 23 countries signed the first version of the GATT. By 1994, the GATT had 123 signatories. As they made progress in tariff reduction, they turned their attention to other perceived 'irritants,' or non-tariff obstacles to liberalization, like subsidies, government procurement, technical barriers to trade and, later, trade in services, intellectual property, and regulatory differences. The expanding number of participating countries, as well as the growing list of issues on the agenda, made the GATT process of ad-hoc rounds of talks challenging and unwieldy. Demands for a proper institution led to the creation of the World Trade Organization (WTO) in 1995. The WTO spawned two key developments for trade and culture. First, it brought into being a powerful dispute settlement body. One of the early cases it would hear concerned the right of the Canadian government to continue its support to domestic periodicals. Canada lost this dispute and had to change its domestic magazine support policies.

The UNESCO Convention on the Protection and Promotion of the Diversity of Cultural Expressions was born out of this surprising (to some) decision against Canada, entering into force in 2007 in part to provide a counterweight to the prominence of the non-discrimination principle. Over 140 countries have ratified the Convention, though notably, the United States is not among them. Several provisions in the Convention are relevant to the current discussion. Importantly, it enshrines that, 'cultural activities, goods and services have both an economic and a cultural nature, because they convey identities, values and meanings, and must therefore not be treated as solely having commercial value.' It also establishes that, 'states have, in accordance with the Charter of the United Nations and the principles of international law, the sovereign right to adopt measures and policies to protect and promote the diversity of cultural expressions within their territory.' At the same time, the Convention cannot trump signatories' other international commitments. Article 20 states that, 'parties recognize that they shall perform in good faith their obligations under this Convention and all other treaties to which they are parties.' It goes on to note that, 'Nothing in this Convention shall be interpreted as modifying rights and obligations of the Parties under any other treaties to which they are parties.' Despite these limits, Richieri Hanania in this volume shows how the EU approach to trade and culture has been directly affected by the advent of the UNESCO Convention.

Complex multilateral negotiations at the WTO would soon stall, prompting governments to shift from the centralized WTO to a more fragmented and growing set of free trade agreements. Many governments are now relying on FTAs to advance liberalization agendas, creating many more opportunities to address the trade and culture debate. Goff describes how the proliferation of trade agreements has had consequences for Canada's approach to cultural industries in trade negotiations. Ryoo and Jin note the impact on Korea's cultural policy of trade agreement negotiations with the

United States. Neuwirth shows how the rise of China has the potential to inject a very different perspective on the relationship between trade and culture into contemporary discussions.

Finally, the third category of factors has precipitated shifts in national approaches to trade and culture. Marshall McLuhan famously observed over fifty years ago that 'the medium is the message' (McLuhan 1964). In many respects, this is still true. Our substantive cultures have evolved in myriad ways in recent decades as fashions shift and tastes change. But, perhaps most significant for the purposes of the present discussion are the changes in how we produce and consume cultural content. Increasingly, we encounter culture on digital platforms. Electronic books, streaming music, and film downloads supplement and, in some instances, eclipse traditional modes of consuming culture for entertainment. At the same time that these digital outlets ease access to a wide variety of cultural experiences, they can provide inadequate safeguards for forms of traditional knowledge and for artists relying on copyright, among others. Digital technology, therefore, changes the context within which we now seek to reconcile cultural policy goals with trade liberalization in at least two ways. If the cultural policy is targeted toward traditional media, but people are not accessing cultural products through those formats, then that domestic policy will be inefficient at best. Furthermore, if traditional media are protected in trade agreements, but new digital media are not, then a lot of the work to protect and promote cultural diversity may be lost. In this volume, Gagné shows that the American position on the trade and culture debate has shifted in recent negotiations to reflect the government's clear commitment to digital trade.

Against the backdrop of these key developments, each contributor explores national or regional strategies to reconcile cultural goals with trade liberalization. They illuminate the preferred approach the government takes to cultural policy where it intersects with trade liberalization, outlining the key cultural sensitivities in play and how the relationship between culture and trade is understood. They then outline how and why an approach might have evolved over time. The volume is comprised of seven cases – Canada and the European Union as leaders in this debate; South Africa, Latin America (with a focus on Mexico), and South Korea provide varying perspectives from developing countries. Finally, we explore the United States as a foil to many other countries making policy in this area, and China, which may bring a fresh perspective and a new approach.

Goff's analysis of Canada shows how that country's approach has evolved through recent trade agreement negotiations. Each trading partner is a bit different, as is each deal. As a result, the Canadian effort to preserve space for domestic cultural policy reflects this. Similarly, Richieri Hanania shows how the EU has shifted its approach, largely due to its embrace of the UNESCO Convention on the Protection and Promotion of the Diversity of Cultural Expressions.

Catteneo and Snowball trace South Africa's efforts to harness cultural industries to promote growth, development and job creation, while also seeking to build a post-apartheid identity. These two objectives can certainly co-exist, depending on the government of the day. Jaramillo takes on the ambitious task of trying to capture trends across Latin America. She shows that policies have evolved along two tracks. One track reflects the export prowess of Latin American television programs; the other describes the concerns of countries rich in traditional knowledge and traditional cultural expressions. Ryoo and Jin paint a similarly complex picture of the South Korean debate, where neoliberal and developmental policies toward culture have alternated with one another, and sometimes coincided, as the country navigated key moments in its export-led model of economic growth and sought to enhance its soft power.

Gagné takes on the case of the United States, whose desire to foreground the commercial value of culture has so shaped the trade and culture debate. He shows that recent US trade agreements reflect a growing embrace of digital trade. Finally, Neuwirth explores the approach of a new entrant in this debate, China. He argues that China brings a much more holistic perspective to a debate that traditionally has been understood as dichotomous. Time will tell if China will influence other countries on this front.

In lieu of a conclusion, the final chapter serves as an afterword to provoke discussion on the way forward. Mangset asks whether cultural policy, especially the post-World War II variants that manifested in Europe, has achieved its goals. Further, he asks whether public cultural policy measures can survive transformative forces, like globalization. His point–counterpoint strategy of presentation offers no definitive answers. Nonetheless, he shifts our gaze toward another critical aspect of the debate over trade and culture. Much of our attention is often on the adjustments that we might make to trade policy to accommodate favoured cultural policy approaches. Yet Mangset encourages us to examine those very cultural policy approaches to see if they should be accommodated or updated to reflect current needs and objectives. In so doing, he points to another aspect of the debate that is worthy of our attention. Indeed, we may also wish to subject trade policy to the same sort of analysis that Mangset provides for cultural policy.

This volume is a timely intervention in the conversation about trade and cultural policy. In some instances, a substantial amount has been written on a particular country or region included here, however in others, considerably less so. Therefore, the added value of the volume is both to offer an analysis of regions that get less attention with regard to this subject and also to assemble these analyses under one cover. We also hope to underline the inherent dynamism in the approaches that governments adopt by tracing their evolution in recent decades.

## Note

1. APEC is a regional economic forum comprised of 21 member countries.

## Disclosure statement

No potential conflict of interest was reported by the author.

## References

Leiva, G., and M. Trinidad. 2017. "Cultural Diversity and Free Trade: The Case of the EU-Canada Agreement." *International Journal of Cultural Policy* 23 (6): 765–781. doi:10.1080/10286632.2015.1119131.

McLuhan, M. 1964. *Understanding Media*. New York, NY: McGraw-Hill.

Sands, C. 2001. "A Chance to End Culture Trade Conflict between Canada and the United States." *The American Review of Canadian Studies* 31 (3): 483–499. doi:10.1080/02722010109481607.

Van Den Bossche, P. 2008. *The Law and Policy of the World Trade Organization: Text, Cases and Materials*. 2nd ed. Cambridge, UK: Cambridge University Press.

# Canada's cultural exemption

Patricia M. Goff

**ABSTRACT**
Certain countries stand out as having distinctive approaches to trade and culture. Canada occupies a key position in this pantheon of distinctive approaches. Since the 1980s, Canada has pursued a 'cultural exemption' in its various trade agreements. The perception is that it has largely maintained this exemption, however I will show in this article that each iteration of the exemption differs from the others in subtle but noteworthy ways. These differences stem in large part from the nature of the particular trade agreement negotiations and the identity of the specific trading partner(s). Ultimately, the aim of this contribution is to show that Canada's cultural exemption strategy has had to evolve alongside key trends in trade, notably the proliferation of free trade agreements.

In conversations about approaches to trade and culture, certain countries stand out as distinctive. For example, as Gagné argues in this special issue, the United States has typically eschewed the view that films, television programs and the like are cultural products, seeing them instead as highly lucrative entertainment industry commodities. France, on the other hand, has promoted a cultural exception for audiovisual industries, informed by a certain understanding of author's rights, as well as a historical legacy with the film industry. France's perspective has deeply influenced the European Union's approach, as Lilian Richieri Hanania shows in her contribution to this issue.

Canada also occupies a key position in this pantheon of distinctive approaches. Since the 1980s, Canada has pursued a 'cultural exemption' in its various trade agreements. The perception is that it has largely maintained this exemption, however I will show in this article that each iteration of the exemption differs from the others in subtle but noteworthy ways. These differences stem in large part from the nature of the particular trade agreement negotiations and the identity of the specific trading partner(s). Therefore, this article proceeds in two main sections. First, I delineate key shifts in trade governance and trade agreement negotiation in the post-World War II period, with special emphasis on the last thirty years. Second, I explore the various forms that the Canadian cultural exemption has taken in bilateral and multilateral fora over that same period. Ultimately, the aim of this contribution is to show that Canada's cultural exemption strategy has had to evolve alongside the proliferation of free trade agreements (FTAs). We expect the cultural exemption strategy to reflect domestic interests or technological developments. We pay less attention to the consequences that shifts in trade governance have for the cultural exemption strategy. I elucidate some of those consequences here.

## Trends in trade

The nature, regulation and governance of trade have undergone significant changes in the post-WWII period. These changes include an embrace of regional and global value chains in some sectors (Ravenhill 2014); the ascent of emerging market countries, like Brazil, India and China as key players in trade (Hopewell 2015); and the proliferation of preferential trade agreements (Dür, Baccini, and Elsig 2013). It is this last trend that is particularly helpful in illuminating the evolution in the Canadian cultural exemption strategy.

Until the 1990s, relatively few countries negotiated preferential trade agreements. Instead, the multilateral system with the General Agreement on Tariffs and Trade (GATT) at its centre, provided the focal point for trade liberalization. However, many scholars point to the mid-1990s as a turning point (Dür and Elsig 2015; Horn, Mavroidis, and Sapir 2009). Every World Trade Organization (WTO) member had negotiated at least one free trade agreement by 2016 and many had negotiated as many as twenty (WTO 2017). The last twenty years have been particularly active on this front. Prior to the founding of the WTO, its predecessor, the GATT, received 124 notifications of FTAs. The WTO received over 450 in just over twenty years (WTO 2018).[1]

The shift toward preferential agreements has had two key effects on Canada's cultural exemption strategy. First, for proponents, it creates new opportunities to extend the exemption found in the North American Free Trade Agreement (NAFTA) to other trading partnerships. (For opponents, it saddles the government with a bargaining position that might require a concession elsewhere). Second, each negotiation requires a slightly different approach. Some trading partners are more sympathetic to the cultural exemption than others. Some negotiating circumstances allow Canada to exert different forms of leverage and influence. Some negotiations will require specific kinds of trade-offs. Each time, the animating principle is arguably the same – to nurture and promote Canadian culture – though the manner in which this gets manifested in a particular agreement can vary. Indeed, the Government of Canada has defended the cultural exemption in every preferential agreement it has signed. However, the actual exemption provisions vary across five axes in the seventeen preferential agreements (fourteen in force, including CETA, which is provisionally applied, the CPTPP, which went into force in December 2018 and USMCA, which is awaiting ratification), in addition to two relevant multilateral agreements, the GATT and the General Agreement on Trade in Services (GATS).

These five axes are the following: the definition of cultural industries used in the agreement; the possibility of retaliation against Canadian efforts to promote cultural industries; whether new relevant domains are mentioned in an agreement, including digital and e-commerce; whether the exemption is a blanket one or a chapter-by-chapter carve-out; and whether there is any mention of cultural diversity or similar language emerging from the UNESCO Convention on the Protection and Promotion of the Diversity of Cultural Expressions process.

In the sections that follow, I explore key agreements along these axes. I show that there is great continuity in Canada's definition of cultural industries. Despite shifts in technology and modes of consuming culture, the definition identifying those technologies covered by the exemption remains the same. The only variation is in the multilateral system where no definition is offered. However, where a definition is included in a trade agreement to which Canada is a party, it is always identical. The cultural industry definition is important because it demarcates the scope of coverage of the exemption. It shows what signatories understand the sector to comprise and can indicate whether there is any explicit acknowledgement for the purposes of the trade agreement of the evolving technological underpinnings of the cultural sector, both in terms of how products are produced and consumed. Whether there is reference to digital trade or electronic commerce elsewhere in an agreement can provide insight into this same issue from another angle.

Reference to the UNESCO Convention on the Protection and Promotion of the Diversity of Cultural Expressions would be an explicit acknowledgement of the socio-cultural dimensions of cultural industries (in addition to the commercial dimensions) and their link to cultural identity and diversity. The last two axes – whether the exemption is chapter-by-chapter or blanket and whether the exemption includes a right to retaliate against use of the exemption in domestic policy – gives some idea of the robustness of the protections afforded by a particular exemption provision. Taken together, the five axes help to illuminate what is distinctive about the Canadian approach to trade and culture, as well as how effectively the Government of Canada has been in enshrining it across a number of FTAs.

## The multilateral system

In the aftermath of WWII, led by Great Britain and the United States, allied powers met in Bretton Woods, New Hampshire to forge an institutional framework that would stabilize the global economy and hopefully avoid the conflagrations of the first part of the twentieth century, including two world wars and a major economic depression. Out of that process ultimately came the GATT, which sought to commit governments to open markets and to the reduction in discriminatory practices, like tariffs, quotas, and subsidies. Through eight rounds of talks over the next fifty years, the GATT progressively expanded its list of signatories to well over 100 and also expanded the list of products and sectors governed by its provisions. By the early 1990s, it became apparent that such an ad hoc arrangement was insufficient for the complexity of economic and political issues that countries were facing. Canada, among others, called for the creation of a brick-and-mortar institution that could provide more substantial support and monitoring of trade practices. The last round of GATT talks to be completed, the Uruguay Round (1986–1994), created the World Trade Organization. The GATT did not disappear with the creation of the WTO. Rather, it remains a key agreement among the several that the WTO oversees.

### *GATT (1947-present)/World Trade Organization (1995-present)*

There is no formal cultural exemption in the multilateral system, although the debate about trade and culture has certainly been part of the conversation. In the first round of talks, signatories included the possibility of limited quotas in Article IV of the GATT on Special Provisions relating to Cinematographic Films to ensure screen time for domestic films. A number of European countries already used such quotas domestically (Galt 2004, 912; Neuwirth 2002) given the pervasive presence of US films, so this provision allowed the continuation of an already established practice. Furthermore, an exception was ostensibly made for cinema 'because its regulation was more related to domestic cultural policies than to economics and trade' (Jackson 1969, 293).

Trade and culture would come to the fore in the GATT system again during the Uruguay Round of negotiations, coming to a head near the end of the round, in 1994. By then, Canada had negotiated what it thought would be reliable protection for its cultural industries in its agreements with the United States. I discuss the Canada-US Free Trade and North American Free Trade Agreements below. Nonetheless, Canada supported France in its efforts to gain a 'cultural exception' in the multilateral system for audiovisual industries, a narrower category of cultural industries, including television and film, but not books, magazines, radio and music, periodicals and newspapers.

In the end, the US and the EU could not reach agreement about audiovisual industries during Uruguay Round GATT negotiations. They 'agreed to disagree' (Galt 2004, 914). No provisions covering audiovisual or cultural industries are contained in the GATT, which governs trade in goods in the trading system. Instead, audiovisual industries can be covered in the GATS. The GATS differs from the GATT in a key way. While the GATT functions according to a negative list – everything is opened to free trade *except* those things that are identified as exceptions – the GATS works mostly on a positive list basis. This means that *nothing* is opened to liberalization except those specific things that WTO members list in their schedule of services commitments. Perhaps not surprisingly, Canada, the EU and others have chosen not to make commitments to opening services sectors related to culture, which has been interpreted by some as amounting to an exemption of sorts for cultural services, but not for goods (Galt 2004, 915; Burri 2014).

In addition to the debates about trade and culture during GATT negotiating rounds, cases have emerged in the WTO dispute settlement system. Of particular importance to the Canadian cultural exemption strategy is Canada-Certain Measures Concerning Periodicals. The Periodicals case grew out of an announcement by the American publication, *Sports Illustrated*, that it would be launching a Canadian edition. This edition would recycle content from the American edition, add some Canadian content, along with Canadian advertisements. The so-called split-run magazine edition threatened to siphon advertising dollars – a critical revenue stream – away from Canadian publications, prompting the Canadian government to impose an excise tax on *Sports Illustrated*.

Over a period of years, the policy spat eventually turned into a WTO dispute. Since other American magazines engaging in the same split-run practices were not subject to the excise tax (e.g. *Reader's Digest*), the US contested this and other discriminatory measures, including favourable postal rates for domestic publications. WTO Panel and subsequent Appellate Body rulings required that Canada change its domestic magazine industry support mechanisms or be in contravention of its commitments to WTO agreements. Both the Panel and Appellate Body reports found that Canada had not met its obligations under Article III of the GATT, which governs National Treatment and Internal Taxation and Regulation. Just ten paragraphs long, this key article prohibits signatories from treating imported products in a discriminatory fashion, including through the application of a tax. The Canadian Government tried to defend the excise tax, which sought to divert advertising dollars toward Canadian magazines, on the grounds that the substantive content of Canadian and American magazines is qualitatively different. In the language of the WTO, they are not 'like products' and, therefore, can be subject to differential treatment. The Panel did not accept this argument. The Appellate Body later questioned the Panel's technical designation of 'like products' in this specific case, however still found the excise tax to be a discriminatory trade practice, applied to 'directly competitive or substitutable products.' The Panel also rejected the Canadian claim that the dispute was really about services, as opposed to goods (WTO 1997).

This outcome prompted discussions that would lead to the UNESCO Convention on the Protection and Promotion of the Diversity of Cultural Expressions, which I examine in the next section. Indeed, the Government of Canada presumed that the exemption negotiated in CUSFTA and subsequently in NAFTA would protect against these sorts of disputes with the United States and allow domestic policies to support cultural industries, like magazines. However, the American choice to pursue this action at the WTO, where there is no cultural exemption, in some ways made the NAFTA provisions moot.

In terms of the five axes identified above, the multilateral agreements – especially GATT and GATS – are exceptional in the pantheon of trade agreements to which Canada is a party because they do not contain a definition of cultural industries. Indeed, there is neither a blanket exemption nor a chapter-by-chapter carve-out in WTO agreements. Ultimately, there is no cultural exemption in the GATT, as the Periodicals case demonstrated. There is, however, some protection for cultural services for countries that choose to exclude the cultural sector from market access and national treatment obligations in their national schedules. Discussions of e-commerce continue at the WTO. In 1998, members agreed not to impose duties on electronic transmissions.[2] Consultations and information gathering continue.

### *UNESCO convention on the protection and promotion of the diversity of cultural expressions (2005)*

The experience with the WTO dispute over periodicals led many to the realization that carve-outs and safeguards in the trading system for cultural industries – even ostensibly blanket exemptions – would likely be insufficient (Grant 2011, 344). Though Canada would point to hard-won provisions in CUSFTA and NAFTA, which I describe below, the United States sidestepped them by using the alternative WTO forum to contest Canadian periodicals policies.

The Sectoral Advisory Group on International Trade (SAGIT) on cultural industries issued a report in 1999 in which they acknowledged the importance of a cultural exemption strategy, but also its limitations. They proposed 'a new strategy that would involve negotiating a new international instrument that would specifically address cultural diversity, and acknowledge the legitimate role of domestic cultural policies in ensuring cultural diversity.'[3] The centrepiece of this new approach would be a separate, legally-binding international instrument. The Government of Canada was one of its key champions.

In October 2005, the Convention on the Protection and Promotion of the Diversity of Cultural Expressions was approved by a vote of 148–2 UNESCO members with four abstentions, entering into force in March 2007. Over 140 parties have ratified the Convention. The United States voted against it and has not ratified it. The Convention affirms governments' sovereign right to make cultural policy, noting that 'cultural activities, goods and services have both an economic and a cultural nature, because they convey identities, values and meanings, and must therefore not be treated as solely having commercial value.' It stipulates that 'states have, in accordance with the Charter of the United Nations and the principles of international law, the sovereign right to adopt measures and policies to protect and promote the diversity of cultural expressions within their territory.'

The hope was that this language would provide a robust counterweight to trade agreements that seek to liberalize trade in cultural products by providing a principled justification for cultural policies that favour domestic cultural industries. However, as Article 20 of the Convention makes clear, the UNESCO instrument does not supersede other government commitments; specifically: 'parties recognize that they shall perform in good faith their obligations under this Convention and all other treaties to which they are parties.' Furthermore, it states, 'Nothing in this Convention shall be interpreted as modifying rights and obligations of the Parties under any other treaties to which they are parties.' Therefore, it exists alongside trade agreements as soft law.

One of the few tests of the Convention came in a WTO dispute launched by the United States in 2007 over Chinese audiovisual policy, China – Measures Affecting Trading Rights and Distribution Services for Certain Publications and Audiovisual Entertainment Products. The Chinese government did not rely on the Convention for its defence. Instead, it made a 'public morals' argument based on Article 20 of the GATT. However, it does mention the UNESCO Convention to assert that audiovisual products have both economic and cultural value. Even if China had based its case on the Convention, the fact that the United States is not a signatory would limit its relevance in this instance (Pauwelyn 2005).

While the UNESCO Convention is not binding on its signatories, it is an important normative instrument (Burri 2013). As I note below, Canada does invoke it in at least one major trade agreement. It is a source of language for some versions of the cultural exemption that can sharpen and reinforce the commitments contained therein.

## Preferential trade agreements

### *CUSFTA (1989)/NAFTA (1994)*

Canada has long adopted strategies to protect its culture. Neathery-Castro dates Canadian government involvement in the cultural sector back to 1849, 'when it instituted a postal subsidy for newspapers, magazines and books' (Neathery-Castro 2012, 78). This policy legacy found its way into the conversation about trade in 1980s negotiations leading to the Canada-US Free Trade Agreement (CUSFTA). For all intents and purposes, Canada's cultural exemption strategy starts with CUSFTA.

When Canada-US free trade talks accelerated in earnest in the 1980s, Canadians targeted those few industries where US tariffs were still high, and also sought to pre-empt the potential negative consequences of growing protectionist sentiments in the US Congress (Morici 1985, 312). Nonetheless, these prospective gains came with accompanying risks, including the inevitable American request that Canada open its market to the US entertainment industry.

At the time, Canadians often pointed to the strong presence of foreign cultural products in the home market, noting for example that, 'foreign firms and products account for: 34% of book sales in Canada; 81% of English-language consumer magazines on Canadian newsstands and over 63% of magazine circulation revenue; 79% (over $910 million) of retail sales of tapes, CDs, concerts, merchandise and sheet music; 85% ($165 million) of the revenues from film distribution in Canada; and between 94 and 97% of screen time in Canadian theatres' (cited in Browne 1999, 364). Canadians interpreted this very strong 'Americanizing' presence as potentially threatening to Canadian identity (Goff 2007).

Negotiations leading to the Canada-US Free Trade Agreement set up a confrontation between dissimilar Canadian and US views regarding trade and culture. Browne characterizes the Canadian policy as geared toward ensuring that Canadians have 'a wide range of choice in cultural products' (1999, 364). For Canadians, cultural industries are linked to sovereignty and mobilized to define and consolidate Canadian identity; they provide a vehicle through which Canadians can communicate with one another, assuming they have access to cultural industries to tell Canadian stories. For Americans, on the other hand, the notion of 'cultural industries' does not resonate. Instead, film and television and, to a lesser degree, book publishing and radio, are entertainment industries and leading exports. Where Canadians emphasize the socio-cultural contribution of cultural industries, Americans focus on the economic importance of entertainment industries. Of course, some Canadian groups seek foreign markets for their cultural products and, likewise, some American groups appreciate the cultural dimension of cultural products. Nonetheless, these groups are in the minority in their respective national contexts (Maule 2003). In policy terms, this has meant that the US has perennially wanted cultural products to be governed by the principles of free trade, while Canada has sought to shield them from those same principles.

The post-WWII trading system hinges on the principle of non-discrimination. Central to this notion is the concept of national treatment, which establishes that trading partners should be treated 'no less favorably' than domestic producers. The cultural exemption is intended to shield the cultural sector from the imperative of national treatment. Canada can then continue with policies that advantage domestic cultural industries, including Canadian content requirements for licensed television and radio broadcasters; limits on foreign ownership of cultural industries; and direct funding support to artists and to public entities, like the Canadian Broadcasting Corporation (CBC). In the absence of the exemption, such policies could be deemed incompatible with key trade agreement principles. Indeed, in their recent submission to the US Trade Representative as part of NAFTA renegotiation consultations, the Motion Picture Association of America (MPAA) calls the NAFTA cultural exemption 'inconsistent with the principles of free and fair trade' (Brennan 2017).

CUSFTA negotiations did lead to a cultural exemption, the first of its kind in Canadian FTAs, which laid the groundwork for subsequent provisions. In trilateral negotiations that brought Mexico to the table for NAFTA negotiations, the exemption was preserved in its entirety. Annex 2106 of NAFTA establishes a cultural industries exemption by reference to CUSFTA.[4]

The relevant provision in CUSFTA, Article 2005, states that

(1) Cultural industries are exempt from the provisions of this Agreement except as specifically provided in Article 401 (Tariff Elimination), paragraph 4 of Article 1607 (divestiture of an indirect acquisition) and Articles 2006 and 2007 of this Chapter.
(2) Notwithstanding any other provision of this Agreement, a Party may take measures of equivalent commercial effect in response to actions that would have been inconsistent with this Agreement but for paragraph 1.

Article 2107 of NAFTA defines cultural industries as 'persons engaged in any of the following activities:

(a) the publication, distribution, or sale of books, magazines, periodicals or newspapers in print or machine readable form but not including the sole activity of printing or typesetting any of the foregoing;

(b) the production, distribution, sale or exhibition of film or video recordings;
(c) the production, distribution, sale or exhibition of audio or video music recordings;
(d) the publication, distribution or sale of music in print or machine readable form; or
(e) radiocommunications in which the transmissions are intended for direct reception by the general public, and all radio, television and cable broadcasting undertakings and all satellite programming and broadcast network services.'

The CUSFTA/NAFTA exemption is not air tight. Critics point out that paragraph 2 allows for retaliation of equivalent commercial effect. This has not occurred to date, but it does drive home the fact that continued cultural policy choices in the North American context are not without risk.

It is not surprising that Canada received a qualified exemption in CUSFTA and NAFTA, given the perspective of the American partner. Powerful lobbies from the US entertainment sector mobilized to ensure that any cultural exemption would be watered down. Jack Valenti, then-MPAA Chairman, became well-known to trade watchers in the 1980s and 1990s as the face of Hollywood opposition to the exemption. The US acquiesced to an exemption in CUSFTA and NAFTA, knowing that it was non-negotiable for Canada (Larrea 1997, 1107), but the prospect of retaliation placated domestic constituencies. The combination of US opposition in principle to the exemption and a strong desire to conclude a deal arguably produced the exemption we see in CUSFTA and NAFTA.

In terms of the five axes that I identify above, the CUSFTA/NAFTA process gave us the cultural industry definition that we find in subsequent free trade agreements to which Canada is a party. The prospect of retaliation also appears in the CUSFTA/NAFTA exemption and, later, exceptionally, in USMCA. Only agreements that include the United States allow for the prospect of retaliation of equivalent commercial effect should Canada use the cultural exemption. The lack of references to digital, e-commerce and cultural diversity reflects the times. These issues had not yet become significant when those agreements were signed. The CUSFTA/NAFTA process also kicks off the blanket exemption strategy that Canada has largely preserved, with the exception of CETA and CPTPP. I turn to these agreements in the following sections.

### *Canada-European Union comprehensive economic and trade agreement (2017)*

CETA in its present incarnation dates to 2007, when Canadian and European leaders proposed a joint study of the costs and benefits of an agreement. In early 2009, Canada and the EU finalized 'Assessing the Costs and Benefits of a Closer EU-Canada Economic Partnership,' which generally suggests that the prospective gains of a deal merited a negotiation. The first round of negotiations took place in October 2009. In October 2013, then-Prime Minister Stephen Harper and then-European Commission President José Manuel Barroso announced that they had reached an agreement in principle. By 2017, the Agreement had been provisionally applied, pending full approval (parliamentary votes or referenda) in EU Member countries. On the Canadian side, Bill C-30, the Canada-European Union Comprehensive Economic and Trade Agreement Implementation Act, has passed through the House of Commons and Senate, and received royal assent.

The CETA does not include a blanket cultural exemption. In fact, it is one of only two trade agreements to which Canada is a party that does not. It is the first of two to adopt a chapter-by-chapter approach. There are two possible explanations for this, which are not mutually exclusive. First, as scoping reports on a Canada-EU agreement suggest, the EU is, in many respects, a like-minded partner. One calls the EU 'a historical and natural trading partner' (Report of the Standing Committee on International Trade 2012) for Canada while another notes 'shared values and special historic links between Canada and the member states of the EU' (Report of the Standing Committee on International Trade 2011). The EU and Canada both supported a cultural exception in Uruguay Round GATT talks; both spearheaded efforts leading to the UNESCO Convention; and both share the view that cultural industries play an important socio-cultural role. Therefore, one could argue that the need for a blanket exemption, which might be perceived to offer stronger protection, was unnecessary.

Second, CETA is a twenty-first century, 'deep' agreement (Hoekman 2015; Hübner, Deman, and Balik 2017). It goes well beyond what many prior trade agreements tried to achieve in the sense that it targets more than just tariffs. It also includes provisions on non-tariff barriers, like government procurement, and tries to harmonize regulatory differences. Deep agreements often go beyond what has been achieved at the WTO. In this context, a chapter-by-chapter approach can make sense. Many of the chapters found in deep agreements may have little relevance to cultural industry concerns. In addition, as Sauvé and Steinfatt note, WTO cases show that 'cultural products are already largely subject to WTO disciplines governing trade and investment in goods, services and trade-related intellectual property matters. From a juridical standpoint, any purported cultural 'exception' or blanket immunity from international trade law, a notion still much in vogue in large segments of some countries' cultural industries, is mere chimera' (Sauvé and Steinfatt 2000, 324). Instead, an approach targeted at specific trade agreement chapters can be more effective.

It is also worth noting that a chapter-by-chapter approach does not necessarily deliver less protection for domestic cultural policy. As provincial and federal government officials contend, the objective in trade negotiations is always to preserve the maximum latitude for domestic cultural policy. It may be more time-consuming to produce this outcome on a chapter-by-chapter basis, requiring more painstaking preparatory work by negotiating teams. But, the same objective can be met in this way and perhaps even be strengthened. Unlike NAFTA and USMCA, for example, which each contain a blanket exemption, CETA does not authorize retaliation of equivalent commercial effect.

The CETA explicitly invokes the parties' strong commitment to cultural diversity and sovereign cultural policy. The Preamble refers directly to the UNESCO Convention: 'RECOGNISING that the provisions of this Agreement preserve the right of the Parties to regulate within their territories and the Parties' flexibility to achieve legitimate policy objectives, such as public health, safety, environment, public morals and the promotion and protection of cultural diversity;'[5] It also says, 'AFFIRMING their commitments as parties to the UNESCO Convention on the Protection and Promotion of the Diversity of Cultural Expressions, done at Paris on 20 October 2005, and recognising that states have the right to preserve, develop and implement their cultural policies, to support their cultural industries for the purpose of strengthening the diversity of cultural expressions, and to preserve their cultural identity, including through the use of regulatory measures and financial support.' This preambular language is unprecedented in any other Canadian trade agreement.

Chapter 1, Article 1.1 preserves the cultural industry definition that originated in CUSFTA. The chapter-by-chapter carve-outs appear in Chapter 7 (Subsidies)[6]; Chapter 8 (Investment)[7]; Chapter 9 (Cross-border Trade in Services)[8]; and Chapter 12 (Domestic Regulation).[9] In addition, Chapter 19 (Government Procurement) contains protections for cultural industries for sub-national governments.[10] Each of these chapters contains quite a sweeping cultural exemption as it pertains to the specific subject matter.

In terms of the five axes, then, CETA maintains the standard definition of cultural industries and it uses a chapter-by-chapter carve-out approach instead of a blanket exemption. It contains specific references to the UNESCO Convention and to cultural diversity, as well as a chapter on e-commerce. It does not authorize retaliation against invocation of cultural protections. In comparison to NAFTA, CETA protections seem quite significant, despite the fact that they are chapter-by-chapter. Nothing seems to have been lost by adopting this alternative approach.

## *TPP (2016)/CPTPP (2018)*

The Trans-Pacific Partnership (TPP) began in 2005 as an agreement between Brunei, Chile, New Zealand and Singapore. By 2016, it had grown to be one of the largest prospective trading blocs, comprising forty percent of world trade. Twelve countries in total, including the United States, Japan, Canada, and Mexico, ultimately signed the agreement. Former US President, Barack Obama, had touted not only TPP's economic potential, but also its potential to influence the rules for doing business in Asia. Despite these features, President Donald Trump chose to withdraw the United States from the agreement shortly after he took office in early 2017. For a time, some thought the TPP was dead, however Japan and others successfully pushed to revive a TPP-11 among the remaining parties. In early 2018, the eleven countries signed a modified TPP – the Comprehensive and Progressive Trans-Pacific Partnership (CPTPP), which retained most features of the original agreement, while suspending twenty-two provisions favoured by the United States.

This trajectory from TPP to CPTPP is important for understanding the Canadian cultural exemption strategy for two reasons. First, the TPP exemption differs in interesting ways from what the government negotiated in NAFTA, CETA and later, USMCA. Second, cultural provisions were among the key modifications that Canada demanded before signing on to CPTPP.

Canada joined TPP in 2012. Nine countries had already negotiated significant chunks of agreement text by that time. Joining the negotiations late and ultimately as one of twelve made it unlikely that Canada could expect a blanket exemption. As I note above, that cultural provisions come on a chapter-by-chapter basis is not necessarily worse than a blanket exemption, though the TPP exemption is weaker than CETA's. CPTPP's chapter-by-chapter carve-outs differ from CETA's in another way. Rather than including the provisions in the text of each chapter, specific non-conforming measures that relate to these chapters are gathered in Annexes.

In Annex 15A, Canada's Schedule on Government Procurement, the Government of Nova Scotia excepts any measure that it 'adopts or maintains with respect to culture or cultural industries.' Similarly, the Government of Québec excludes 'procurement ... (a) of cultural or artistic goods and services' and 'any measure of Québec adopted or maintained with respect to culture or cultural industries.' In a later section, Section E: Services, Annex 15A excludes '(f) Services related to culture or cultural industries,' apparently for the federal and provincial/territorial levels of government.

Canada's Schedule in Annex I Non-Conforming Measures contains cultural exceptions pertaining to Investment[11] and relatedly, Ownership.[12] In Annex II Non-Conforming Measures (16–17), 'Canada reserves the right to adopt or maintain a measure that affects cultural industries and that has the objective of supporting, directly or indirectly, the creation, development or accessibility of Canadian artistic expression or content, except:

(a) discriminatory requirements on service suppliers or investors to make financial contributions for Canadian content development; and
(b) measures restricting the access to on-line foreign audio-visual content.'

Some read Articles a) and b) as limiting the scope of the TPP cultural exemption (ACTRA 2017; Geist 2016). Others read the provisions as allowing some flexibility since they only preclude discriminatory action (Grant in Sookman blog 2016; Jackson 2018). It is arguably standard practice in any trade agreement to seek to ensure that any advantage extended to a local producer also be extended to a foreign one. Non-discrimination is, after all, the animating principle of the world trading system. Yet critics make just this point. The exemption is not intended solely to permit non-discriminatory practices. It is intended to allow practices that favour Canadian cultural industries. This provision would prove to be quite important.

In the aftermath of US withdrawal from TPP, Canada (like other signatories) set about working to suspend unpalatable provisions that the US had championed. Culture was top of mind for Canada and for some key provincial players, like Québec. The Canadian government proceeded to sign side letters with all remaining TPP signatories moderating the effects of the original TPP cultural provisions. The side letters targeted the language in Annex II of TPP, in particular the non-conforming measures pertaining the cultural industries. Each letter is identical in its proposed modification. The relevant passage reads as follows:

'Canada and [CPTPP signatory] agree that, in continuing to give effect to the Agreement, notwithstanding the following language in Annex II – Canada – 16 and 17 – under the Cultural Industries Sector, first paragraph under the subheading "Description," that states "except: (a) discriminatory requirements on service suppliers or investors to make financial contributions for Canadian content development; and (b) measures restricting the access to on-line foreign audio-visual content", *Canada may adopt or maintain discriminatory requirements on service suppliers or investors to make financial contributions for Canadian content development and may adopt or maintain measures that restrict access to on-line foreign audio-visual content*' (emphasis added). Successfully including this revision in side letters with the other signatories suggests that Canada might have strengthened the cultural exemption as compared to what would have been in place had TPP gone ahead as negotiated by the United States. It is hard to know the outcome of the counterfactual. At a minimum, the Trudeau government sent an important political signal to key constituencies. Indeed, some commentators examine this turn of events through a partisan lens. There is no doubt that the Liberals have been outwardly supportive of cultural policies in domestic debates in ways that the Conservatives have not and, furthermore, the Conservatives negotiated the weaker TPP provisions while the Liberals negotiated the side letters that may have strengthened the CPTPP exemption. We will never know if a Conservative government would have sought to suspend the same provisions were they still in power for CPTPP's signature. It is plausible that they would have, not because they have a principled commitment to culture, but because they, too, would have felt the weight of Québec's desire to get the strongest outcome on culture. In the end, only the withdrawal of the United States provided the permissive condition for the side letters. It is likely that the American presence at the TPP negotiating table – not Conservative leadership in Canada – explains the weaker outcome in TPP.

In addition to specific provisions in the agreement, some commentators have noted the distinctive language in the TPP Preamble (Maltais 2016). One passage promises to 'RECOGNISE the importance of cultural identity and diversity among and within the Parties, and that trade and investment can expand opportunities to enrich cultural identity and diversity at home and abroad.' Maltais criticizes this for emphasizing the 'opportunities for the promotion of culture and diversity through trade and investment, [while failing] to acknowledge the threats and challenges in the agreement' (Maltais 2016, 10). Indeed, it is starkly different from the preambular language in CETA.

Article 14.4 of CPTPP contains a provision on the Non-Discriminatory Treatment of Digital Products. The text sounds quite familiar to observers of USMCA negotiations. As I discuss below, very similar text surfaces in the trilateral agreement. The CPTPP passage reads as follows:

(1) No Party shall accord less favourable treatment to digital products created, produced, published, contracted for, commissioned or first made available on commercial terms in the territory of another Party, or to digital products of which the author, performer, producer, developer or owner is a person of another Party, than it accords to other like digital products.
(2) Paragraph 1 shall not apply to the extent of any inconsistency with the rights and obligations in Chapter 18 (Intellectual Property).
(3) The Parties understand that this Article does not apply to subsidies or grants provided by a Party, including government-supported loans, guarantees and insurance.
(4) This Article shall not apply to broadcasting.

Given this provision, it is not clear that digital cultural products receive protection in CPTPP. A similar provision appears in USMCA, but government officials argue that digital is protected in that later agreement precisely because there is a blanket exemption in the deal with the US and Mexico, which trumps this provision on digital. We do not find a blanket exemption in the CPTPP. Future litigation may tell the tale.

In terms of the five axes, CPTPP contains the same cultural industries definition that we find in other Canadian trade agreements. It uses a chapter-by-chapter approach. There are no references evocative of UNESCO Convention language. There is an e-commerce chapter. Since there is no blanket exemption, there is no provision authorizing retaliation of equivalent commercial effect. One might have expected such a measure here since it only appears in agreements that include the United States. But, the chapter-by-chapter approach and the specific exceptions delineated in the original Annex arguably made that a moot point.

### *Other FTAs*

In addition to the high-profile trade agreements examined here, Canada is party to several more with partners including Chile, Colombia, Costa Rica, Honduras, Israel, Jordan, Panama, Peru, South Korea and Ukraine. There is remarkable consistency across these agreements with respect to cultural industries. All agreements contain a blanket exemption, usually found in a General Exceptions chapter. The relevant Article is typically short and sweet.[13] Unlike the blanket exemption made famous in CUSFTA, later preserved in NAFTA and USMCA, these blanket exemptions include no provision authorizing retaliation of equivalent commercial effect. It is worth noting that even the most permissive blanket exemption still requires tariff elimination. Furthermore, trading partners can follow the lead of the United States and contest cultural policies in the multilateral forum, where no cultural exemption exists for goods. Nonetheless, the choice of a strong blanket exemption in this series of FTAs is noteworthy.

Many of the agreements contain language in their Preamble that references cultural diversity. Canada's agreement with Chile is exceptional in this regard. Its Preamble does not include such a reference. However, several other agreements include almost identical language. The Preambles of Canada's agreements with Colombia, Honduras, Israel, Jordan, Panama, Peru contain the following passage: 'Recognizing that states must maintain the ability to preserve, develop and implement their cultural policies for the purpose of strengthening cultural diversity, given the essential role that cultural goods and services play in the identity and diversity of societies and the lives of individuals.' Language in the Preamble of Canada's agreement with Ukraine is almost identical.

Agreements with Costa Rica[14] and South Korea[15] capture a similar sentiment in their respective Preambles through somewhat different formulations. The Agreement with South Korea contains a unique provision on cultural cooperation, cultural exchanges, and co-production.[16]

Therefore, in terms of the five axes, the other FTAs to which Canada is a party are quite consistent in their approach to the cultural exemption. They rely on the same definition of cultural industries found in CUSFTA, which underpins a blanket exemption in all cases with no authorization for retaliation. Many of these agreements contain language in their Preambles that references cultural diversity and national identity, though none specifically references the UNESCO Convention. Most agreements contain chapters on e-commerce.

### *US Mexico Canada agreement (2018)*

Canada's latest engagement in the trade and culture debate came during negotiations to modernize NAFTA. Donald Trump campaigned on a promise to improve the trilateral agreement. Not long after taking office, he notified Congress that he would be reopening the deal to seek better terms for American workers, among others. In early October, 2018, the terms of the United States-Mexico-Canada Agreement (USMCA) were made public. Several provisions are relevant to a discussion of trade and culture.

Notably, USMCA generally preserves NAFTA's blanket cultural exemption language in the chapter on general exceptions. Article 32.6 on Cultural Industries preserves the CUSFTA/NAFTA definition of cultural industry. Paragraph 2 preserves the blanket exemption, '2. This Agreement does not apply to a measure adopted or maintained by Canada with respect to a cultural industry, except as specifically provided in Article 2.3 (National Treatment and Market Access for Goods – Tariff Elimination) or Annex 15-D (Simultaneous Substitution).' Paragraph four preserves the possibility of retaliation, '4. Notwithstanding any other provision of this Agreement, a Party may take a measure of equivalent commercial effect in response to an action by another Party that would have been inconsistent with this Agreement but for paragraph 2 or 3.'

USMCA contains some new provisions pertaining to culture for Canada. Paragraph five of the exemption article specifies the parameters for any dispute that arises from use of paragraph four, authorizing retaliation of equivalent commercial effect.

Annex 15-D (Chapter 15 is Cross-Border Trade in Services) tries to resolve some longstanding differences. Notably, it requires Canada to resume simultaneous substitution of Canadian ads for American ones during transmission in Canada of American sports games. Millions of dollars in revenue are in play for owners of the Canadian rights to the Super Bowl, for example. The Canadian broadcasting regulation that banned simultaneous substitution had the effect of redirecting Canadian watchers to American channels broadcasting in Canada. As of this writing, the Canadian regulatory authority is awaiting ratification of USMCA before rescinding the relevant regulation. USMCA also allows the transmission of American home shopping stations in Canada.

Among the more debated new provisions in USMCA is Article 19.4 from the chapter on Digital Trade. It pertains to Non-Discriminatory Treatment of Digital Products and reads as follows:

> (1) No Party shall accord less favorable treatment to digital products created, produced, published, contracted for, commissioned or first made available on commercial terms in the territory of another Party, or to digital products of which the author, performer, producer, developer or owner is a person of another Party, than it accords to other like digital products.
> (2) The Parties understand that this Article does not apply to subsidies or grants provided by a Party, including government-supported loans, guarantees and insurance.

This passage received a lot of attention when the text of USMCA was published, sparking a debate as to whether the blanket exemption extended to digital platforms. Government officials have repeatedly confirmed that the exemption is broadly inclusive. The Global Affairs Canada website offers a similar assurance in its Cultural Industries Summary, noting that USMCA 'maintains Canada's existing cultural industries exception under NAFTA, a key provision designed to preserve Canada's cultural sovereignty, *including in the online environment*' (emphasis added).

In terms of the five axes, then, USMCA contains the standard cultural industry definition, as well as a blanket exemption that permits retaliation of equivalent commercial effect. That exemption ostensibly extends to digital platforms and there is a chapter on digital trade in USMCA. There is no language referencing cultural diversity or evocative of the UNESCO Convention in the Preamble. However, it is worth noting that Mexico also negotiated cultural exceptions in USMCA, contained in an Annex to the chapter on Cross-Border Trade in Services. Annex 15E, entitled Mexico's Cultural Exceptions, includes a Preamble emphasizing the importance of culture to human development, the right to freedom of expression, and 'recognizing that states have the sovereign right to preserve, develop and implement their cultural policies, to support their cultural industries for the purpose of strengthening the diversity of cultural expressions, and to preserve their cultural identity.' Mexico's exceptions are specific carve outs from the Investment and Services chapters relating to broadcasting, newspaper publishing, cinema and audiovisual services, including local ownership requirements, minimum cinema screen time, and provisions for broadcasting concessions relating to Indigenous people and women.

## Conclusion

Despite the notion of a 'Canadian cultural exemption strategy,' there is notable variation across the trade agreements to which Canada is a party. The phenomenon of proliferating trade agreements helps us to understand this variation. Had the trade focus remained on the multilateral system, which had been the case immediately after WWII until roughly the mid-1990s, domestic cultural policy toward cultural services might have preserved some room for manoeuvre via the GATS, something that would not have been possible for cultural goods under the GATT. However, Canada and the United States arguably started something of a trend in the 1980s by including a cultural exemption in CUSFTA and NAFTA. These agreements were turning points in that they were negotiated among a subset of GATT signatories and they contained provisions not typically seen in the multilateral system. Canada's cultural exemption originated there and evolved as Canada negotiated subsequent trade agreements with different partners. With smaller partners, Canada was always able to maintain a relatively strong, blanket exemption. With larger and more powerful partners, the Government of Canada pursued a cultural exemption strategy, but the outcomes varied. At a minimum, then, the proliferation of free trade agreements outside of the multilateral system created opportunities for cultural exemptions that otherwise would not have been forthcoming.

Attention to the five axes that I identify above suggests other ways that the proliferation of trade agreements has affected the cultural exemption provisions that Canada has negotiated in the last thirty years. Canada's definition of 'cultural industry' has not changed since CUSFTA. Canadian domestic interests, especially driven by technological shifts toward digital platforms, might have wanted an updated or expanded definition. However, at least two attributes of the trade negotiations would mitigate against that. First, trading partners like the United States would resist this. Second, the co-existence of multiple trade agreements almost requires a uniform definition. Expansion of the definition in one trade agreement would call into question the scope of coverage in another.

In all but two instances, Canada has negotiated a blanket exemption for culture. In CETA and TPP, later CPTPP, we find a chapter-by-chapter exemption. Neither the demands of Canadian domestic interests nor technological developments would explain this latter approach. Instead, the nature of the trade negotiations offer some insight. Both are complex, 'deep' agreements. As trade agreements become more extensive, targeted exemptions can provide greater predictability for partners offering the concession. Furthermore, both agreements also have a relatively large number of participants.[17] Especially in the case of TPP, while the US might have been willing to give a cultural exemption of some sort to Canada, they were likely alert to the broader consequences that a blanket, in-text exemption might have beyond that specific trading partner. The targeted, chapter-by-chapter exemption can circumscribe their concession. One more aspect of the phenomenon of proliferating trade agreements is relevant here. Canada's trading partners in CETA and TPP were at that time (or soon to be) negotiating FTAs with other partners. In a trading landscape thick with trade agreements, governments recognize that the substance and form of concessions in one agreement can provide a model for another agreement.

The blanket exemption paired with a right to adopt measures of equivalent commercial effect only appears in agreements with the United States. As I note above, this formulation is a middle ground that gives Canada a cultural exemption while at the same time reassuring American domestic interests who oppose it. Why did the United States deviate from this formulation in TPP? Only the negotiators in the room know for sure. However, as I note above, the nature of the negotiation with several more parties must be part of the answer. Though the TPP exemption's form differs, the US approach is arguably quite consistent across the four agreements that include Canada. In all instances, it is a qualified exemption. CUSFTA, NAFTA, and USMCA include the exemption with the right to retaliate. TPP includes an exemption, but limited to specific areas. By the time USMCA negotiations rolled around, Canada had already suspended the limiting provisions in TPP, signaling their unwillingness to accept such a formulation. The USMCA exemption, then, reverts to the status quo ante.

Mention of the UNESCO Convention also suggests ways that the proliferation of trade agreements can affect the formulation of cultural exemptions. Though several of Canada's trading partners are parties to the Convention, it goes unmentioned in their trade agreements with Canada.[18] In these same agreements, however, we find language evocative of the commitment to cultural diversity in the Preamble, suggesting that the EU may have driven the choice of including clear references to the Convention in CETA. Different trading partners bring different approaches to the negotiating table.

Finally, for the purposes of the current discussion – to show that the proliferation of trade agreements can affect the form that the Canadian cultural exemption has taken over the years – I merely flag the increasingly common inclusion of chapters on electronic commerce or digital trade. The WTO has not managed to incorporate e-commerce into its agreements, though members are trying. However, this topic, which dovetails with the cultural exemption in important ways as we produce and consume cultural products with new technologies, has become a staple in FTAs. It is perhaps this last issue that is most ripe for future research as we work to understand how the cultural exemption will evolve in the future.

## Notes

1. WTO members must notify the organization should they enter into a free trade agreement.
2. https://www.wto.org/english/thewto_e/minist_e/mc11_e/briefing_notes_e/bfecom_e.htm.
3. http://www.international.gc.ca/trade-agreements-accords-commerciaux/topics-domaines/ip-pi/sagit-gcsce.aspx?lang=eng.
4. Notwithstanding any other provision of this Agreement, as between Canada and the United States, any measure adopted or maintained with respect to cultural industries, except as specifically provided in Article 302 (Market Access – Tariff Elimination), and any measure of equivalent commercial effect taken in response, shall be governed under this Agreement exclusively in accordance with the provisions of the Canada – United States Free Trade Agreement.
5. CETA references can be found here: http://www.international.gc.ca/trade-commerce/trade-agreements-accords-commerciaux/agr-acc/ceta-aecg/text-texte/PRE.aspx?lang=eng.
6. Article 7.7 – Exclusion of subsidies and government support for audio visual services and cultural industries: 'Nothing in this Agreement applies to subsidies or government support with respect to audio-visual services for the European Union and to cultural industries for Canada.'
7. Section D – Investment protection ARTICLE 8.9 Investment and regulatory measures: '1. For the purpose of this Chapter, the Parties reaffirm their right to regulate within their territories to achieve legitimate policy objectives, such as the protection of public health, safety, the environment or public morals, social or consumer protection or the promotion and protection of cultural diversity.'
8. Article 9.2 Scope "2. This Chapter does not apply to a measure affecting: ...(b) for the European Union, audio-visual services;(c) for Canada, cultural industries;".
9. Article 12.2 Scope "2. This Chapter does not apply to licensing requirements, licensing procedures, qualification requirements, or qualification procedures: a. pursuant to an existing non-conforming measure maintained by a Party as set out in its Schedule to Annex I; or b. relating to one of the following sectors or activities: for Canada, cultural industries and, as set out in its Schedule to Annex II, social services, aboriginal affairs, minority affairs, gambling and betting services, and the collection, purification, and distribution of water; and for the EU Party, audio-visual services and, as set out in its Schedule to Annex II, health, education, and social services, gambling and betting services, and the collection, purification, and distribution of water."
10. Annex 19.7 General Notes '1. This chapter does not cover procurement: i. by Québec entities of works of art from local artists or to procurement by any municipality, academic institution or school board of other provinces and territories with respect to cultural industries. For the purpose of this paragraph, works of art includes specific artistic works to be integrated into a public building or a site;'.
11. '4. An investment subject to review under the Investment Canada Act may not be implemented unless the Minister responsible for the Investment Canada Act advises the applicant that the investment is likely to be of net benefit to Canada. This determination is made in accordance with six factors described in the Act, summarised as follows: (e) the compatibility of the investment with national industrial, economic and cultural policies, taking into consideration industrial, economic and cultural policy objectives enunciated by the government or legislature of any province likely to be significantly affected by the investment;'.
12. "7. The review thresholds set out in paragraphs 1 and 3 do not apply to an acquisition of a cultural business. 8. In addition, the specific acquisition or establishment of a new business in designated types of business activities relating to Canada's cultural heritage or national identity, which are normally notifiable, may be subject to review if the Governor-in-Council authorises a review in the public interest. 9. An indirect 'acquisition of control' of a Canadian business by an investor of a Party in a sector other than a cultural business is not reviewable."
13. For example, Article 2205 in Canada-Peru says, 'nothing in this FTA, shall be construed to apply to measures adopted or maintained by either Party with respect to cultural industries except as specifically provided in Article 203 (National Treatment and Market Access for Goods – Tariff Elimination).'

14. 'Recognize that States have the ability to preserve, develop and implement their cultural policies for the purpose of strengthening cultural diversity;'.
15. 'Promote cultural cooperation and recognise that the Parties have the right to preserve, develop, and implement their cultural policies and to support their cultural industries for the purpose of strengthening the diversity of cultural expressions;'.
16. Article 1.6: Cultural Cooperation "1. The Parties agree to promote cultural cooperation in order to increase mutual understanding and benefit from each other's competitive strengths in the development of content for the global market. In this regard, the Parties endeavour to promote cultural exchanges and carry out joint initiatives in various cultural spheres, such as audiovisual coproductions. 2. Recognising that audiovisual coproduction agreements can significantly contribute to the development of the audiovisual industry and to an intensification of cultural and economic exchange, the Parties agree to consider the negotiation of an audiovisual coproduction agreement. Such a future audiovisual coproduction agreement shall form an integral part of this Agreement."
17. The EU negotiates as a bloc, representing its 28 members.
18. Honduras, Jordan, Panama, Peru, Korea and Ukraine all signed onto the Convention before concluding trade negotiations with Canada.

## Disclosure statement

No potential conflict of interest was reported by the author.

## References

Alliance of Canadian Cinema, Television and Radio Artists (ACTRA). 2017. "How to Protect Canada's Right to Support Our Storytellers." ACTRA Submission to Global Affairs Canada on the Canada-Pacific Trade Consultations (Formerly Trans-Pacific Partnership), Ottawa, October 30th.

Brennan, A. 2017. "Letter from the MPAA to the Office of the USTR." June 12.

Browne, D. 1999. "Canada's Cultural Trade Quandry (Sic)." *International Journal* Summer 54(3): 363–374.

Burri, M. 2013. "The UNESCO Convention on Cultural Diversity: An Appraisal Five Years after Its Entry into Force." *International Journal of Cultural Property* 20: 357–380. doi:10.1017/S0940739113000209.

Burri, M. 2014. "Trade versus Culture: The Policy of Cultural Exception and the WTO." In *The Palgrave Handbook of European Media Policy*, edited by K. Donders, C. Pauwels, and J. Loisen, 479–492. New York, NY: Palgrave Macmillan.

Dür, A., L. Baccini, and M. Elsig. 2013. "The Design of International Trade Agreements: Introducing a New Dataset." *Review of International Organizations* 9 (3): 353–375. doi:10.1007/s11558-013-9179-8.

Dür, A., and M. Elsig. 2015. "Introduction: The Purpose, Design, and Effects of Preferential Trade Agreements." In *Trade Cooperation: The Purpose, Design, and Effects of Preferential Trade Agreements*, edited by A. Dür and M. Elsig, 1–22. Cambridge, UK: Cambridge University Press.

Galt, F. S. 2004. "The Life, Death, and Rebirth of the "Cultural Exception" in the Multilateral Trading System: An Evolutionary Analysis of Cultural Protection and Intervention in the Face of American Pop Culture's Hegemony." *Washington University Global Studies Law Review* 3 (3): 909–935.

Geist, M. 2016. "The Trouble with the TPP, Day 18." http://www.michaelgeist.ca/2016/01/the-trouble-with-the-tpp-day-18-failure-to-protect-canadian-cultural-policy/

Goff, P. M. 2007. *Limits to Liberalization: Local Culture in a Global Marketplace*. Ithaca, NY: Cornell University.

Grant, P. S. 2011. "The UNESCO Convention on Cultural Diversity: Cultural Policy and International Trade in Cultural Products." In *The Handbook of Global Media and Communication Policy*, edited by R. Mansell and M. Raboy, 336–352 Oxford, UK: Wiley-Blackwell

Grant, P. S. 2016. "Does the TPP Protect Canadian Cultural Policy?" Barry Sookman blog. https://www.barrysookman.com/2016/02/07/does-the-tpp-protect-canadian-cultural-policy/

Hoekman, B. 2015. "Fostering Transatlantic Regulatory Cooperation and Gradual Multilateralization." *Journal of International Economic Law* 18: 609–624. doi:10.1093/jiel/jgv028.

Hopewell, K. 2015. "Different Paths to Power: The Rise of Brazil, India and China at the World Trade Organization." *Review of International Political Economy* 22 (2): 311–338. doi:10.1080/09692290.2014.927387.

Horn, H., P. C. Mavroidis, and A. Sapir. 2009. *Beyond the WTO? An Anatomy of EU and US Preferential Trade Agreements.* Brussels: Bruegel.

Hübner, K., A.-S. Deman, and T. Balik. 2017. "EU and Trade Policy-Making: The Contentious Case of CETA." *Journal of European Integration* 39 (7): 843–857. doi:10.1080/07036337.2017.1371708.

Jackson, E. 2018. "CPTPP Side Deals Leave Door Open for Canada to Regulate Netflix, Experts Say." *Financial Post*, March 8.

Jackson, J. H. 1969. *World Trade and the Law of GATT*. Indianapolis, IN: Bobbs-Merrill Company.

Larrea, T. A. 1997. "Eliminate the Cultural Industries Exemption from NAFTA." *Santa Clara Law Review* 37 (4): 1107–1150.

Maltais, A. L. 2016. *The TPP and Cultural Diversity*. Ottawa, ON: Canadian Centre for Policy Alternatives.

Maule, C. 2003. "State of the Canada-US Relationship: Culture." *The American Review of Canadian Studies* 33 (1): 121–142. doi:10.1080/02722010309481152.

Morici, P. 1985. "U.S.-Canada Free Trade Discussions: What are the Issues?" *American Review of Canadian Studies* 15 (3): 311–323. doi:10.1080/02722018509480821.

Neathery-Castro, J. 2012. "Canada as Multilateral Player: Trade in Cultural Products." *Canadian Foreign Policy Journal* 18: 76–91. doi:10.1080/11926422.2012.674377.

Neuwirth, R. 2002. "The Cultural Industries and the Legacy of Article IV GATT: Rethinking the Relation of Culture and Trade in Light of the New WTO Round." Paper presented at Cultural Traffic: Policy, Culture, and the New Technologies in the European Union and Canada Conference, Ottawa, ON, Carleton University, November 22–23. doi:10.2139/ssrn.1352171.

Pauwelyn, J. 2005. "The UNESCO Convention on Cultural Diversity, and the WTO: Diversity in International Law Making?" *ASIL Insights* 9 (35): 1–3.

Ravenhill, J. 2014. "Global Value Chains and Development." *Review of International Political Economy* 21 (1): 264–274. doi:10.1080/09692290.2013.858366.

Report of the Standing Committee on International Trade. 2011. *Fact-Finding Mission to the European Union on the Benefits and Challenges of a Possible Comprehensive Economic and Trade Agreement between Canada and the European Union.* (February 9). 40th Parliament, 3rd Session. http://www.parl.gc.ca/HousePublications/Publication.aspx?Language=e&Mode=1&Parl=40&Ses=3&DocId=4928552

Report of the Standing Committee on International Trade. 2012. *Negotiations toward a Comprehensive Economic and Trade Agreement (CETA) between Canada and the European Union*. 41st Parliament, 1st Session, March 12. http://www.parl.gc.ca/HousePublications/Publication.aspx?Language=e&Mode=1&Parl=41&Ses=1&DocId=5431905 doi:10.1094/PDIS-11-11-0999-PDN.

Sauvé, P., and K. Steinfatt. 2000. "Towards Multilateral Rules on Trade and Culture: Protective Regulation or Efficient Protection?" Achieving Better Regulation of Service Conference Proceedings. Canberra: Australian National University.

World Trade Organization. 1997. *Canada-Certain Measures Concerning Periodicals*. WT/DS31/AB/R.

World Trade Organization. 2017. *Regional trade agreements: an introduction*. https://www.wto.org/english/tratop_e/region_e/scope_rta_e.htm

World Trade Organization. 2018. *Regional Trade Agreements: Facts and Figures*. https://www.wto.org/english/tratop_e/region_e/region_e.htm#facts

# Trade, culture and the European Union cultural exception

Lilian Richieri Hanania

**ABSTRACT**
The article examines how the European Union has addressed the 'trade and culture debate' in its international trade agreements. From a cultural exception approach based on an attempt to detach culture from trade provisions, the European Union economic agreements seem to evolve to a broader and more holistic position aiming to promote cultural exchanges through cooperation, while still safeguarding policy space in cultural matters through its traditional cultural exception. The article provides an overview of the European positions to defend the specificity of the audio-visual services sector at the multilateral (World Trade Organization Agreements), regional and bilateral levels. It also examines how the implementation of the 2005 UNESCO Convention on the Protection and Promotion of the Diversity of Cultural Expressions has led the European Union to negotiate cultural cooperation provisions in parallel to some of its recent bilateral and regional trade agreements and the way this Convention may impact the understanding of the 'trade and culture debate'.

## I. The 'trade and culture debate': from opposition to integration

The 'trade and culture debate' connects with the explicit or implicit recognition of the dual nature, commercial and cultural, of cultural goods and services. This dual nature implies a complexity of interests and actors. The manifold interests of these different stakeholders complexify decision-making regarding the legal treatment to be applied to cultural goods and services in international trade agreements.

Countries with economically strong cultural sectors, such as the audio-visual sector (e.g. the United States), have naturally tended to highlight the commercial aspect of those goods and services when negotiating international trade agreements. Other countries (e.g. France, Spain and Belgium, within the European Union) which perceive some of their cultural sectors as economically sensitive or vulnerable and/or whose societies express a stronger concern for the social and cultural impact of those goods and services on cultural diversity and the exercise of democracy have tended to emphasise their cultural dimension. However, both the economic and cultural interests involved are intricately linked, and cultural goods and services may only be defined by these two complementary, despite sometimes conflictual, aspects.

Complex thinking as described by Edgar Morin seems particularly interesting when examining the 'trade and culture debate' (Morin 2005). Cultural exchanges 'require an integrated diversity, paradoxically conceived both in human unity and diversity and which cannot be understood without its different contexts and the interactions occurring in them' (Richieri Hanania and Norodom 2016). Strategies designed to pursue cultural diversity need, therefore, to go beyond simplifications and polarisations. They must build upon conflict among differing and complex concerns to find innovative solutions. Especially in the extremely dynamic and continuously changing and disrupting digital environment, they must be capable to evolve while addressing uncertainty, indetermination and random phenomena (Morin 2005, 48–49). Flexibility, transformation and ability to grow are thus fundamental when it comes to establishing cultural policies or initiatives. And there is no single and rigid solution or model to follow.

This need for flexibility may, nevertheless, become problematic with respect to international trade agreements – as with legal provisions in general, as precisely highlighted by Neuwirth (2016). International trade agreements crystallize commitments for market liberalization which may later prevent a country from adopting specific cultural policies which, according to the country's historical, economic, administrative or social circumstances, might be considered the most suitable. The paradox and complexity behind the 'trade and culture debate' stand particularly out in this field, since, while cultural diversity cannot flourish without cultural exchanges, those specific commitments might deter policymakers from adopting cultural policies particularly appropriate for their countries at a certain point in time.

The legal treatment applied to the exchanges of cultural goods and services has historically differed in international agreements containing trade provisions. While those agreements may in certain cases refer in their Preambles or general statements to an incentive to cultural cooperation among the parties, together with other cooperation objectives, distinct approaches can be observed regarding the legal provisions governing how cultural goods and services are to be traded. For instance, when negotiating international trade liberalization provisions, Canada has since the 1980s required the exclusion of cultural industries from its agreements' scope by inserting a cultural exception clause for those industries. In agreements signed with the United States (US), the commercial dimension of cultural goods and services often prevails. Even though subsidies to traditional cultural sectors are usually authorized under those agreements, US trade partners had to negotiate specific reservations to maintain cultural measures and policies. While some partners were able to include more comprehensive reservations in the annexes to the agreements with the US (e.g. Australia), in several cases, reservations have not been drafted in a way that is sufficiently flexible to allow for an evolving strategy regarding cultural policies. Finally, as will be presented in the following sections of this article, the European Union (EU) traditional position in international trade agreements has consisted of excluding the audio-visual services sector from the chapter on trade in services and establishment by drafting a cultural exception for that sector only, based on the magnitude of the social, cultural and economic importance of audio-visual content in modern societies (see, for instance, Richieri Hanania 2009, 2012).

When observed from an isolated perspective focused on the international trade agreement in question, this EU cultural exception translates an oppositional logic between trade and culture. This exception has, nevertheless, allowed for cultural policy space of EU Member States and specifically designed cultural cooperation among them and with third countries, in accordance with article 167 of the Treaty on the Functioning of the European Union (TFEU).[1]

At the end of the day, those approaches in international trade agreements reflect the combination of the commercial partners' views on the importance of (certain or all) cultural industries, on how they affect cultural diversity, cultural identity and the practice of democracy and, ultimately, to which extent State intervention might be desirable in cultural sectors because of the cultural and social interests involved. For instance, within the EU, countries such as the United Kingdom and the Netherlands have often been reluctant to the very logic of cultural exception. Differences among EU Member States result in practical difficulties in determining and sustaining a common position when negotiating with a trade partner.

The decision on which sectors are to be excluded also reveals how a country measures the contribution of specific cultural industries to cultural diversity, as well as how it assesses the competitiveness of those industries in the international market. Indeed, the perceived relationship of opposition and contradiction between trade and culture illustrated by the Canadian and European positions often came from a feeling of vulnerability and need of defence when faced with countries such as the United States, willing to open markets in cultural sectors and notably in the audio-visual sector. The opposition between trade and culture deriving from cultural exception techniques, confronting economic and trade agreements on the one side with cultural policies on the other, does not necessarily imply, however, contradiction between cultural policies and cultural exchanges. The latter may perfectly be part of a country's strategy and policies in favour of cultural diversity – and they should be, through a coordinated approach of these two elements.

The conflictual nature of the 'trade and culture debate' was at the origin of the discussions which led to the adoption of the UNESCO Convention on the Protection and Promotion of the Diversity of Cultural Expressions (CDCE) in 2005. The CDCE overcomes opposition through an integrative and systemic approach of the cultural and economic interests involved in the creation, production, dissemination, distribution of and access to cultural activities, goods and services (Richieri Hanania 2014a). It acknowledges both the specificity of cultural goods and services – possibly translated into cultural exceptions in international trade agreements when needed and/or legally feasible – and international cultural cooperation for better and more balanced exchanges, as two necessarily complementary elements conducive to cultural diversity (Richieri Hanania 2009, 2014b).

The European Union was, together with Canada, a leading promoter of this convention, extremely active during its negotiations and a strong advocate of its ratification once the CDCE was adopted. Even though the CDCE contains mostly non-binding provisions and provides mainly political support for its Parties, its integrated perspective has been embraced by the European Union when negotiating legal frameworks for cultural cooperation in parallel to some of its bilateral and regional trade and economic agreements since the adoption of the CDCE. From a rather isolated cultural exception approach based on an attempt to detach culture from trade provisions, the European Union economic agreements seem to evolve to a broader and more holistic position aiming to promote cultural exchanges through cooperation, while still safeguarding policy space in cultural matters through its traditional exception. With the objective of demonstrating this evolution of perspective, the present article presents an overview of the EU approach to the 'trade and culture debate' in the World Trade Organization (WTO) (Section II), as well as in its regional and bilateral agreements negotiated since the adoption of the CDCE (Section III), before providing some conclusive remarks.

## II. Cultural exception in the 'trade and culture debate'

Considering that market liberalization commitments may threaten cultural policy space and flexibility, several WTO members, including the European Union (initially the 'European Communities'), employed legal techniques allowing to limit their commitments in the audio-visual services sector and other cultural sectors when becoming a member to the WTO. In the case of the EU, efforts were focused on the audio-visual sector. Other services sectors, despite having sometimes a strong cultural component, have not been addressed in the same way.

### *A. Limited commitments coupled with exemptions for audio-visual services*

The first recognition of the difficulty in establishing a balance between trade liberalization goals and the need to promote national cultural production appears in the 1947 General Agreement on Tariffs and Trade (GATT), which contains in its article IV an exception allowing for national screen quotas for cinematographic films under certain conditions. When the services sector was brought to the multilateral trade negotiations during the Uruguay Round, which led to the creation of the WTO in 1995, a similar problem was highlighted by negotiating Parties such as the EU and Canada regarding the audio-visual services sector, causing some countries to decide not to undertake liberalization commitments (national treatment[2] and market access obligations) and to include exemptions to the most-favoured-nation treatment[3] in this sector.

Since the WTO members' commitments under the General Agreement on Trade in Services (GATS) are undertaken through 'positive lists' of commitments (if a member does not include a sector in its schedule of commitments, no national treatment or market access obligation applies for that sector), not mentioning the audio-visual services sector in its schedule of commitments (WTO 1994b) was the solution found by the EU at the time to ensure that the EU Member States would retain sufficient flexibility in the audio-visual sector to create and apply cultural policies. Moreover, the contracting parties were authorized to define exemptions to the most-favoured-nation obligation of article II GATS when becoming members of the WTO. Several of those exemptions relate to the audio-visual sector and refer to cultural objectives when safeguarding the possibility for the concerned member to establish preferential relationships with other countries in the audio-visual sector. For instance, the EU list of exemptions pull out of the GATS' most-favoured-nation obligation certain support measures for audio-visual works meeting European origin criteria, as well as measures allowing to extend national treatment to audio-visual works meeting certain criteria under the Council of Europe Convention on Transfrontier Television or bilateral and plurilateral audio-visual co-production agreements (WTO 1994a, 1–3).

### *B. Incentive for liberalization in other cultural sectors*

When defining their list of commitments under the GATS during the Uruguay Round, the European Communities undertook commitments in sectors which might be considered as having a strong cultural dimension. While those commitments may be restricted by limitations and differentiation according to specific sectors and EU Member States, they demonstrate the difficulty, even within the European Union, to reach an agreement on the cultural sectors in which flexibility and policy space are to be pursued in international trade negotiations. For example, the EU has accepted commitments at the WTO regarding recreational and cultural services other than audio-visual services, comprising entertainment services (including theatre, live bands and circus) and news and press agency services (WTO 1994b, 85), as well as in sectors also presenting a strong cultural – or at least creative – facet, but classified separately in the Services Sectoral Classification List (WTO 1991), such as printing and publishing services (WTO 1994b, 47), architectural services (20) and advertising services (38). As mentioned earlier, the economic significance of some of those sectors for certain Member States (e.g. press agency and publishing services for Spain) and the perception of vulnerability, also from a cultural standpoint, by other Members usually explain the different levels of commitments in each of those sectors.

Regarding exemptions to the most-favoured-nation treatment in other cultural sectors, only three requirements for reciprocity regarding market access and foreign participation – one in Italy for publishing services and two in France for news agency and press agency services – are mentioned in the EU list of exemptions to article II of the GATS (WTO 1994a, 6). Moreover, under these three exemptions, the reason indicated for their existence does not relate to cultural objectives. The document mentions the '[n]eed to ensure effective market access and equivalent treatment' (WTO 1994a, 6), illustrating once again the difficulty in recognizing the specificity and dual nature of those sectors as a shared position among EU Member States.

When, at the beginning of the years 2000's, WTO members started exchanging requests and offers for further liberalization in services and modification of their lists in the framework of the Doha Round, the European Union also seemingly requested from other WTO members enhanced commitments in sectors such as advertising and architectural services. The negotiations leading to the CDCE had just started and such requests were interpreted by certain WTO members, such as Brazil, as contradictory to the advocating by the EU of the specificity of cultural goods and services at UNESCO. Indeed, the CDCE does not distinguish between different cultural sectors when it acknowledges the legitimacy of public cultural policies and measures. However, when countries like France tried to defend a cultural exception comprising other sectors than the audio-visual services sector after the adoption of the CDCE, the European Commission often referred to the coherence with commitments already undertaken in previous agreements (including at the WTO) to reject such proposal.

With the deadlock of the Doha Round multilateral negotiations on services, parallel bilateral and plurilateral negotiations have taken place at the WTO, such as those, starting in 2013 among 23 WTO members[4] known as the 'Really Good Friends of Services' and including the EU. The presence of the US in the negotiations of this Trade in Services Agreement (TiSA),[5] as well as of several countries having signed an agreement with the US and/or having already undertaken trade commitments in the audio-visual and other cultural sectors under the GATS can foreshadow general pressure for liberalization in all services sectors under such initiative – and difficulties in potential attempts to acknowledge the specificity of cultural services by the members of that group having ratified the CDCE, including the EU (Vlassis and Richieri Hanania 2014, 35).

In addition, trade principles established between the US and the EU in 2011 on information and communication technology services (TEC 2011) might also have an impact on ongoing and future negotiations on services related to digital cultural content involving the United States and the European Union, whether at the bilateral (in the event that negotiations of a Transatlantic Trade and Investment Partnership (TTIP) are resumed[6]), plurilateral or multilateral levels. The TEC Trade Principles for Information and Communication Technology Services expressed the intention of both parties 'to promote the implementation of these principles within their bilateral economic relationship and in their trade negotiations with third countries.' While they are presented as 'a set of non-binding trade-related principles' acknowledging the importance of technological neutrality[7] and not aiming directly at audio-visual services, they contain non-discrimination and market access principles that may have a strong impact on the audio-visual sector or any other sector having a cultural dimension and being affected by new technologies. The text is quite understandable in the framework of the continuous US efforts to improve liberalization in the digital field and the economic potential of this new environment for American media industries.

The TEC principles are put forward as being without prejudice 'to the policy objectives and legislation of the European Union and the United States', comprising, following a request by the EU during negotiations, 'the enhancement of cultural diversity (including through public funding and assistance).' While an explicit reference to cultural diversity is undoubtedly positive, and public funding and assistance are mentioned without exclusion of other means for promoting cultural diversity, from a legal standpoint such reference has no potential to hinder liberalization in digital media sectors *per se*. In addition, the difference in perspective between the US and the EU on how the enhancement of cultural diversity should be pursued has been flagrant in the last decades (Richieri Hanania and Ruiz Fabri 2014, 498). Furthermore, there is no definition of 'information and communication technology services' in the text, and no distinction between services which may be a vehicle for cultural content and services which transport such content. This is not reassuring, neither from a legal certainty perspective, nor from a cultural diversity perspective.

This may be problematic in view of the discrepancies between the US and the EU in their bilateral and regional trade agreements regarding trade in digital cultural goods and services. In its bilateral agreements concluded in the last two decades, the US has established a specific legal regime for 'digital products', which are defined as 'computer programs, text, video, images, sound recordings, and other products that are digitally encoded and transmitted electronically, regardless of whether a Party treats such products as a good or a service under its domestic law'. The EU has adopted an approach that seems more respectful of the specificity of cultural and particularly audio-visual services in the digital era, by maintaining its traditional and technologically neutral exception for audio-visual services in its agreements. Since the adoption of the CDCE, the EU has comforted its traditional position when negotiating its bilateral and regional trade agreements, while endeavouring to apply the CDCE provisions and principles to promote cultural exchanges.

## III. Cultural exception for better cultural exchanges

The CDCE provisions may be grouped into two main facets: (i) the acknowledgement of the specificity of cultural goods and services and, consequently, the legitimacy of the adoption of cultural policies and measures by States, mainly enshrined in articles 5 and 6 of the CDCE; and (ii) the promotion of international cultural cooperation 'for the creation of conditions conducive to the promotion of the diversity of cultural expressions', as stated under articles 12 and following of the CDCE. Both aspects are recognized as necessary or at least useful towards the objective of cultural diversity.

Article 16 of the CDCE adds complexity to international cultural cooperation when it states that '[d]eveloped countries shall facilitate cultural exchanges with developing countries by granting, through the appropriate institutional and legal frameworks, preferential treatment to artists and other cultural professionals and practitioners, as well as cultural goods and services from developing countries'. The expression 'preferential treatment' followed by a reference to 'cultural goods and services' conveys a trade-related connotation to this clause. Allowing for or encouraging cultural goods and services originating from countries with economically-weaker cultural industries to enter international markets has certainly a trade and economic dimension. However, they do not necessarily require the consolidation of market access commitments in trade agreements. Other cultural cooperation strategies may allow to reinforce the cultural industries of countries facing difficulties in reaching the international market or the market of specific partners.

The EU experience since the adoption of the CDCE illustrates the evolving search for a balance between, on the one hand, the need to safeguard the largest and most flexible policy space as possible for the exercise of the sovereign right to adopt and maintain cultural policies, notably in the audio-visual sector, and, on the other hand, the objective of promoting cultural cooperation that can contribute to more balanced international cultural exchanges. While continuous assessment of the effectiveness of EU agreements on this matter is necessary and much could undoubtedly be done to improve them, the EU experience remains an interesting case in the transformation of the 'trade and culture debate' by the CDCE.

### *A. Allowing for cultural policies in the audio-visual sector*

The EU traditional exception for audio-visual services in its bilateral and regional economic agreements is technologically neutral in its drafting. The entire sector is excluded from the chapter on trade in services, without specific reference to technological means of supply. Unless commitments have been undertaken at the WTO or under other trade agreements, the EU trade partners remain authorized under the agreements with the EU to adopt cultural policies in favour of both traditional and digital audio-visual services.

The changes operated by the digital economy in the audio-visual sector have, nevertheless, strengthened the opposition by countries like the United States against cultural exceptions. According to such countries, there would be no need to establish quotas or other restrictive cultural policy measures in favour of national cultural productions in an era in which the Internet allows for limitless storage space. However, while certain traditional cultural policies may seem progressively outdated, their rationale remains relevant. Storage space is by no means a guarantee of cultural diversity online. Recent research has indeed demonstrated the many difficulties in measuring diversity online (Marenghi, Hernández Prieto, and Badillo 2016; Ranaivoson 2016), the lack of 'exposure diversity' (Burri 2016) and of 'discoverability' of a diversified cultural offer, as well as the threats on cultural diversity resulting from market concentration in the hands of the so-called 'net giants' (Kulesz 2015, 2016).

By establishing a distinct category of 'digital products' in their bilateral free trade agreements, the United States has defined a specific legal regime based on non-discrimination (national treatment and most-favoured-nation treatment obligations) for many services that would likely fall under the definition of audio-visual services, such as video, images and sound recordings available online. For instance, under article 15.4 § 1 of the US-Chile Free Trade Agreement (FTA) (USTR 2003), no discriminatory treatment shall be applied on the basis that a digital product has been 'created, produced, published, stored, transmitted, contracted for, commissioned, or first made available on commercial terms in the territory of the other Party; or (b) the author, performer, producer, developer, or distributor of such digital products is a person of the other Party.' In other FTAs that chronologically followed the one with Chile, it has been added that discrimination is also prohibited 'so as otherwise to afford protection to the other like digital products that are created, produced, published, stored, transmitted, contracted for, commissioned, or first made available on commercial terms in its territory' (see, for instance, article 14.3, § 3 of CAFTA-DR FTA (USTR 2004)). When the US partners did not establish specific reservations to those obligations (e.g. Central American countries and Morocco), the US was able to guarantee liberalized exchanges of digital products with those countries and access to their digital markets, often to the detriment of the cultural policy space of these partners (Richieri Hanania 2019).

In the case of the EU agreements, the e-commerce chapter has focused on cooperation, without prejudice to the traditional and technologically neutral cultural exception for audio-visual services. Those agreements generally require cooperation on subjects relating to e-commerce (e.g. electronic signature certification, liability of service suppliers in information transmission and storage, consumers' protection, security of electronic transactions), no custom duties on electronic delivery or transmissions, and high international standards on data protection. In some of the agreements, the prohibition regarding custom duties is explicitly explained by the fact that electronic delivery is to be considered as the supply of a service (Richieri Hanania 2019). No market liberalization obligations are undertaken regarding e-commerce and in certain agreements the cultural exception is explicitly extended to the e-commerce provisions. For example, article 16.7 of the Comprehensive Economic and Trade Agreement (CETA) concluded between the European Union and Canada (EU 2016) states that, in case of contradiction between the chapter on e-commerce and the other chapters of the agreement (e.g. the chapter on trade in services), the latter shall prevail, together with the cultural exceptions indicated therein. The agreement with Singapore (EU 2015) also affirms under article 8.59 that 'measures related to the supply of a service using electronic means falls within the scope of the obligations contained in the relevant provisions of this Chapter [on trade in services, establishment and e-commerce] subject to any exceptions applicable to such obligations'.

The maintenance of a cultural exception for the audio-visual sector allows the EU authorities and Member States to continuously improve policies and measures aiming at cultural diversity along with technological evolution. One example is the recent review of the European Audio-visual Media Services Directive (AVMSD) (EU 2010) which adapts the existing European audio-visual rules to new audio-visual services and actors. The new rules will apply, for instance, to video-sharing platforms and user-generated videos on platforms such as Facebook. The rationale of traditional quotas, aiming at reserving a certain space for European audio-visual production, has been adapted to the digital context through the obligation for video-on-demand catalogues to promote European works by proposing at least 30% of European content (EC 2018).

A remaining question relates to other cultural sectors. For instance, in the CETA agreement, Canada maintained its cultural exception for cultural industries in general (through chapter-by-chapter exceptions), while the EU only excluded its audio-visual services sector. The argument of coherence with previously adopted commitments in other cultural sectors than the audio-visual services sector prevailed once again on the EU side. Arguably, in that specific agreement, negotiated between parties to the CDCE that have historically been strong promoters of that convention, could not both parties have adopted the larger Canadian exception? Despite previous EU commitments under the GATS or in other bilateral agreements for other cultural sectors covered by the Canadian exception (commitments that remain applicable in any case), a larger cultural exception would have had a stronger political meaning, demonstrating the Parties' commitment to the CDCE, its visibility and the specificity of all cultural sectors (Richieri Hanania and Ruiz Fabri 2014, 495–496; Richieri Hanania 2019). The clear intent of the EU to implement the CDCE appears, nevertheless, with respect to international cultural cooperation.

### *B. While promoting cultural exchanges*

Since the adoption of the CDCE, the European Commission has attempted, in parallel to some of its trade agreements, to strengthen cultural cooperation provisions with some of its partners and promote a more integrative approach based on the CDCE regarding culture and trade (Richieri Hanania 2012, 2019; Souyri-Desrosier 2014).

In a search for this new approach (EC 2009), when negotiating the 2008 Economic Partnership Agreement (EPA) with the Caribbean Forum (CARIFORUM) States[8] (EU 2008), the Commission proposed to attach to the EPA a Protocol on Cultural Cooperation (PCC) inspired by the CDCE. A lot of discussions were raised within the civil society regarding the appropriateness of such a protocol attached to an economic agreement, the fact that it contained market access provisions for audio-visual co-production works, and its link with the cultural exception for audio-visual services established elsewhere in the agreement. Criticism came mainly from the impression that the EU had somehow softened its commitment to the specificity of the audio-visual sector and to its traditional cultural exception for audio-visual services in trade agreements (Richieri Hanania 2012, 2019). The EU CARIFORUM PCC focused, moreover, on market access for co-produced audio-visual works, which, according to specific criteria, may qualify as works of European origin and have facilitated access to the European market through the quotas established under the AVMSD. The use of a protocol attached to and part of an economic agreement to cover this type of market access provision was legally justified: not all CARIFORUM States were authorized to establish a preferential relation with the EU in the audio-visual services sector because of obligations already undertaken in that sector under the GATS. A protocol attached to a regional trade agreement allowed the parties to define a preferential (by essence discriminatory) relation through Article V of the GATS, according to which economic integration agreements may be withdrawn from the GATS most-favoured-nation treatment obligation under certain conditions.

Considering the development level of the audio visual industries in the CARIFORUM States, the Commission aimed precisely to apply article 16 of the CDCE. In this case, preferential treatment implied market access for the parties to the PCC, even though the audio-visual services sector had been excluded from liberalization in the trade part of the agreement. The type of market access granted to the CARIFORUM States differed, nevertheless, from a general commitment by the parties to grant market access or non-discriminatory treatment to the other party in the audio-visual services sector. The commitment contained in the PCC was rather inspired from a common feature of bilateral co-production agreements: establishing specific conditions for co-produced works to be considered as 'national works' under both parties' national legislation and support schemes. It does not prevent, therefore, the parties from adopting, maintaining or modifying national measures or policies, nor limits them with respect to the types of measures and policies that may be adopted.

A few years later, a protocol was also negotiated with the Republic of Korea (EU 2011b).[9] The EU-CARIFORUM PCC, based on non-reciprocal treatment due to the differences in the audio-visual industries of the parties, was proposed as the template to start negotiations with South Korea. Such approach raised concerns, not only because the use of a single model would be inappropriate considering the specific circumstances of the cultural sectors in EU trade partners, but also South Korea already had a prosperous audio-visual industry that did not require the implementation of article 16 of the CDCE. A link made to the exception for audio-visual services established in the trade part of the agreement also seemed problematic, since it was drafted as limiting that exception: according to article 1.2 of the EU-Korea PCC, '[t]he exclusion of audio-visual services from the scope of Chapter Seven (Trade in Services, Establishment and Electronic Commerce) is without prejudice to the rights and obligations derived from this Protocol. (...)'.

During negotiations and thanks to comments received from civil society and the French government (France 2009), the PCC draft evolved and incorporated a clearer distinction between the cultural cooperation provisions and trade provisions. A specific 'Committee on Cultural Cooperation', composed of cultural experts, was created and oversees any dispute arising under the PCC, with the exclusion of jurisdiction by the Trade Committee created under the free trade agreement (articles 3.1, 3.3 and 3bis). The EU-Korea PCC also made market access provisions reciprocal, allowing co-productions meeting the requirements of the PCC to benefit from promotional schemes for local/regional cultural content existing in both parties (article 5). Finally, the grounding of the cultural cooperation provisions on the CDCE principles, objectives and definitions was also positive: while the CDCE provisions establish very limited obligations for its Parties, clear references to this convention contribute to its visibility, credibility and the strengthening of the political support it may offer to its Parties regarding their cultural policies. It was also agreed henceforth that a protocol attached to a trade agreement would only be necessary when (i) cultural cooperation established a preferential treatment that could be assimilated to market access and (ii) commitments already undertaken under the GATS required making use of a regional trade agreement.

The attempt to more clearly distinguish cultural cooperation from trade and market access to preserve the cultural exception for audio-visual services and their specificity in trade agreements was later observed in another protocol, signed in 2010 between the EU and Central American countries under the umbrella of the Association Agreement signed in June 2012 (EU 2012a). The PCC was not directly attached to the trade chapter of the Association Agreement.[10] The same approach was transposed to a stand-alone Agreement on Cultural Cooperation with Peru and Colombia in 2011 (EU 2011a), legally disconnected from the trade agreement negotiated in parallel with those partners and signed in 2012.[11]

Considering the difference in economic power of the parties' cultural industries, in those two last cultural cooperation frameworks, as well as with the CARIFORUM States, technical assistance by the EU was foreseen, aiming at the development of cultural industries and cultural policies, as well as the production and the exchange of cultural goods and services. Contrary to the EU-CARIFORUM PCC though, they do not include preferential treatment through market access and rather focus on fostering preferential relations through 'festivals, seminars and similar initiatives' (article 5.2 of the PCC with Central American countries and article 7.2 of the Cultural Cooperation Agreement with Peru and Colombia). The objective was to establish a framework to promote cultural cooperation among the partner countries based on 'pure' cultural cooperation, rather than market liberalization measures that would crystallize commitments and rigidify the scope and form of potential cultural policies and measures in the sectors concerned. As such, it respects the letter of the CDCE and its objectives under the two facets identified earlier, i.e. the specificity of cultural goods and services (possibly implying cultural exceptions in trade agreements) and the promotion of international cultural cooperation.

The focus of the cultural cooperation provisions also shifted from the audio-visual sector (with co-productions, festivals, seminars, exchange among broadcasting industries and on broadcasting policy and regulation) to address, at an equal level, the mobility of/and exchanges among artists and cultural practitioners; performing arts (exchanges, joint productions and training for practitioners); publishing (dissemination of publications, organisation of events, co-publishing and translation, and professional exchanges and training for librarians, writers, translators, booksellers and publishers); and the protection of cultural heritage and historic monuments (exchanges of expertise and best practices). Indeed, the objective being to contribute to new opportunities for the partner countries' cultural goods and services, cultural cooperation should be attentive to their needs and priorities in a diverse range of cultural sectors.

While specific cooperation regarding the promotion of exchanges of digital cultural content was not particularly addressed, technical assistance with technology transfer and know-how among the parties was foreseen in the three non-reciprocal cultural cooperation frameworks negotiated with the CARIFORUM countries, Central American countries, as well as Peru and Colombia (article 4 in each of those frameworks). The use of international and regional standards for compatibility and interoperability of audio-visual technologies was also seen as a factor contributing to cultural exchanges in the PCCs with the CARIFORUM States (article 5) and with South Korea (article 6.3). The EU-CARIFORUM and EU-Korea PCCs, as well as the Agreement on Cultural Cooperation with Colombia and Peru also address the digitalisation of audio-visual archives (articles 5, 6.3 and 7.5, respectively), and the four frameworks on cultural cooperation 'encourage the development of international theatre technology standards and the use of theatre stage signs' (article 7.3 in the EU-CARIFORUM PCC, article 8.3 in the PCC with the Republic of Korea, article 6.3 in the PCC with Central American countries and article 8.3 under the Agreement with Peru and Colombia). With respect to the publishing sector, only the Agreement with Peru and Colombia explicitly mentions digital publications.

Although not expressly mentioned in those frameworks, their implementation in the digital economy will necessarily need to target digital media market opportunities and audio-visual diversity online. For instance, this could be pursued through technical and financial assistance, online festivals aiming at developing audience for the partners' cultural productions, the creation of common platforms for the distribution of content resulting from collaborative projects, partnership with private online platforms (including the 'net giants') providing cultural content, collaboration in the preparation of the countries' digital strategies, online platforms to promote exchange of knowledge, experiences and best practices, as well as collaborative work, and capacity-building projects involving access and use of digital technologies (Richieri Hanania 2017).

Admittedly, the effectiveness of the cultural cooperation provisions negotiated by the EU still needs to be demonstrated. For example, in the case of the CARIFORUM countries, difficulties cover organizational weakness and structural difficulties of the Caribbean cultural sector, lack of awareness about the PCC and its practical application by cultural practitioners, lack of information on the requirements for market access to the EU, and difficulties in complying with the conditions defined in the protocol for an audio-visual work to be considered co-produced and allowed to benefit from European rules (KEA European Affairs 2011). However, all the four frameworks are still recent and the effectiveness of the cultural cooperation provisions they foresee and their long-term impact on the cultural industries of each partner will be better assessed with the benefit of hindsight. In any case, by fostering cultural cooperation without limiting the parties' cultural policy space with stiff liberalization commitments, those frameworks conciliate the specificity of cultural (notably audio-visual) goods and services and the necessary search for more balanced exchanges of those goods and services through international cultural cooperation.

## IV. Concluding remarks

The 'trade and culture debate' stems from the need for flexibility in cultural policymaking. Faced with the constant evolution of the digital economy, strategies need to be even more flexible and dynamic. Undertaking trade liberalization commitments in cultural sectors, which are highly affected by the unfolding of new technologies, may limit such flexibility.

The European traditional position when negotiating trade agreements (at the multilateral, regional and bilateral levels) has consisted of keeping the largest cultural policy space possible for the audio-visual sector by inserting a cultural exception in those agreements. By applying the principle of technological neutrality, such an exception makes no distinction with respect to the technological means for providing audio-visual services. The parties to those agreements do not need, therefore, to continuously modify the text of the agreement to adapt it to new digital products and services – the technologically neutral cultural exception guarantees enough flexibility on that. The recognition of the specificity of the audio-visual sector in its trade agreements has, nevertheless, not prevented the European Union from promoting international cultural cooperation and exchanges, which are seen, since the CDCE, as necessarily complementary to attain cultural diversity. Cultural cooperation has been addressed in specific normative frameworks, either in the form of stand-alone agreements, or attached to trade agreements when required by existing trade commitments of partner countries.

The digital economy is an opportunity for the EU to engage in permanent consultations with stakeholders in cultural and creative sectors (also other than the audio-visual sector) with the objective of setting up evolving measures and policies that most appropriately pursue the objective of cultural diversity in the digital context. The means to attain such an objective cannot be thought without considering the complexity of actors and interests in the cultural market, as well as the specific circumstances of the digital media market in Europe. Those policies will necessarily affect varied political fields and branches of law having, directly or indirectly, an influence on the operation of cultural industries.

With its systemic and integrative vision of the exchanges of cultural goods and services and of the governance of the cultural industries (Richieri Hanania 2014b, 299ff., 2015a, 2015b), the CDCE articulates divergent interests relating inter alia to trade, culture, sustainable development and international cooperation. It can work as a tool to improve coherence and coordination among different fields of action. The CDCE should, therefore, remain an important legal framework for consistent and coherent EU action in favour of cultural diversity, regardless of the technological means employed to convey cultural expressions. Its political support for the Parties to secure their policy space in international trade agreements is not limited by types of policies nor specific cultural sectors, provided those policies mainly target culture and cultural expressions and comply with the CDCE principles and objectives (Richieri Hanania 2015b, 4). Indeed, in its article 4.6, the CDCE defines largely the notion of cultural policies and measures as those relating to culture, either focused on culture as such or designed to have a direct effect on cultural expressions. Being open to changes when pursuing cultural diversity implies constantly assessing its cultural market and the different sectors having a direct or indirect link with culture, in order to prepare and influence the dynamics of the market. Reflecting upon possible future exceptions in trade agreements to come is an essential part of such preparation.

## Notes

1. Article 167 TFEU (former article 151 of the TEC introduced by the Maastricht Treaty) prescribes that
2. The national treatment obligation implies non-discrimination between foreign and national products and services, which means applying to partner countries the same treatment as to its own products and services.
3. The most-favoured-nation treatment requires non-discrimination in the treatment applied to different foreign trade partners.
4. The US, Australia, Canada, Chile, Chinese Taipei, Colombia, Costa Rica, the EU, Hong Kong, Iceland, Israel, Japan, Liechtenstein, Mauritius, Mexico, New Zealand, Norway, Pakistan, Panama, Peru, South Korea, Switzerland and Turkey (EC (European Commission) 2018b).
5. Negotiations of this agreement have been paused 'since the US Presidential elections in November 2016, pending clarity in the US trade policy' (EC (European Commission) 2018a, 10).
6. The EU Member States agreed in June 2013 to exclude audio-visual services from the European Commission negotiations mandate for the TTIP. Commitments in sectors covered under the information and communication technology services could possibly be used to circumvent to a certain extent this exception in the digital context. The TTIP negotiations halted indefinitely in late 2016, despite some willingness to resume the negotiations expressed since mid-2017.
7. Technological neutrality implies that regulation and international provisions do not impose or discriminate based on the use of a technology (EU (European Union) 2002), thus not requiring that a party renegotiate its international commitments along with technological developments.
8. The CARIFORUM is a subgroup of the African, Caribbean and Pacific Group of States comprising the 15 Caribbean Community states and the Dominican Republic.

9. The PCC with South Korea has been provisionally applied since 2011. The trade agreement is in force since December 2015.
10. The European Union – Central America Association Agreement (EU (European Union) 2012a) was signed on 29 June 2012 with Costa Rica, El Salvador, Guatemala, Honduras, Nicaragua and Panama. The trade part of the agreement has been provisionally applied since 2013.
11. The Agreement on Cultural Cooperation with Colombia and Peru (EU (European Union) 2011a) is not yet in force but was negotiated in parallel to a trade agreement signed on 26 July 2012 and provisionally applied since 2013 (EU (European Union) 2012b).

## Disclosure statement

No potential conflict of interest was reported by the author.

## References


Burri, M. 2016. "Exposure Diversity as a New Cultural Policy Objective in the Digital Age." In *Diversity of Cultural Expressions in the Digital Era*, edited by L. Richieri Hanania and A.-T. Norodom, 209–236. Buenos Aires: Teseo. https://www.teseopress.com/diversityofculturalexpressionsinthedigitalera/

EC (European Commission). 2009. *Commission Staff Working Document on the External Dimension of Audiovisual Policy.* SEC (2009) 1033 Final. 14 July 2009. http://ec.europa.eu/archives/information_society/avpolicy/docs/ext/external_swp.pdf.

EC (European Commission). 2018. "Audiovisual Media Services: Breakthrough in EU Negotiations for Modern and Fairer Rules." *European Commission - Press release*, Brussels. Accessed 26 April 2018. http://europa.eu/rapid/press-release_IP-18-3567_en.htm

EC (European Commission). 2018a. "Overview of FTA and Other Trade Negotiations." Accessed October 2018. http://trade.ec.europa.eu/doclib/docs/2006/december/tradoc_118238.pdf

EC (European Commission). 2018b. "TiSA in a Nutshell." *in Trade in Services Agreement.* http://ec.europa.eu/trade/policy/in-focus/tisa/

EU (European Union). 2002. "Directive 2002/21 on a Common Regulatory Framework for Electronic Communications Networks and Services." *(Framework Directive) [2002] OJ L108/33.* https://eur-lex.europa.eu/legal-content/EN/TXT/PDF/?uri=CELEX:32002L0021&from=en

EU (European Union). 2008. "Economic Partnership Agreement between the CARIFORUM States, of the One Part, and the European Community and Its Member States, on the Other Part Including its Protocol III on Cultural Cooperation [2008] OJ L 289/3-1955." Accessed 30 October 2008. http://ec.europa.eu/world/agreements/downloadFile.do?fullText=yes&treatyTransId=12969

EU (European Union). 2010. "Directive 2010/13/EU of the European Parliament and of the Council of 10 March 2010 on the Coordination of Certain Provisions Laid down by Law, Regulation or Administrative Action in Member States Concerning the Provision of Audio-Visual Media Services (Audio-visual Media Services Directive)." https://eur-lex.europa.eu/legal-content/EN/ALL/?uri=celex%3A32010L0013

EU (European Union). 2011a. "Agreement on Cultural Cooperation between the European Union and Its Member States, of the One Part, and Colombia and Peru, of the Other Part." http://ec.europa.eu/assets/eac/culture/policy/strategic-framework/documents/agreement-cultural-colombia-peru_en.pdf

EU (European Union). 2011b. "Free Trade Agreement between the European Union and Its Member States, of the One Part, and the Republic of Korea, of the Other Part [2011] OJ L 127." Accessed 14 May 2011. http://eur-lex.europa.eu/legal-content/EN/TXT/PDF/?uri=OJ:L:2011:127:FULL&from=EN

EU (European Union). 2012a. "Agreement Establishing an Association between Central America, on the One Hand, and the European Union and Its Member States, on the Other, Including Its Protocol on Cultural Cooperation." *[2012] OJ 15 December 2012*. http://trade.ec.europa.eu/doclib/press/index.cfm?id=689

EU (European Union). 2012b. "Trade Agreement between the European Union and Its Member States, of the One Part, and Colombia and Peru, of the Other Part." http://trade.ec.europa.eu/doclib/press/index.cfm?id=691

EU (European Union). 2015. "Free Trade Agreement between the European Union and the Republic of Singapore." http://trade.ec.europa.eu/doclib/press/index.cfm?id=961

EU (European Union). 2016. "Comprehensive Economic and Trade Agreement between Canada, of the One Part, and the European Union and Its Member States, of the Other Part." http://ec.europa.eu/trade/policy/in-focus/ceta/ceta-chapter-by-chapter/

France. 2009. "For a New European Union External Cultural Strategy - Communication by France." https://www.diplomatie.gouv.fr/IMG/pdf/2009-12-21_Communication_France_Strategie_culturelle_exterieure_ENG.pdf

KEA European Affairs. 2011. "Implementing Cultural Provisions: How Do They Benefit the Caribbean Cultural Sector?" *(ECDPM Discussion Paper 118)*. Maastricht: ECDPM.

Kulesz, O. 2015. "Challenges of the Digital Age." In *Re/Shaping Cultural Policies – A Decade Promoting the Diversity of Cultural Expressions for Development, 2005 Convention Global Report*, edited by UNESCO, 75–87. Paris: UNESCO. http://unesdoc.unesco.org/images/0024/002428/242866e.pdf

Kulesz, O. 2016. "Challenges and Opportunities for Cultural Diversity in the Digital Era (Video)." In *Diversity of Cultural Expressions in the Digital Era*, edited by L. Richieri Hanania and A.-T. Norodom. Buenos Aires: Teseo. https://www.youtube.com/watch?v=0kt87FjSeCA

Marenghi, P., M. Hernández Prieto, and Á. Badillo. 2016. "Diversity of the Audiovisual Industry in the Digital Age: The Challenges Entailed in Its Measurement." In *Diversity of Cultural Expressions in the Digital Era*, edited by L. Richieri Hanania and A.-T. Norodom, 183–207. Buenos Aires: Teseo. https://www.teseopress.com/diversityofculturalexpressionsinthedigitalera/

Morin, E. 2005. *Introduction À La Pensée Complexe*. Paris: Editions du Seuil. Essais. Points.

Neuwirth, R. J. 2016. "The UNESCO Convention and Future Technologies: A Journey to the Centre of Cultural Law and Policymaking." In *Diversity of Cultural Expressions in the Digital Era*, edited by L. Richieri Hanania and A.-T. Norodom, 85–111. Buenos Aires: Teseo. https://www.teseopress.com/diversityofculturalexpressionsinthedigitalera/

Ranaivoson, H. 2016. "The Internet Platforms' Impact on the Diversity of Cultural Expressions: To the Long Tail, and Beyond!" In *Diversity of Cultural Expressions in the Digital Era*, edited by L. Richieri Hanania and A.-T. Norodom, 337–263. Buenos Aires: Teseo. https://www.teseopress.com/diversityofculturalexpressionsinthedigitalera/

Richieri Hanania, L. 2009. *Diversité Culturelle Et Droit International Du Commerce*. Paris: La Documentation française.

Richieri Hanania, L. 2012. "Cultural Diversity and Regional Trade Agreements: The European Union Experience with Cultural Cooperation Frameworks." *Asian Journal of WTO & International Health Law and Policy* 7 (2): 423–456. https://papers.ssrn.com/sol3/papers.cfm?abstract_id=2087639

Richieri Hanania, L., and H. Ruiz Fabri. 2014. "European Media Policy and Cultural Diversity at the International Level: The EU's Role in Fostering the Implementation of the 2005 UNESCO Convention." In *The Palgrave Handbook on European Media Policy*, edited by K. Donders, C. Pauwels, and J. Loisen, 493–508. Basingstoke: Palgrave Macmillan.

Richieri Hanania, L., ed. 2014a. *Cultural Diversity in International Law: The Effectiveness of the UNESCO Convention on the Protection and Promotion of the Diversity of Cultural Expressions*. London/New York: Routledge.

Richieri Hanania, L. 2014b. "General Conclusions and Recommendations." In *Cultural Diversity in International Law: The Effectiveness of the UNESCO Convention on the Protection and Promotion of the Diversity of Cultural Expressions*, edited by L. Richieri Hanania, 297–305. London/New York: Routledge.

Richieri Hanania, L. 2015a. "The UNESCO Convention on the Diversity of Cultural Expressions as a Coordination Framework to Promote Regulatory Coherence in the Creative Economy." *The International Journal of Cultural Policy* 1–20. doi:10.1080/10286632.2015.1025068.

Richieri Hanania, L. 2015b. "Le Débat Commerce-Culture À L'ère Numérique: Quelle Application Pour La Convention De l'UNESCO Sur La Diversité Des Expressions Culturelles Au Sein De L'économie Créative?" http://papers.ssrn.com/sol3/papers.cfm?abstract_id=2600647

Richieri Hanania, L., and A.-T. Norodom. 2016. "Introduction - Diversity of Cultural Expressions in the Digital Era." In *Diversity of Cultural Expressions in the Digital Era*, edited by L. Richieri Hanania and A.-T. Norodom, 17–30. Buenos Aires: Teseo. https://www.teseopress.com/diversityofculturalexpressionsinthedigitalera/

Richieri Hanania, L. 2017. "L'action Culturelle Dans La Politique Commerciale Extérieure De l'UE: Assurer La Spécificité Des Biens Et Services Culturels À L'ère Du Numérique." *Politique Européenne*: 124–145 Special Issue 56. doi:10.3917/poeu.056.0124.

Richieri Hanania, L. 2019. "European Union Trade Agreements and Cultural Exception in the Digital Age." In *Audio Visual Industries and Diversity: Economics and Policies in the Digital Era*, edited by L. A. Albornoz and M. T. García Lelva, 136-151. London: Routledge.

Souyri-Desrosier, C. 2014. "EU Protocols on Cultural Cooperation. An Attempt to Promote and Implement the CDCE within the Framework of Bilateral Trade Negotiations." In *Cultural Diversity in International Law: The Effectiveness of the UNESCO Convention on the Protection and Promotion of the Diversity of Cultural Expressions*, edited by L. Richieri Hanania, 209–224. London/New York: Routledge.

TEC (Transatlantic Economic Council). 2011. "European Union-United States Trade Principles for Information and Communication Technology Services." Accessed 4 April 2011. http://trade.ec.europa.eu/doclib/docs/2011/april/tradoc_147780.pdf

USTR (United States Trade Representative). 2003. "US-Chile Free Trade Agreement." *(FTA)*. https://ustr.gov/trade-agreements/free-trade-agreements/chile-fta/final-text

USTR (United States Trade Representative). 2004 "Dominican Republic-Central America FTA (CAFTA-DR)." https://ustr.gov/trade-agreements/free-trade-agreements/cafta-dr-dominican-republic-central-america-fta/final-text

Vlassis, A., and L. Richieri Hanania. 2014. "Effects of the CDCE on Trade Negotiations." In *Cultural Diversity in International Law: The Effectiveness of the UNESCO Convention on the Protection and Promotion of the Diversity of Cultural Expressions*, edited by L. Richieri Hanania, 25–39. London/New York: Routledge.

WTO (World Trade Organization). 1991. "Services Sectoral Classification List." *MTN.GNS/W/120*. Accessed 10 July 1991. https://www.wto.org/english/tratop_e/serv_e/serv_sectors_e.htm

WTO (World Trade Organization). 1994a. *European Communities and Their Member States – Final List of Article II (MFN) Exemptions*. General Agreement on Trade in Services, GATS/EL/31. 15 April 1994. doi:10.3168/jds.S0022-0302(94)77044-2.

WTO (World Trade Organization). 1994b. *European Communities and Their Member States – Schedule of Specific Commitments*. General Agreement on Trade in Services, GATS/SC/31. 15 April 1994. doi:10.3168/jds.S0022-0302(94)77044-2.

# South Africa's trade in cultural goods and services with a focus on cultural trade with BRICS partners

Nicolette Cattaneo and Jen Snowball

**ABSTRACT**
As the potential for cultural and creative industries to drive growth and job creation is increasingly recognised, developing countries like South Africa are examining their cultural goods and services trade in a new light. This article investigates the pattern of South Africa's cultural trade, with a focus on the strategically important BRICS trading bloc. Results show that, like many small, open developing countries, South Africa has a significant cultural goods trade imbalance, especially with China and India. While cultural trade policy is still somewhat fragmented, there are indications that where policies have been put in place, such as in the crafts and audio-visual sectors, progress in reducing significant deficits has been made. At the same time, the pattern of CCI trade preferences currently favours SADC, the EU and EFTA over BRICS partners. Finally, South Africa performs well in a number of services sectors for which cultural trade is important.

## 1. Introduction

South Africa's re-integration into the global economy following the 1994 democratic transition was accompanied by a rapid opening up to international trade both unilaterally and as part of the country's obligations under the Uruguay Round of trade negotiations (Bell 1997). Supply-side incentives accompanied trade liberalisation with a view to improving the competitiveness of South African industries. International trade was seen as an important potential driver of development and job creation for the post-apartheid economy. A more comprehensive trade and industrial policy emerged in the late 2000s, following the difficulties of industrial restructuring in a context of rapid liberalisation. A central tenet of the new policy trajectory was to orientate trade and industrial policy to encourage the development of sectors with the potential to stimulate higher value added growth and employment. These included the cultural and creative industries (CCIs) (the dti (Department of Trade and Industry) 2010b).

South Africa's Trade Policy and Strategy Framework has, since 2010, emphasised trade policy as a tool of industrial policy, within the confines of the country's WTO and other international obligations (the dti (Department of Trade and Industry) 2010a, the dti (Department of Trade and Industry) 2012). South Africa is part of the Southern African Customs Union (SACU)[1] and effectively administers the common external tariff. It has comprehensive trade agreements with the EU and EFTA, and the country is a member of the Southern African Development Community (SADC)[2] free

This article is based on a report (Cattaneo and Snowball 2018) prepared for the South African Department of Arts and Culture under the South African Cultural Observatory.

trade area. A limited preferential trade agreement exists between SACU and MERCOSUR. South Africa recently signed the African Continental Free Trade Area (AfCFTA) Agreement which is an African Union (AU) initiative to create a continental market of 55 countries and over 1.2 billion people. South Africa is also a member of the BRICS grouping which is of strategic geo-political and economic importance to the country and includes two of its largest trading partners, China and India. While there is no formal trade agreement between the BRICS countries, South Africa and Brazil are members of the SACU-MERCOSUR agreement.[3]

There is no specific trade policy for the CCIs set out in South Africa's Trade Policy and Strategy Framework documents (the dti (Department of Trade and Industry) 2010a, the dti (Department of Trade and Industry) 2012). While a number of cultural product categories are fully liberalised, more sensitive product categories continue to attract tariffs on an MFN basis. South Africa's CCI trade is also affected by the differential preferences granted under its various trade agreements and it is interesting to consider the implications of these differences for the direction of its CCI trade. South Africa is also a signatory to the UNESCO (2005) Convention on the Protection and Promotion of the Diversity of Cultural Expressions and the SADC Protocol on Culture, Information and Sport, both of which emphasise the need for the protection and promotion of cultural diversity. It is therefore important to consider the tensions that may arise between the liberalisation provisions of trade agreements and the need to protect cultural expressions in developing countries like South Africa.

According to Hadisi and Snowball (2017), cultural occupations in South Africa account for about 3% of total employment in the country. This translated into a larger number of jobs than the mining sector in 2014. The first Industrial Policy Action Plan (IPAP) following the release of the 2007 National Industrial Policy Framework (NIPF) explains the prioritisation of cultural industries in terms of their 'potential contribution to nation-building and South Africa's international image and because they can support employment creation in tourism as well as in production of cultural goods and services' (the dti (Department of Trade and Industry) 2007, 29). This perspective informs the development of key action programmes for the film and television and crafts sectors, as well as other cultural industries, in subsequent iterations of the IPAP.

Against this background, this article explores the growth and structure of South Africa's cultural and creative industries trade, with a focus on the country's trade with its BRICS partners. The paper uses the trade classification system set out in the UNESCO (2009) Framework for Cultural Statistics (FCS). More particularly, the study uses UN Comtrade data at the 6-digit level of the 2007 Harmonised System (HS) for the goods trade analysis. This allows for a direct mapping to the HS codes used to define cultural goods trade in the UNESCO (2009) FCS. It also allows for an investigation of intra-industry trade by domain. Increased intra-industry specialisation within particular sectors or domains can better harness the potential benefits of trade expansion and promote more balanced value added trade. Tariff differentials between South Africa's main trade agreements can also be examined at the 6-digit HS level.

While the focus of the paper is on South Africa's cultural goods trade, it is important to recognise the role and significance of trade in cultural services. As noted in UNESCO 2016, 12), there has been significant 'dematerialisation' of certain categories of cultural goods as a result of digitisation, with noteworthy impacts on sectors such as music, film and books.

The remainder of the article is structured as follows. Section 2 highlights some of the theoretical debates related to the promotion of international trade in cultural products, while Section 3 considers previous research related to South Africa's CCI trade. Section 4 discusses trade and industrial policy for the CCIs in South Africa. Section 5 explains the issues involved in defining and measuring cultural trade and the data and methods used in the paper. Section 6 discusses the results of the analysis on South Africa's CCI trade, with a focus on trade with BRICS partners. This includes an examination of differential tariff preferences affecting CCI product categories under the country's main trade agreements and South Africa's GATS commitments in sub-sectors relevant for cultural services trade. Section 7 concludes.

## 2. The theory and debates in international cultural trade

According to UNESCO (2013), the creative economy is now one of the most rapidly growing sectors of the world economy. World trade of creative goods and services more than doubled between 2002 and 2011 with an overall average annual growth rate of 8.8%. The developing country share of this trade has grown steadily, with export growth rates between 2002–11 averaging 12.1% annually (UNESCO 2013). A more recent UNESCO report (2016) shows that the world flow of cultural trade doubled between 2003 and 2014, despite the 2008/9 financial crisis.

Many authors have noted the tension between trade liberalisation and the desire to develop and protect culture, heritage and identity through managed trade. This is especially the case in post-colonial developing countries (Mulcahy 2017) like South Africa. The question arises as to what extent cultural and creative industry (CCI) trade should be protected and subsidised, as expressed in many cultural policy documents. There are also questions about whether some cultural sectors are more important for trade than others, and the impact of the online environment and digital distribution.

Early discussions on trade and culture in the context of international trade negotiations leading up to the 1947 General Agreement on Tariffs and Trade (GATT) noted that 'cultural specificity' meant that some cultural goods did not have much demand outside of their domestic market, often because of language differences. However, it was soon determined that some products, especially in the audio-visual sectors, were highly tradeable, and the danger of US dominance was noted. An early study by Marvasti (1994) showed that, particularly for books and films, trade flowed from rich to poor countries. There was also evidence of the dominance of English-speaking countries in these sectors, and that the size of the domestic market mattered. Ultimately, in the case of cinematographic film, 'screen quotas' were included in the 1947 GATT (Marvasti 1994). According to Neuwirth (2002), Article IV of the GATT, which allows screen-time quotas for films, was 'designed to recognise the importance of the media for the Contracting Parties' sovereignty, cultural cohesion and identity, as well as their economic force in the stimulation of domestic production'.

Mas-Colell (1999) contrasts the arguments in favour of free trade with those of protection for cultural goods and services. On the free trade side, each country would specialise in producing those cultural goods and services in which they have a comparative advantage, and trade these for other products. However, a counter argument is that comparative advantage is a dynamic rather than static phenomenon, and needs to be nurtured and created through learning by doing. This may require some initial protection, together with performance requirements (often referred to as reciprocal control mechanisms) to ensure that the recipients of incentives and subsidies improve their competitiveness or forgo the protection (Amsden 2005). This infant industry argument applies to both cultural and non-cultural production (Marvasti 1994). Learning by doing can also facilitate the exploitation of both economies of scale and scope in particular industries, resulting in benefits to consumers in the form of lower prices and wider choice.

However, there are also arguments relating to what is often referred to as the 'cultural exception', that is, that cultural goods and services are different from other goods and services in that they have some public good value related to the protection and promotion of national cultural heritage and identity (Mas-Colell 1999). If consumer demand for national cultural products is weak, there may be arguments for stimulating this demand. Mas-Colell (1999, 89) explains that 'there might well be public good and network externalities, issues that might create a failure in the transmission to the market of a demand that really exists'.

Footer and Graber (2000) note that few countries ever committed to the full market access aimed for under WTO agreements, with many reserving the right to cultural promotion through subsidies, domestic content quotas, licensing restriction and taxes on foreign productions. Neuwirth (2002) explains that in the Uruguay Round of trade negotiations leading up to the formation of the WTO, discussions on how to treat audiovisual media, for example, were so controversial that it was decided to leave the issue to future negotiating rounds.

Another source of conflict is the differing levels of intellectual property (IP) protection through systems like copyright, royalty fee payments and performers rights. On the one hand, the 'idea' is a public good, while the 'expression' can be copyrighted.

> "It is due to this public/private dichotomy to which cultural works give rise that they may be equated both with the notion of the public good and with the intensification of cultural commodification and hence, the market retains an ambivalent position with respect to these public/private spheres" (Footer and Graber 2000, 127).

Mas-Colell (1999) also points out that some countries restrict the export of unique cultural goods or artefacts, on the grounds that they are part of the cultural capital of that particular country. This is also related to the ideas around the status of copies and mass-produced cultural goods and what is sometimes seen as the 'commodification' of culture.

Shin (2015) argues that trade in cultural goods and services can also have implications for cultural diversity. While economists have tended to focus on the variety of choice as a measure of cultural diversity, scholars from the humanities have also included 'fair' distribution or representation of different cultures in cultural diversity measures. For example, cultural diversity should not only include the number of films available to South African consumers to choose from, but also the presence of diverse, local South African films in, for example, different indigenous languages. If one accepts this latter description of cultural diversity, Shin (2015) argues that protection of local cultural production could be justified in terms of its impact on current and future cultural diversity.

Shin (2015) also finds evidence of a 'hub effect', namely that cultural hubs produce cultural goods that are more attractive to their trading partners than the products of the trading partner are to the hub country. In this case, the hub country becomes the dominant trading partner (a net exporter). On the other hand, evidence that trade in cultural goods and services is increasing worldwide provides an opportunity for growth and job creation in the CCIs. A study conducted by Disdier et al. (2010), found that countries are more likely to trade in cultural goods if they share a common language, have past colonial links, and have similar 'cultural tastes'. In addition, they found that 'cultural trade has a facilitating impact on non-cultural trade', which suggests that bilateral cultural goods trade and non-cultural goods trade move together, although causality was not proven (Disdier et al. 2010, 592).

## 3. South Africa's cultural trade: previous research

A 2013 research report on CCI trade between South Africa and the EU (EU-SA Trade Report 2013) uses the UNCTAD definition of CCI trade and UNCTADstat trade statistics to investigate total South African CCI exports and imports between 2002 and 2010, as well as specific trade patterns with the EU, one of South Africa's main trading partners. The UNCTADstat database (UNCTAD 2017) distinguishes seven main groupings for cultural goods trade that differ slightly from the six UNESCO (2009) cultural domains.

Findings suggest that South Africa's total CCI goods exports rose slightly from R2.42bn in 2002 to R3.12bn in 2010 in nominal terms – a compound annual growth rate of 0.65% per year. However, during this same period, imports grew at 15.62% per annum in nominal terms (from R4.13bn to R15.26bn). CCI goods exports made up just 0.005% of total South African exports in 2010, while CCI imports made up 0.021% of total South African imports in the same year (EU-SA Trade Report 2013). South Africa's CCI trade imbalance with the rest of the world widened considerably between 2002 and 2007, then narrowed marginally in 2008–2009, before widening again in 2010.

The 2013 EU-SA report finds that significant changes in the direction of South Africa's CCI trade took place between 2002 and 2010. The data suggest that South African CCI goods exports to the EU and North America fell in this period, but rose 'significantly' to other African countries. However, imports from the EU increased, while imports from Africa and South America remained 'negligible'. In both 2002 and 2010, South Africa's largest source of CCI imports was China. By 2010, CCI imports from China had increased from just over US$100m to US$700m in nominal terms, while imports from the UK (the next most important source) also increased, but by a far smaller amount (EU-SA Trade Report 2013). The report notes that this is likely to be a result of the financial crisis, which reduced trade with developed countries more significantly than with some emerging markets. The increase in CCI trade with China also reflects the rapid growth in the importance of China as a trading partner for South Africa more generally.

The report (EU-SA Trade Report 2013, 38) explains that services trade data is generally more limited than data on goods trade. However, it identifies a number of broad services categories (specified by UNCTAD) as relevant for CCI services trade, based on the Extended Balance of Payments Services (EBOPS) classification system.[4] These include: Computer and information services; Royalties and license fees; Business and professional services (which includes architectural consultancy), and Personal, cultural and recreational services. Findings indicate that, although South Africa still has a negative trade balance with the EU in CCI services trade, exports to the EU increased at a compound annual growth rate of 11.61%, significantly faster than goods exports. However, in the important category of intellectual property (captured in Royalties and license fees), there was a substantial trade deficit with the EU (EU-SA Trade Report 2013, 44).

A 2014 mapping study commissioned by the South African Department of Arts and Culture (DAC), based on data collected from a random sample of about 2500 CCI firms, along with a database of CCI firms in the country, used a partial equilibrium economic impact model to estimate the direct, indirect and induced impact of the CCIs (defined using the UNESCO FCS) on the South African economy. Results suggested that the CCIs accounted for 2.9% of GDP and 1.08% to 1.28% of employment in South Africa. Cultural exports and spending by foreign cultural tourists contributed R35.57bn to the balance of payments account. Interview data indicated that only 17.6% of CCIs interviewed reported selling their goods or services to international markets. Of those CCI organisations which did sell their products internationally, international markets accounted for 23.7% of their sales. SADC and the EU were most frequently reported as the international markets for organisations, but small sample sizes prevented more detailed analysis (DAC 2014).

A 2016 UNESCO report on world cultural trade flows between 2004 and 2013 shows some interesting changes in world cultural trade patterns. Using the UNESCO FCS (UNESCO 2009) to define cultural goods and services trade, the report indicates that cultural trade is largely dominated by developed countries, with North America and Europe accounting for 49% of world cultural exports, and 61.7% of world cultural imports. Sub-Saharan Africa exported only 0.3% of world cultural goods and services, and imported 0.9% (UNESCO 2016).

However, upper middle income countries (including South Africa) more than doubled their share of cultural exports between 2004 and 2013. Most of this growth results from the phenomenal increase in cultural goods exports from China, which began in 2009. Within a year, China was the largest exporter of cultural goods in the world (having overtaken the USA). By 2013, China exported ten times more cultural goods than it imported. India also experienced rapid growth in cultural exports and had a positive cultural trade balance by 2013. The report found that Zambia and South Africa were amongst the top 20 exporters in the 'Cultural and Natural Heritage' Domain, with 0.5% and 0.4% of the world export share, respectively. The value of South Africa's exports in Domain A doubled between 2004 and 2013 (UNESCO 2016, 42).

CCI trade depends heavily on economic conditions, especially in developed countries. UNESCO (2016) suggests that the financial crisis decreased world cultural exports by 13.5% and cultural imports by 22% in the 2008/9 period. However, it is also noted that exports of all goods fell by 22.4%, and imports fell by 23% in 2008/9, perhaps suggesting that cultural trade is not as volatile as trade overall. This interesting question is examined further later in this paper. UNESCO (2016) reports, however, that despite a quick recovery cultural trade growth rates were significantly lower by 2013 than before the financial crisis.

## 4. Trade and industrial policy for the CCIs in South Africa

Tsegaye (2016) points out that the CCI discourse has a relatively long history in African policy-making, going back to the 1980 Lagos Plan of Action. In the more recent 2008 Nairobi Plan of Action on Cultural and Creative Industries in Africa (AU 2008), as in previous plans, globalisation and international trade are seen as both an opportunity to develop cultural industries, and a threat to cultural diversity and cultural capital. Proposals include expanding intra-AU trade in cultural products through, for example, reducing or removing taxes on 'works of culture', payments made in national currencies, and specific trade agreements to facilitate global market access. At the same time, it is acknowledged that support for the enforcement of copyright is central to the improvement of the livelihoods of cultural producers and the further development of the sector.

At the regional level, South Africa as a member of SADC is bound by a number of protocols that are relevant for CCI trade, including the SADC Protocol on Culture, Information and Sport (2001), the SADC Trade Protocol (SADC 1996), and the more recent SADC Trade in Services Protocol (2012). The Protocol on Culture, Information and Sport calls for the development of the CCIs in the SADC region while encouraging measures necessary to 'nurture, protect and promote' infant industries (SADC 2001). Under the SADC Trade Protocol, South Africa's imports from the region are already tariff-free. However, the Trade Protocol also provides for infant industry protection, as well as measures 'for the protection of national treasures of artistic, historic or archaeological value' (SADC 1996). The SADC Trade in Services Protocol signals the intent to liberalise six key services sectors in the first phase of negotiations (SADC 2012). These include two sectors which are particularly important for the CCIs, namely communications and tourism services. The SADC Protocol on Culture, Information and Sport and the SADC Protocol on Trade both emphasise the importance of harmonising legislation on copyright protection in SADC and encourage accession to the relevant international conventions. The former also calls for measures to ensure the protection of intellectual property more broadly in the region (SADC 2001).

The first post-Apartheid policy on the cultural sector in South Africa was the White Paper on Arts, Culture and Heritage (DACST 1996). Coming out of a period where only the English and Afrikaans culture of the white population had been supported by the state, the focus of the 1996 White Paper was primarily on broadening the definition of culture to support and fund black African cultural forms and practitioners, and to provide access to arts and culture for the majority of the black population which had been excluded. While the economic potential of the cultural sector was acknowledged in passing, arts, culture and heritage were seen primarily as a way to reclaim African identity and to build social cohesion. The role of government was seen as providing supportive sponsorship, rather than directed investment, and funding was made available at 'arm's length' via panels of experts through new institutions like the National Arts Council (DACST 1996). In this, South Africa followed the UK model of direct arts funding from the public sector, rather than the US model of providing incentives for private sector funding via tax rebates (Mulcahy 2017).

In 2013, the DAC released a new White Paper that had a radically different approach (DAC 2013). It focused almost entirely on the 'cultural and creative industries', rather than on any other cultural values, and described the 1996 White Paper as 'outdated'. In the era of budget cuts following the global financial crisis of 2008/9, and given growing unemployment and inequality in South Africa, the DAC changed emphasis to the potential of the sector to generate jobs and income. There was a shift from seeing public sector support as subsidies primarily to non-profit organisations producing social and cultural value, to seeing it as investment in a sector that would generate economic returns. Rather than continuing with the 'arm's length' funding, direct funding from the DAC itself was proposed.

However, the 2013 version of the White Paper was poorly received by cultural practitioners and civil society. The sudden and dramatic change in focus towards the cultural and creative industries was seen as politically opportunistic and exclusionary. The DAC was criticized for a lack of consultation and for ignoring the valuable work of non-profit organisations, such as museums and archives. One commentator observed: 'Instead of asking how government can best create the conditions and structures for the citizens to engage with arts, culture and heritage in a way that gives life to the values and principles of our Constitution, it asks how government can use arts, culture and heritage to drive its own agenda' (Archival Platform 2013). In addition, one of the DAC's mandates is to report on Outcome 14 of the National Development Plan that relates to nation building and social cohesion, an aspect that the 2013 White Paper downplayed dramatically. The 2013 version of the White Paper was ultimately withdrawn in the face of strong criticism.

A new version of the White Paper was released in 2016 and has since been through a number of iterations. It attempts to balance the view of the arts, culture and heritage sector as providing public goods with social and cultural value with the role of the CCIs in creating jobs and growth. The Revised White Paper (DAC 2017) seems likely to be adopted by Parliament, but given the shrinking budget of the DAC, a focus on funding and support for the creative industries necessarily implies less funding for the non-profit arts.[5] There has thus been quite significant disagreement on the role of the cultural sector and how it should be viewed and funded by government. This is evident to a lesser degree in the trade policy space, where cultural goods trade is recognized for its potential to generate income, but where the need to protect cultural products (especially in the case of unique cultural artifacts) is also emphasised.

In terms of CCI trade policy in South Africa, the third draft of the country's revised White Paper on Arts, Culture and Heritage (DAC 2017) recognises barriers to trade (particularly market access for small, medium and micro CCIs) as a factor constraining the growth and transformation of the sector. With respect to proposals for the funding and financing of the CCIs, the draft White Paper (DAC 2017, 75) particularly mentions the establishment of a 'regional fund … to invest in cultural and creative industries that are, or are wanting to, trade in the African region'. The draft White Paper also emphasises the importance of inter-departmental co-operation in financing and managing the CCIs, with the Department of Trade and Industry referred to as one of the 'key' ministries for taking the sector forward. There is also a proposal to treat CCI trade differently from other goods and services trade to enable 'the movement of cultural products, publications of cultural works' and 'the partial or total removal of taxes on works of culture and payment in national currencies for the trade in cultural goods' (DAC 2017, 82). South Africa's import tariffs on CCI product categories are considered further in Section 6 below.

South Africa's trade strategy since the late 2000s has reflected an orientation towards the country's BRICS partners and the African market while maintaining relations with traditional trading partners (the dti (Department of Trade and Industry) 2012). While the country's most recent trade policy framework documents do not explicitly discuss a trade strategy for the CCIs, current trade policy is seen as a tool of industrial policy, and South Africa's CCIs were prioritised in the country's rolling Industrial Policy Action Plans (IPAPs) between 2007 and 2014. The early IPAPs focused on key action programmes for the Film and Television and Crafts sectors. The 2010 IPAP explains the designation of Film and Television as a strategic sector with reference to its employment, investment and export generating potential, as well as prospects for beneficial spillover effects into the domestic economy (the dti (Department of Trade and Industry) 2010b, 77). The sector's importance in generating synergies with the tourism sector, in education, and in protecting and sustaining cultural heritage are noted as important considerations. In subsequent IPAPs, the need for a music industry strategy has also been emphasised.

The Film and Television Production and Co-production Incentive Programme subsidises local, co-produced and international film and television production. To qualify for the Programme, the content of the film or television production is largely irrelevant, although some categories (such as game shows and documentaries) are excluded (Collins and Snowball 2015). The Film and Television Incentive initially contained two categories: a foreign film and television production and post production incentive and a South African production and co-production incentive (the dti (Department of Trade and Industry, South Africa) 2015, 52). In 2014, the Emerging Black Filmmakers' Incentive was instituted as a third sub-programme of the Film and Television Production Incentive Scheme (the dti (Department of Trade and Industry) 2014). The objective is to support black filmmakers to develop the capabilities necessary to undertake large scale productions that will generate employment. The incentive takes the form of a 50% rebate on the first R6 million of qualifying expenditure and 25% on remaining qualifying costs.

The Crafts sector was identified as a strategic IPAP sector due to its importance for economic growth and the rural economy, and for providing a link between formal and informal sector activity, as well as creative design for other sectors. The 2010 IPAP notes the sector's ability to 'contribute to nation building ... through the expression of creativity and exploration of culture and heritage' (the dti (Department of Trade and Industry) 2010b, 75). The sector is seen as important for broad-based black economic empowerment and the development of small businesses. The IPAP highlights the export market as a key opportunity for South Africa's Crafts sector, together with the tourism market. Policies to promote the commercial development of the sector for the local market and export include the establishment of Craft hubs and the development of synergies with the Tourism sector. More recent IPAPs (2015–2017) have continued to focus on the Film and Television sector, although the Creative Industries Unit at the dti has moved to the Department of Small Business Development since that Ministry's creation in 2014.

Despite the controversy surrounding the earlier version of the DAC's White Paper with respect to the balance between cultural values and the economic potential of the CCIs, it seems that in the trade and industrial policy space there is a broader perspective in the Department of Trade and Industry policy documents that emphasises both the CCIs employment, export and income earning potential as well as their contribution to nation-building, social cohesion and the protection of cultural heritage.

## 5. Defining and measuring cultural trade in goods and services

South Africa does not currently have an official framework for cultural statistics that defines what is included in the CCIs. However, some discussion documents are available on developing such a framework (Snowball 2016). South African policy documents refer to the CCIs based on the UNESCO (2009) FCS. Although the UNESCO (2009) FCS is not the only possible framework (see Throsby 2008), it incorporates many of the features of other models and attempts to provide a useful template that can be adapted to the needs of individual countries. Most importantly, it can use existing data to measure the CCIs.

The UNESCO Framework provides a breakdown of the CCIs into a set of sub-sectors, or cultural domains, and links these to data sets and classifications available in many countries. The six domains that the UNESCO FCS identifies are as follows: Cultural and Natural Heritage, Performance and Celebration, Visual Arts and Crafts, Books and Press, Audio-visual and Interactive Media and, finally, Design and Creative Services. The domains include all the cultural activities, goods and services that are involved in the phases of the culture cycle model (creation; production; dissemination, exhibition/reception/transmission; and consumption/participation) and are mutually exclusive.

The UNESCO (2009) FCS provides guidance on how existing trade data can be used to identify cultural trade in both goods and services. For goods trade, the FCS specifies which categories of the 2007 Harmonised Commodity Description and Coding System (HS) and the Standard International Trade Classification Revision 4 (SITC4) can be used to measure cultural goods trade. Of the two classification systems, the 2007 HS provides greater detail, with 85 six-digit HS codes identified as relevant for cultural goods trade across the six domains. More specifically, the UNESCO FCS defines the HS six-digit codes that are included in each of the six cultural domains. Data for South Africa's total and bilateral trade is readily available from a number of sources at the HS six-digit level. For this reason the more detailed HS classification system is used in this article. In particular, UN Comtrade data organised according to the 2007 version of the HS is used to allow for a direct alignment with the 2009 UNESCO FCS.

It is important to understand that the aspect of cultural trade captured using the HS codes is somewhat limited. As noted in UNESCO (2009, 37), the HS 'classifies goods by their observable physical characteristics and not according to the status of national content, cultural value or other similar criteria'. Furthermore, for categories such as film, customs data may simply capture the import or export of the master copy, while copyright charges are recorded in services trade data (UNESCO 2009, 38). In addition, as noted in the introduction, the impact of digitisation is significant in sectors such as music, film and books, increasing the importance of taking account of cultural services trade.

Trade in cultural services can be measured using the EBOPS Classification System, based on the sixth edition of the Balance of Payments and International Investment Position Manual (BPM). The services trade data that is recorded via the balance of payments is primarily cross-border supply of services (known as Mode 1 supply of services under the WTO). Under this mode of supply, the service provided 'moves across' the border while the consumer and service supplier remain in their own countries. UNESCO (2009) explains that isolating cultural services trade categories precisely in the EBOPS classification system is not straightforward, but that the categories indicated provide an important guide to measuring cultural services trade. The difficulty is that for many developing countries services trade data is not presently available at the required level of disaggregation to identify the country's cultural services trade.

This article uses statistical and graphical analysis to explore the growth and structure of South Africa's CCI trade from 2007 to 2016, with a focus on the country's trade with its BRICS partners. The study computes the shares and growth rates of South Africa's cultural goods trade relative to total trade to explore the extent to which cultural goods trade moves together with total trade. The relative value of trade by domain in the aggregate and with each of the country's BRICS partners is calculated. This facilitates a discussion of the domains and sectors that drive the trade balance with each partner which in turn has implications for policy and future research at the sector level.

Grubel-Lloyd indices of intra-industry trade are computed to explore the extent of two-way trade within particular domains and sectors for the most recent period.[6] International trade is *inter-industry* in nature when it takes place between two different sectors and *intra-industry* when it occurs within a sector. The expansion of trade that is intra-industry in nature (that is, two-way trade within a sector) is associated with higher value added manufacturing trade and lower adjustment costs for industries and workers (Cattaneo and Fryer 2002).[7]

The goods trade analysis concludes by considering differences in the scheduled tariffs on CCI imports across South Africa's main trade agreements. Existing tariff preferences have implications for the growth of CCI trade with different partners, particularly the BRICS countries.

South African services trade data is not presently available at the required level of disaggregation to identify cultural services trade at the EBOPS sub-sector level. However, an indication of South Africa's cultural services trade is provided by looking at the more disaggregated services trade data that became available since 2014 following the Reserve Bank's move from BPM5 to BPM6. In addition, information from the ITC services database is used where applicable, as the ITC provides a breakdown of South Africa's services trade into eighteen BPM6 categories, some of which are relevant for cultural services trade at a broad level. UNCTADstat provides only six sub-groupings in its creative services database, with data only up to 2012, while the World Bank Trade in Services Database only has data until 2010. Bilateral services trade data between South Africa and its BRICS partners is not currently available for the CCIs, although some indication is given in the paper of key relevant services sectors traded bilaterally within BRICS, based on a recent ITC report on the BRICS services sectors (ITC 2017).

## 6. Results and discussion

### *6.1. South Africa's total cultural goods trade*

In 2016, South Africa's cultural goods exports as a share of total commodity exports stood at 0.46%, while cultural goods imports as a share of total commodity imports were 0.66% (UN Comtrade 2017). Figure 1 depicts annual growth rates of South Africa's cultural goods exports and imports in

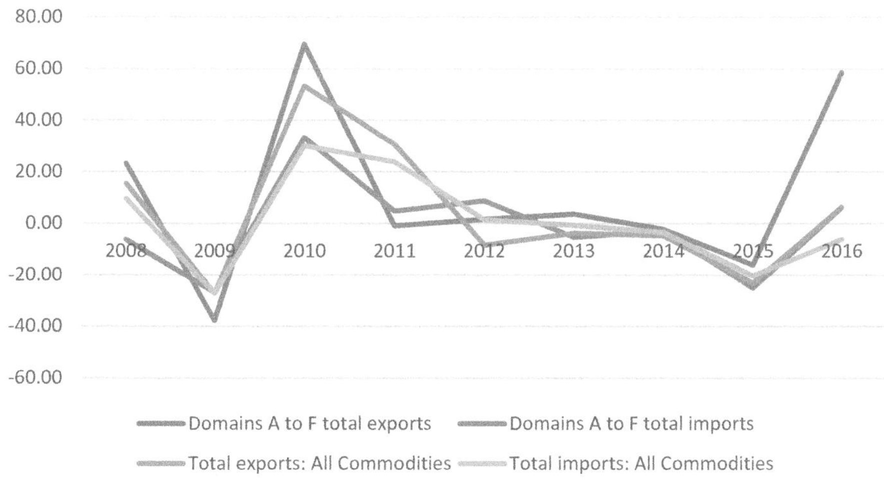


**Figure 1.** Annual growth rates of South Africa's total cultural goods trade relative to total trade (Source: Authors' computations from UN Comtrade 2017).

nominal terms for the period 2008 to 2016. Annual growth rates of total exports and imports for all commodities are included for comparative purposes. Cultural goods export growth reflects a sharp recovery following the global financial crisis but collapses again in 2011 remaining low but stable until 2014 before falling quite sharply again in 2015. A similar pattern is seen with respect to the growth rates of cultural goods imports. It is interesting to note that import growth is more muted in the recoveries than export growth, however the latter takes place off a significantly lower base (see Figure 1).

Focusing on the most recent period, it is evident that there was a significant slowdown in South Africa's total cultural goods trade in 2015. Hadisi and Snowball (2017) find a similar phenomenon in the cultural occupations employment data. In the economy more broadly, GDP growth slowed to 1.3% in 2015 from 1.5% in 2014 following a modest post-crisis recovery during the commodity boom. According to SARB (2015), this was the slowest GDP growth in the past 17 years, except for 2009 (during the financial crisis).

The 2014–2015 trend in CCI trade is therefore unsurprising, particularly since the CCIs are known to be quite volatile and sensitive to economic growth (Grodach and Seman 2013). Interestingly export and import growth for all commodities tracks cultural trade growth fairly closely, as Figure 1 indicates. While total trade growth did not fall as sharply in 2011 as cultural trade growth, it is evident that, for the period since 2012, cultural good export growth has performed better than total export growth, especially in the 2016 recovery period. This is reflected in Figure 2, which depicts the shares of South Africa's cultural trade in the country's total commodity trade for both exports and imports. The rising share of cultural exports in total exports since 2012 (reflecting the faster growth of the former) is clearly evident. Figure 2 also shows that cultural imports are a greater share of total commodity imports throughout the period under study compared to cultural exports as a share of total commodity exports. However, this gap in the export and import shares is narrowing, with cultural imports as a share of total imports at 0.66% in 2016 and cultural exports as a share of total exports rising to 0.46% that year.

Figure 3 shows South Africa's total cultural goods exports and imports in nominal US$ values from 2007 to 2016. The extent of the trade imbalance is stark, but it is also evident that the trade imbalance has fallen in a number of periods, most markedly since 2014. Cultural goods imports show greater downward sensitivity in bad times, while cultural goods exports appear to have been more resilient during the downturns, particularly during the contraction associated with the global financial crisis and during the 2015 downturn. It is not unusual for cultural trade to reflect a significant negative trade balance in the case of small, open developing economies such as South Africa.

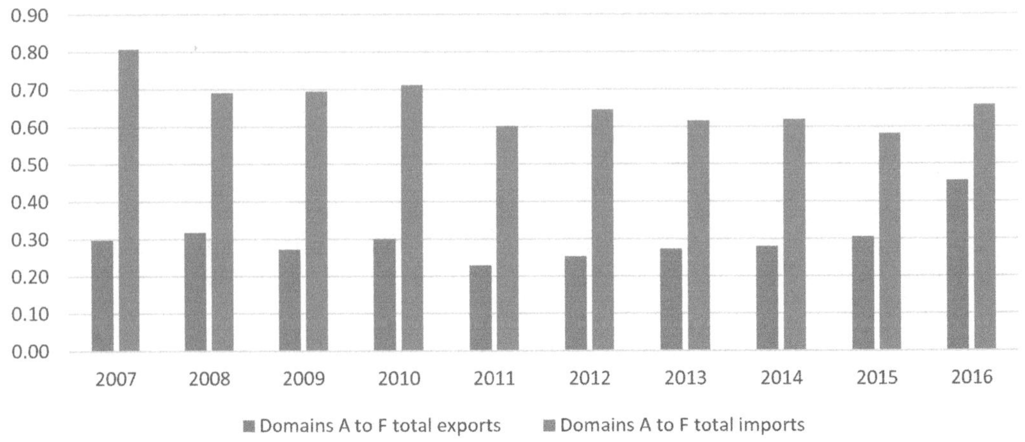


**Figure 2.** South Africa: shares of cultural trade in total commodity trade (Source: Authors' computations from UN Comtrade 2017).

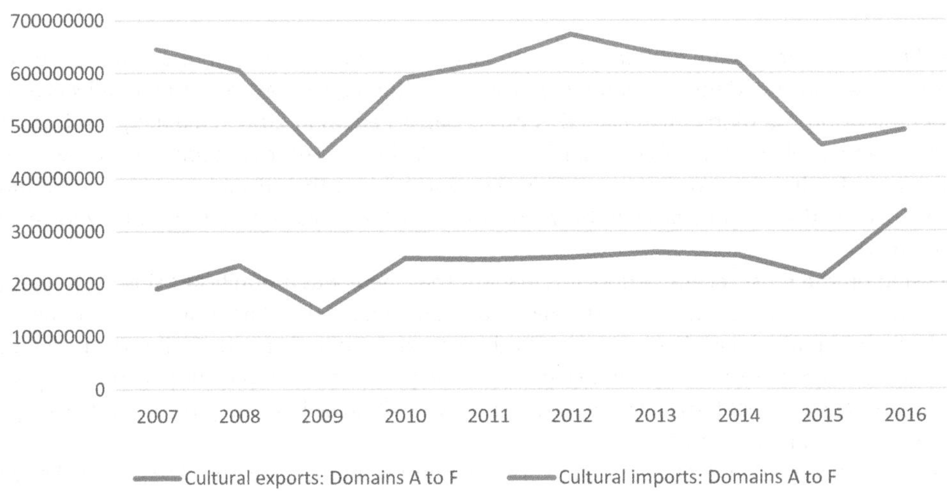


**Figure 3.** South Africa's total cultural trade: all domains (Source: Authors' computations based on data from UN Comtrade 2017).

The interesting question to examine is which domains are driving the level of the trade balance as well as trends in the trade balance over the period under discussion. On the export side, there has been rapid growth of the Visual Arts and Crafts domain and a small but positive upward trend in Performance and Celebration. Books and Press, together with Cultural and Natural Heritage exports, appear to be more volatile, while Audio-visual and interactive media exports are very low.

The importance of the Visual Arts and Crafts domain in South Africa's total cultural goods exports can be linked back to the Craft sector's designation as a priority sector in the various Industrial Policy Action Plans (see Section 4). The sector was noted to be particularly important for employment, economic growth and the rural economy, broad-based black economic empowerment and the development of small businesses. The export market was highlighted as a key opportunity for South Africa's Crafts sector. The film and television sector, as part of the Audio-visual and Interactive Media domain, does not appear have a significant export profile as yet. This may be partly because the longstanding Film and Television Incentive programme provides incentives to foreign companies, so that the final production would not show up in South Africa's exports. As the Emerging Black Filmmakers' Initiative takes effect, this may change in the future.

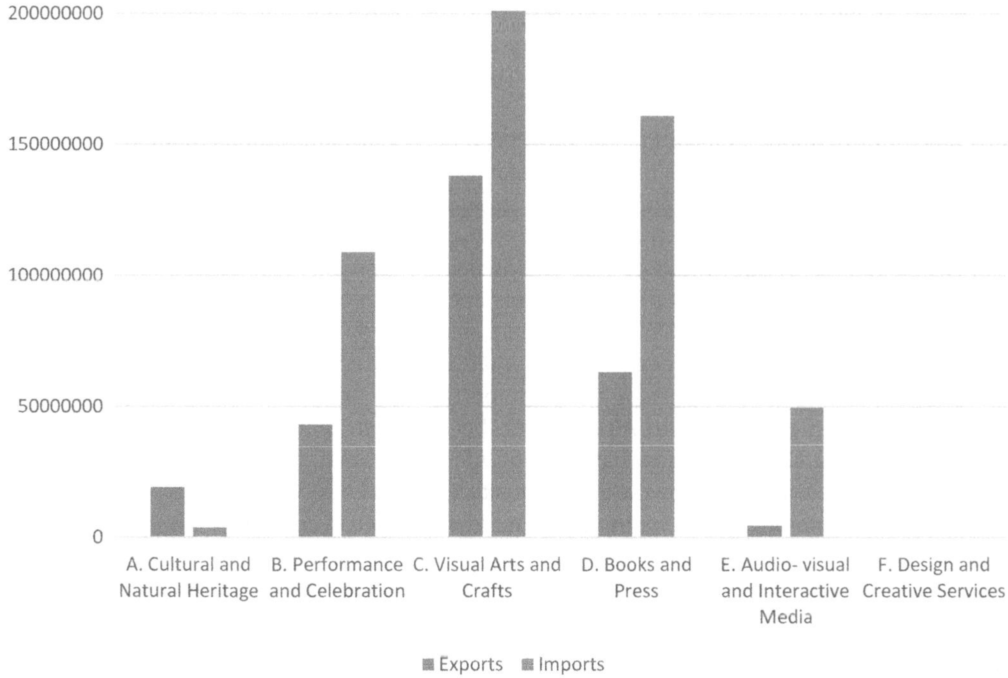


**Figure 4.** South Africa's total cultural trade by domain: 2014–2016 averages (US$) (Source: Authors' computations based on data from UN Comtrade 2017).

There are low levels of imports in Domains A and F (Cultural and Natural Heritage, and Design and Creative Services). Imports of Audio-visual and Interactive Media are much more significant than exports (but still fairly volatile). These imports are driven by the Video games sub-sector which has a distortionary effect on cultural goods trade on the import side in particular. Imports in the Performance and Celebration domain show a downward trend, as do Books and Press. While Visual Arts and Crafts imports have grown in the most recent period, exports in this domain have done very well. The reduction in the overall trade imbalance in South Africa's total cultural goods trade has therefore largely been driven by the strong performance of Visual Arts and Crafts exports and the better growth of Performance and Celebration exports, alongside a reduction in imports mainly in Books and Press in the recent period, but also Performance and Celebration and Audio-visual and Interactive Media imports.

Nevertheless, the trade balance in the most recent period, from 2014 to 2016, was positive only for Domain A (Cultural and Natural Heritage). The trade imbalance was most significant in Books and Press and Performance and Celebration and least in Visual Arts and Crafts and Audio-visual and Interactive media (see Figure 4). If the distorting effect of the Video games sub-sector is removed from Audio visual and Interactive media, the trade imbalance improves significantly in this domain.

### *6.2. South Africa's cultural goods trade with its BRICS partners*

South Africa became a member of the BRICS group of emerging markets at the end of 2010. While the country's much smaller economy makes it the group's outlier in terms of its contribution to global trade and GDP, it sits comfortably within the group in terms of GDP per capita, trade as a proportion of GDP, and indices such as the World Bank's ease of doing business index and the World Economic Forum's Global Competitiveness Index. South Africa's growth performance has been most similar to that of Brazil, although both South Africa and Brazil have significantly worse growth performances than China and India.

As noted in Section 4, since 2012 South Africa's trade policy documents have emphasised an orientation towards the country's BRICS partners and the African market while maintaining relations with traditional trading partners (the dti (Department of Trade and Industry) 2012). From a foreign policy perspective, participation in the BRICS grouping has been of key importance to South Africa. Furthermore, China and India have become significant individual trading partners for the country, while trade with Brazil has grown steadily, albeit off a much lower base. It is therefore interesting to examine the extent and nature of cultural goods trade between South Africa and its BRICS partners.

An examination of South Africa's cultural goods trade in nominal US$ values shows that China and India are South Africa's largest trading partners in cultural products within the BRICS grouping. The trade imbalances with both China and India are, however, enormous, and largely increase over time. The exception is the most recent period, when imports fell sharply in 2015, narrowing the trade imbalance in both partnerships. While imports failed to recover in 2016, exports rose marginally, further improving South Africa's trade balance with China and India that year. As in the aggregate cultural goods trade data, South Africa's cultural goods imports show greater volatility in general and more downward sensitivity in bad times, while cultural goods exports appear to have been more stable. South Africa's trade imbalance in cultural goods trade with Brazil narrowed noticeably during the period of the global financial crisis and from 2015, but widened considerably from 2011 to 2014. Russia is the only BRICS country with which South Africa records a consistent trade surplus in cultural goods trade, except for 2013.

Although it is important to examine which domains are driving the level of, and trends in, South Africa's trade balance with its various BRICS partners, once aggregate trade by domain is decomposed by partner the reliability of the data can become less certain. Data gaps and significant outliers are evident in the bilateral direction of trade data. Nonetheless, it is evident that Visual Arts and Craft is a significant traded domain on both the export and import side in South Africa's trade with its BRICS partners. Cultural and Natural Heritage is an important export domain, followed by Books and Press. Performance and Celebration is an important cultural export domain in South Africa's trade with Russia. On the import side, Visual Crafts and Arts, Performance and Celebration, and Books and Press are prominent import domains. In the case of South Africa's trade with China, Audio-visual and Interactive Media is a key import domain.

An investigation of the extent of matching trade between partners can also be important. Inter-industry trade refers to the exchange of products in different industries, while intra-industry trade refers to two-way trade within a particular sector. Intra-industry trade (IIT) is associated with greater value added manufacturing trade. It can be beneficial as trade expands, since it is easier for firms and workers to move to activities within the same broad industry with specialisation than to shift between industries (Cattaneo and Fryer 2002).

Table 1 depicts South Africa's intra-industry trade by domain and partner, based on average trade values for 2014–2016. IIT is measured using the simple Grubel-Lloyd index which ranges from 0 to 100%, with higher percentages reflecting greater two-way trade within a particular domain.

There is intra-industry trade of at least 30% in South Africa's total cultural goods trade in all domains except for Audio-visual and Interactive Media. It is most useful to consider intra-industry trade in domains where the value of trade is relatively significant. This is the case for Performance and Celebration, Visual Arts and Crafts, and Books and Press. In these domains there may be scope for further intra-industry specialisation with its associated trade benefits.

However it is important to note that the small size of existing trade in a particular domain does not mean that the sector in question should not be important from a policy point of view. For example, Domain A (Cultural and Natural Heritage) is the only domain where there is a trade surplus in overall cultural goods trade. It is therefore important in containing the trade imbalance that is pervasive in the other domains, even to a small degree. South Africa's Cultural and Natural Heritage domain also records a trade surplus in cultural goods trade with Brazil, China and especially with Russia.

**Table 1.** South Africa's intra-industry trade (%) by domain and partner (2014–2016 averages).

| | World | Brazil | China | India | Russia |
|---|---|---|---|---|---|
| A. Cultural and Natural Heritage | 32.6 | 0.7 | 41.5 | 4.4 | 0.9 |
| B. Performance and Celebration | 56.5 | 1.6 | 0.3 | 8.5 | 5.3 |
| C. Visual Arts and Crafts | 81.4 | 30.9 | 0.4 | 4.1 | 10.2 |
| D. Books and Press | 56.3 | 12.9 | 1.4 | 1.1 | 13.4 |
| E. Audio- visual and Interactive Media | 16.6 | | 0.0 | 1.1 | |
| F. Design and Creative Services | 78.4 | 0.0 | 88.0 | 22.9 | |

(Source: Authors' computations based on UN Comtrade 2017)

Another issue that is important when considering intra-industry trade is that an improvement in the IIT index in sectors where imports exceed exports (i.e. where there is a negative trade balance from South Africa's perspective) can be brought about through export promotion in that domain. For example, an increase in the exports of Visual Arts and Crafts with slower growth in imports would improve the level of IIT.

The picture Table 1 provides of IIT between South Africa and its BRICS partners is very different to the IIT levels of at least 30% evident in South Africa's total cultural goods trade in most domains. In the case of Brazil, there is notable IIT in Visual Arts and Crafts of 30.9% in the period 2014–2016. The only other domain that shows some IIT of any magnitude in South Africa's trade with Brazil is Books and Press with 12.9% of matching trade.

In South Africa's trade with China, there is 41.48% IIT in the Cultural and Natural Heritage domain but the value of trade is quite small (although important for South Africa's trade balance). IIT in the Books and Press domain is low at 1.44%. While exports were growing and imports tapering off, the trade imbalance with China is very high. There would have to be significant export growth across Domains B to E to improve the level of IIT with China. The Design and Creative Services domain shows high IIT, but only US$2274 of export trade and US$1786 of import trade is involved.

IIT with India is not significant in South Africa's cultural goods trade. It is highest in Performance and Celebration at 8.5%. IIT with Russia stands at 13.4% for Books and Press in 2014–2016, and 10.2% for Visual Arts and Crafts. In this case, however, the trade balance is significantly in South Africa's favour.

Given the potential benefits of intra- versus inter-industry specialisation export growth in sectors with some two-way trade could be promoted. The promotion of higher value added CCI trade with South Africa's BRICS partners would fit well into the country's current trade and industrial policy framework. In the case of South Africa's relations with China, for example, the 2010 Comprehensive Strategic Partnership Agreement between the two countries explicitly calls for investment and other strategies to promote more balanced value adding trade between South Africa and China. It is important for the CCI sector to develop a higher profile in these kinds of discussions in order to benefit from trade promotion strategies that could advance the sector.

### *6.3. South Africa's import tariffs on CCI product categories*

There are some significant differences in the scheduled tariffs on CCI imports across South Africa's main trade agreements. An examination of South Africa's tariff book (SARS 2018) indicates that of the 85 HS 6-digit product categories that are identified as part of cultural goods trade in the UNESCO (2009) FCS, 46 (or 54%) are already tariff-free across the board (irrespective of the trading partner). Therefore imports into South Africa in more than half of the cultural product categories face no duties.

As far as the preferential trade agreement with MERCOSUR is concerned, 84 out of the 85 CCI product categories fall outside of the agreement, meaning that cultural goods imports from MERCOSUR (and hence Brazil) largely face the general (MFN) tariff as far as cultural goods trade is concerned.[8] The only cultural goods sub-sector that is included in the agreement (Cinematographic film of a width >35 mm) faces a general (MFN) tariff of zero in any case, so the preference granted MERCOSUR is currently meaningless. Effectively, then, the MERCOSUR preferential trade agreement does not provide any meaningful preferences for CCI imports from MERCOSUR (including Brazil) over and above the MFN tariffs. As noted above, however, for South Africa's trading partners in general, imports in 54% of cultural product categories are currently tariff-free across the board.

By contrast, in the case of CCI imports into South Africa from SADC, all 85 CCI product categories are duty-free under the SADC FTA, although provision is made for the protection of infant industries and national treasures of cultural value. In the case of South Africa's trade agreements with the EU and EFTA, there are no specific provisions concerning cultural industries. However the preferences granted to the EU and EFTA in CCI product categories are more extensive than those granted to MERCOSUR. For the EU and EFTA, 63 of the CCI product lines at the 6-digit level (74%) enter South Africa tariff-free and the remaining product lines have duties that are much lower than the MFN (and hence MERCOSUR) tariffs.[9] The EU and EFTA preferences are therefore quite significant relative to the MFN tariffs, with the EFTA countries enjoying a small margin of preference over the EU in 18 of the CCI product lines that attract duties.

In sum, the current pattern of CCI tariff preferences favours SADC, the EU and EFTA quite significantly over South Africa's BRICS partners. This reflects two issues. Firstly, the policy emphasis on expanding trade relations with BRICS countries is more recent, while there is a long history of trade preferences with the SADC region and European partners. Secondly, South Africa's trade strategy since 2009 has emphasised a more cautious approach to signing FTAs, preferring limited preferential trade agreements which provide an initial basis from which to promote mutually beneficial value added trade.

The tariffs that exist on the CCI product categories which do attract duties range from 5% to 30% and give an indication of which cultural product sub-sectors South Africa considers to be most sensitive. All sub-sectors in Domains A (Cultural and Natural Heritage), E (Audiovisual and Interactive Media) and F (Design and Creative Services) are tariff-free across the board. The highest tariffs on CCI imports into the country are found in Domain C (Visual Arts and Crafts), in the Craft, Jewellery and Other visual arts sub-domains (SARS 2018).

### *6.4. Trade in cultural services*

Digitisation is increasingly impacting on cultural trade in certain product categories such as music, film and books. Although South African services trade data is not available at the required level of disaggregation to identify the country's cultural services trade at the EBOPS sub-sector level set out in UNESCO (2009), some indication of South Africa's cultural services trade in 2016 is provided in this section, based on data from the South African Reserve Bank (SARB). Furthermore, the ITC breakdown of South Africa's services trade for the period 2007 to 2016 into eighteen BPM6 categories gives an idea of trends in the relevant services sectors.

Table 2 depicts services trade data from SARB (2017). While the categories shown are significantly more aggregated than the EBOPS categories, they provide a picture of the value of trade in a number of the services sectors that contain cultural services exports and imports, as well as their relative importance (shares) in South Africa's total services trade. Other (non-business) travel, Architectural, engineering and other technical services, and Telecommunications, computer and information services are key export and import categories, while Charges for the use of intellectual property is a significant import sector.

ITC data for 2007 to 2016 indicates that while South Africa has an overall trade deficit in the services categories in which cultural services trade is important, three out of the five relevant services sectors have trade surpluses, namely Personal travel services, Audio-visual and related services, and Other personal and cultural services. However, growing trade deficits exist in Charges for the use of intellectual property and Telecoms, computer and information services. In the former, the deficit is particularly driven by software and audio-visual licenses. Figures 5 and 6 illustrate the

**Table 2.** South Africa's trade in broad sectors relevant for cultural services trade in 2016.

| | Exports Rmn | Share (%) | Imports Rmn | Share (%) |
|---|---|---|---|---|
| Other (non business) travel | 106,513 | 50.5 | 30,301 | 13.8 |
| Charges for the use of intellectual property | 1601 | 0.8 | 29,375 | 13.4 |
| Telecommunications, computer and information services | 8424 | 4.0 | 16,325 | 7.5 |
| Personal, cultural and recreational services | 2898 | 1.4 | 267 | 0.1 |
| Advertising and market research services | 2282 | 1.1 | 2362 | 1.1 |
| Architectural, engineering and other technical services | 10,667 | 5.1 | 17,910 | 8.2 |
| Total services | 210,852 | | 219,056 | |

(Source: Authors' computations from SARB 2017)

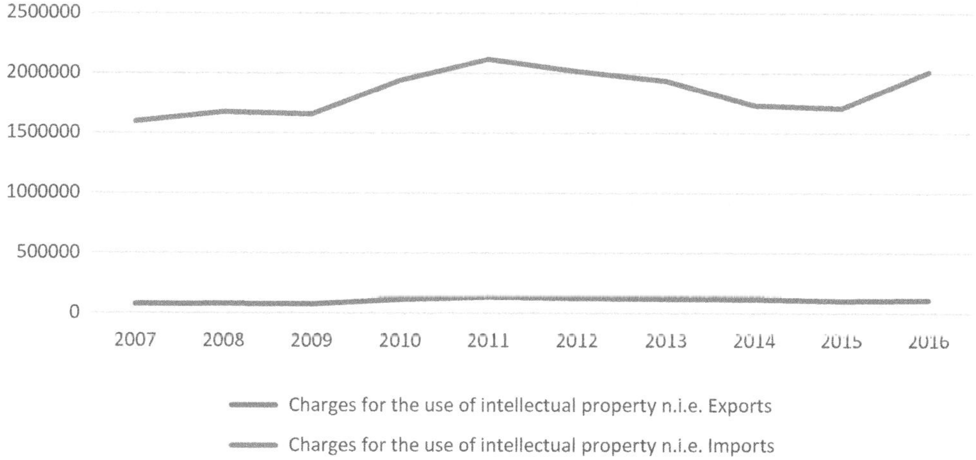


**Figure 5.** South Africa: Charges for the use of intellectual property (US$ 1000s) (Source: ITC, UNCTAD and WTO 2017).

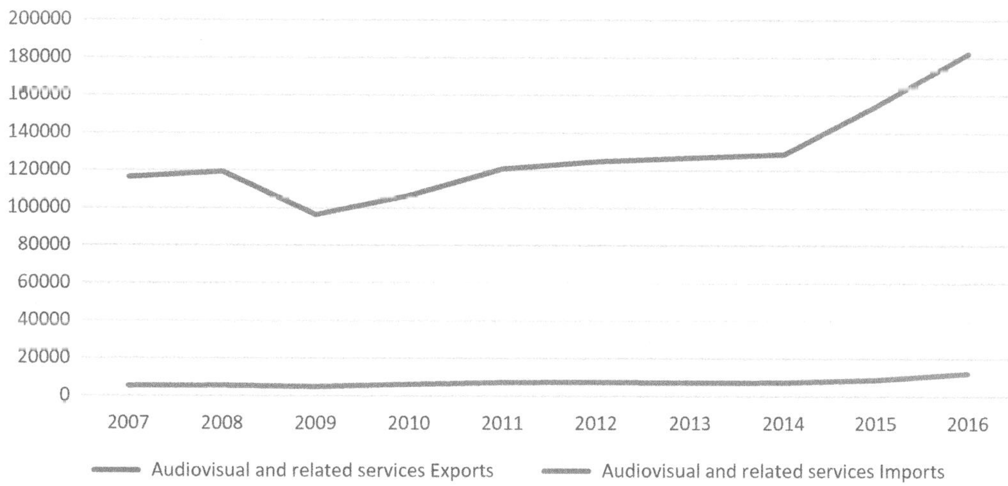


**Figure 6.** South Africa: Audio-visual and related services (US$ 1000s) (Source: ITC, UNCTAD and WTO 2017).

trends for Charges for the use of intellectual property and Audio-visual and related services respectively, the first depicting an increasing deficit and the second a growing surplus.

A recent report on the services sectors of the BRICS countries (ITC 2017, 19) finds that intra-BRICS services trade is most prominent in sectors related to growing goods trade such as transport and logistics and increasingly in tourism. For South Africa, intra-BRICS services trade is estimated to account for nearly 30 per cent of the country's total services exports, largely due to trade with China and India (ITC 2017, 20). This suggests that there is potential for increased trade with BRICS countries in tourist-related service activities in particular.

The General Agreement on Trade in Services (GATS) governs multilateral commitments on trade in services at the WTO. A picture of South Africa's approach to the liberalisation of cultural services can be obtained from an examination of the country's GATS schedule.[10] With the GATS 'positive list approach' a country's schedule only specifies those sectors in which that country has made commitments. The classification of services in the GATS is based on 12 main services sectors and 155 sub-sectors (WTO 1991). Of these 155 sub-sectors, 23 are particularly relevant for cultural services trade. These include nine sub-sectors under Business Services, six under Audiovisual Services, four under Tourism and Travel Services, and four under Recreational, Cultural and Sporting Services.

Out of the 23 relevant sub-sectors, 12 are unlisted on South Africa's GATS schedule, meaning no commitments were made in these areas (they are 'unbound'). The unlisted sub-sectors include all of Audiovisual services and Recreational, Cultural and Sporting Services, as well as Advertising, and Printing and publishing (which both fall under Business Services). Eight sub-sectors are fully liberalised for Modes 1 to 3 of service supply, but have Mode 4 restrictions. The remaining three are partially liberalised. It thus appears that South Africa had a more cautious approach to the liberalisation of cultural services trade at the conclusion of the Uruguay Round, relative to its approach to tariff liberalisation in cultural product trade categories.

## 7. Conclusions and recommendations

This article examined the growth and structure of South Africa's CCI trade between 2007 and 2016, with a focus on the country's trade with its BRICS partners. It also investigated the country's intra-industry trade by domain with each partner. Findings show that cultural goods exports accounted for 0.46% of South Africa's total commodity exports in 2016, while cultural goods imports accounted for 0.66% of total commodity imports. Growth in South Africa's total cultural goods trade slowed significantly in 2015, followed by a comfortable recovery in 2016. Exports grew faster than imports for much of the post-crisis period, reducing the trade imbalance in cultural goods markedly. The Visual Arts and Crafts domain is a significant driver of this trend, alongside weaker import performance in a number of domains. The trade balance by domain is only positive in the case of Cultural and Natural Heritage.

South Africa has large cultural goods trade deficits with China and India, although these have narrowed slightly in the more recent period. Russia is the only BRICS country with which South Africa has a cultural goods trade surplus. Visual Arts and Craft is a significant traded domain on both the export and import side with BRICS partners. On the export side, Cultural and Natural Heritage is an important domain, together with Books and Press. Performance and Celebration is an important export domain in South Africa's trade with Russia. With respect to imports, Visual Crafts and Arts, Performance and Celebration, and Books and Press are significant domains. Imports of Audio-visual and Interactive Media are significant in South Africa's trade with China.

Intra-industry trade by domain in South Africa's aggregate cultural goods trade reached at least 30% in most cases. Notable IIT was recorded between South Africa and Brazil in the case of Visual Arts and Crafts in the period 2014–2016, while in South Africa's trade with China, there was 41.48% IIT in the Cultural and Natural Heritage domain, although the value of trade was comparatively low. Apart from these sectors, IIT was not very high in South Africa's trade with its BRICS partners in sectors with notable trade flows.

The paper provided a picture of trade trends in selected broad services sectors within which cultural services trade is prominent and for which data were available. It was found that South Africa performed quite well in a number of these sectors and there was evidence of growing Audio-visual services exports, suggesting that the Film Incentive programme could be taking effect.

An important recommendation that follows from these findings is the improvement of data collection for CCI trade in both goods and services. This would facilitate further research on IIT within sub categories of particular domains, such as the Jewellery sub-sector, which is potentially an important focus area for South Africa. More comprehensive services trade data for the CCI sector at an appropriate level of disaggregation is particularly important.

From a policy perspective, while South Africa has no explicit trade strategy for the CCIs, particular sectors have been supported in the country's industrial policy framework which emphasises the promotion of greater value added trade. It is recommended that the profile of the CCI sector be raised in trade negotiations within Africa and elsewhere. Initiatives such as the AfCFTA Agreement and the BRICS trade and investment cooperation framework provide opportunities for expanding CCI trade with new partners. CCI trade policy appears fragmented at present, however, with greater coordination needed across relevant ministries and institutions with respect to incentives and export promotion.

South Africa's existing trade agreements incorporate CCI trade preferences which favour SADC, the EU and EFTA over BRICS partners. The large trade imbalances in CCI trade with China and India suggest that careful consideration will have to be given to the nature of future CCI trade and investment cooperation between South Africa and the rest of BRICS. Recent work on the potential for a BRICS CCI agenda that supports and promotes cultural diversity to further the contribution of BRICS to global governance (Hanania and Vlassis 2017) provides an encouraging basis for future research on cultural diversity and trade in the BRICS context.

## Notes

1. Other SACU members are the neighbouring states of Botswana, Lesotho, Namibia and Swaziland.
2. SADC is a southern African regional organisation with 15 member states (Angola, Botswana, DRC, Lesotho, Madagascar, Malawi, Mauritius, Mozambique, Namibia, Seychelles, South Africa, Swaziland, Tanzania, Zambia and Zimbabwe). A free trade area is in place among a subset of member states, including South Africa.
3. South Africa is engaged in ongoing limited PTA negotiations with India and signed a Comprehensive Strategic Partnership Agreement with China in 2010. A BRICS trade and investment cooperation framework also exists.
4. This system is based on the sixth edition of the Balance of Payments and International Investment Position Manual (BPM).
5. Indeed, there have already been significant budget shifts: in 2017, nearly 20% of the budget for funding cultural festivals and events (essentially performing arts) was 'reprioritized' to a venture capital fund for support of small, medium and micro cultural enterprises (National Treasury 2017).
6. The Grubel-Lloyd index is given by $Bi = (1 - (|Xi - Mi|)/(Xi + Mi))) \times 100$.
7. The intra-industry trade index ranges from 0 to 100%, with higher percentages reflecting greater two-way trade within a sector. An index of 0 indicates no overlapping trade within that sector, while an index of 100% reflects exports and imports of the same value within that sector.
8. The limited PTA between SACU and MERCOSUR, signed in 2009, provides for preferences on approximately 1000 product lines in each direction.
9. Authors' calculations based on SARS (South African Revenue Service) (2018) and UNESCO (2009).
10. See https://www.wto.org/english/tratop_e/serv_e/serv_commitments_e.htm. It should be noted, however, that these GATS obligations came into effect at the beginning of 1995. The current domestic reality in most countries is significantly different, with a greater degree of openness in many cases.

## Acknowledgments

Part of the research in this article was produced for the South African Cultural Observatory (SACO) Mapping Study of the Cultural and Creative Industries in South Africa. The financial assistance of SACO is gratefully acknowledged.

## Disclosure statement

No potential conflict of interest was reported by the authors.

## Funding

This work was supported by the South African Cultural Observatory.

## References

Amsden, A. H. 2005. "Promoting Industry under WTO Law." In *Putting Development First: The Importance of Policy Space in the WTO and International Financial Institutions*, edited by K. Gallagher, 216-232. London: Zed Books.

Archival Platform (2013). "Comment on the Revised Draft White Paper on Arts, Culture and Heritage." [Online]. http://www.archivalplatform.org/blog/entry/comment_on_the_revised_draft_white_paper/

AU (African Union). 2008. "Nairobi Plan of Action for Cultural Industries in Africa (2008)." Conference of African Union Ministers of Culture, Algiers, Algeria. [Online]. http://ocpa.irmo.hr/resources/docs/AU_POA_Industries_2005-en.pdf

Bell, T. 1997. "Trade Policy." In *The Political Economy of South Africa's Transition*, edited by J. Michie and V. Padayachee, 71–88. London: Dryden Press.

Cattaneo, N., and D. Fryer 2002. "Intra- versus Inter-Industry Specialisation, Labour Market Adjustment and Poverty: Implications for Regional Integration in Southern Africa." *Trade and Industrial Policy Strategies Working Paper No. 15*, TIPS, Johannesburg.

Cattaneo, N., and J. Snowball. 2018. South Africa's trade in cultural goods and services with a focus on cultural trade with BRICS partners. South African Cultural Observatory, Port Elizabeth. [Online]. www.southafricanculturalobservatory.co.za.

Collins, A., and J. Snowball. 2015. "Transformation, Job Creation and Subsidies to Creative Industries: The Case of South Africa's Film and Television Sector." *International Journal of Cultural Policy* 21 (1): 41–59.

DAC (Department of Arts and Culture, South Africa). 2013. *White Paper on Arts, Culture and Heritage*. Pretoria: Department of Arts and Culture. [Online]. http://www.dac.gov.za/sites/default/files/REVISEDWHITEPAPER04062013.pdf

DAC (Department of Arts and Culture, South Africa). 2014. *National Mapping Study of the Cultural and Creative Industries*. Prepared for the Department of Arts and Culture by Plus 94 Research, Johannesburg.

DAC (Department of Arts and Culture, South Africa). 2017. *Revised White Paper on Arts, Culture and Heritage 2017, 3rd Draft*. Pretoria: Department of Arts and Culture.

DACST (Department of Arts, Culture, Science and Technology, South Africa). 1996. *White Paper on Arts, Culture and Heritage*. Pretoria: Department of Arts, Culture, Science and Technology. [Online]. http://www.dac.gov.za/content/white-paper-arts-culture-and-heritage-0

Disdier, A., S. Tai, L. Fortagne, and T. Mayer. 2010. "Bilateral Trade of Cultural Goods." *Review of World Economics* 145: 575–595. doi:10.1007/s10290-009-0030-5.

EU-SA Trade Report. 2013. "Trade in Creative and Cultural Goods and Services, in the Context of EU-South Africa Development of the Creative Industries in South Africa." EuropeAid/131270/L/ACT/ZA.

Footer, M., and C. Graber. 2000. "Trade Liberalisation and Cultural Policy." *Journal of International Economic Law* 3: 115–144. doi:10.1093/jiel/3.1.115.

Grodach, C., and M. Seman. 2013. "The Cultural Economy in Recession: Examining the US Experience." *Cities* 33: 15–28. doi:10.1016/j.cities.2012.06.001.

Hadisi, S., and J. Snowball. 2017. *Cultural and Creative Industries Mapping Study: Employment in the Cultural and Creative Industries in South Africa*. South African Cultural Observatory, Port Elizabeth. [Online]. www.southafricanculturalobservatory.co.za

Hanania, L. R., and A. Vlassis. 2017. "For a BRICS Agenda on Culture and the Creative Economy." In *The BRICS-Lawyers' Guide to Global Cooperation*, edited by R. Neuwirth, A. Svetlicinii, and D. D. C. Halis, 333-351. Cambridge: Cambridge University Press.

ITC (International Trade Centre). 2017. *BRICS Countries: Emerging Players in Global Services Trade*. Geneva: ITC.

ITC, UNCTAD and WTO, 2017. "Trade in Services Database." [Online]. http://www.trademap.org/Index.aspx

Marvasti, A. 1994. "International Trade in Cultural Goods: A Cross-Sectional Analysis." *Journal of Cultural Economics* 18: 135–148. doi:10.1007/BF01078936.

Mas-Colell, A. 1999. "Should Cultural Goods Be Treated Differently?" *Journal of Cultural Economics* 23: 87–93. doi:10.1023/A:1007527801113.

Mulcahy, K. 2017. *Public Culture, Cultural Identity, Cultural Policy: Comparative Perspectives*. New York: Palgrave Macmillan.

National Treasury (2017). "Estimates of National Expenditure." *Budget 2017: Vote 37 Arts and Culture*. [Online]. http://www.treasury.gov.za/documents/national%20budget/2017/enebooklets/Vote%2037%20Arts%20and%20Culture.pdf

Neuwirth, R. J. 2002. "The Cultural Industries and the Legacy of Article IV GATT: Rethinking the Relation of Culture and Trade in Light of the New WTO Round." Conference on Cultural Traffic: Policy, Culture, and the New Technologies in the European Union and Canada, Carleton University, November 22-23. doi:10.2139/ssrn.1352171.

SADC (Southern African Development Community) 1996. "Protocol on Trade". [Online]. https://www.sadc.int/files/4613/5292/8370/Protocol_on_Trade1996.pdf

SADC (Southern African Development Community) 2001. "Protocol on Culture, Information and Sport." [Online]. https://www.sadc.int/files/3213/5292/8362/Protocol_on_Culture_Information_and_Sport2001.pdf
SADC (Southern African Development Community) 2012. "Protocol on Trade in Services". [Online]. https://www.sadc.int/files/7313/6439/6118/Protocol_on_Trade_in_Services_-_2012_-_English.pdf
SARB (South African Reserve Bank) 2015. *South African Reserve Bank Quarterly Bulletin*. December.
SARB (South African Reserve Bank) 2017. *South African Reserve Bank Quarterly Bulletin*. September.
SARS (South African Revenue Service) 2018. "Customs and Excise Tariff Schedule." [Online]. http://www.sars.gov.za/AllDocs/LegalDoclib/SCEA1964/LAPD-LPrim-Tariff-2012-04%20-%20Schedule%20No%201%20Part%201%20Chapters%201%20to%2099.pdf
Shin, S. 2015. "Cultural Diversity and International Trade in Cultural Products." PhD thesis, Department of Economics, Faculty of Business and Economics, Macquarie University
Snowball, J. 2016. *Towards the Development of a Framework for Cultural Statistics for South Africa*. South African Cultural Observatory, Port Elizabeth. [Online]. https://www.southafricanculturalobservatory.co.za/download/324
the dti (Department of Trade and Industry). 2007. *Implementation of Government's National Industrial Policy Framework: Industrial Policy Action Plan*. Pretoria: the dti. August.
the dti (Department of Trade and Industry). 2010a. *South Africa's Trade Policy and Strategy Framework*. Pretoria: Department of Trade and Industry.
the dti (Department of Trade and Industry). 2010b. *2010/11-2012/13 Industrial Policy Action Plan*. Pretoria: Department of Trade and Industry. February.
the dti (Department of Trade and Industry). 2012. *South Africa's Trade Policy and Strategy Framework: An Update*. Pretoria: Department of Trade and Industry.
the dti (Department of Trade and Industry). 2014. *The South African Emerging Black Filmmakers Incentive*. Pretoria: Department of Trade and Industry. September.
the dti (Department of Trade and Industry, South Africa). 2015. *2014/15 Incentive Performance: Highlights*. Pretoria: Department of Trade and Industry. September.
Throsby, D. 2008. "Modelling the Cultural Industries." *International Journal of Cultural Policy* 14 (3): 217–232. doi:10.1080/10286630802281772.
Tsegaye, K. 2016. "The Cultural Agenda of the OAU/AU since 1963." *Africology: the Journal of Pan African Studies* 9 (7): 37–50.
UN Comtrade, 2017. "International Trade Statistics Database." [Online]. https://comtrade.un.org/
UNCTAD, 2017. "UNCTADstat Creative Economy Database." [Online]. http://unctadstat.unctad.org/wds/TableViewer/tableView.aspx?ReportId=14773
UNESCO. 2005. *Convention on the Protection and Promotion of the Diversity of Cultural Expressions*. Paris: UNES.
UNESCO. 2009. *UNESCO Framework for Cultural Statistics*. Montreal: UNES.
UNESCO. 2013. *Creative Economy Report 2013*. New York and Paris: UNDP and UNES.
UNESCO. 2016. *The Globalisation of Cultural Trade: A Shift in Consumption*. Montreal: UNES.
WTO (World Trade Organization). 1991. "Services Sectoral Classification List", MTN.GNS/W/120. [Online]. July 10. https://www.wto.org/english/tratop_e/serv_e/mtn_gns_w_120_e.doc

# Latin America: trade and culture at a crossroads

Grace Jaramillo

**ABSTRACT**

Trade liberalization took the cultural community in Latin America by surprise, forcing a defensive reaction that took years to generate adequate public policy responses. However, cultural policy has changed unevenly in the region. Two issues became the center of culture and trade debates after the 1990s: cultural industry production and traditional indigenous knowledge. Mexico, by far the largest producer of audiovisual content on the continent, has been reluctant to adopt defensive approaches or red lines during trade negotiations. In fact, Chile is the only country that negotiated a 'cultural reserve' in its FTA with the United States. Regarding traditional knowledge, only states with large indigenous populations like Guatemala, Panama but especially Peru, Bolivia and Ecuador in the Andean Region dedicated significant efforts to fight for intellectual property protection for traditional knowledge, including benefit-sharing for the commercial use of genetic resources, derived through indigenous collective knowledge.

How have cultural policies intersected with trade policies in Latin America? What different approaches have governments used to reconcile cultural goals with those of trade liberalization? How has the relationship between culture and trade evolved over time? These are the guiding questions of this article dedicated to the region. The task is extremely difficult due to the diversity and complexity of Latin American identities. Even though the subcontinent is strongly united by its common colonial heritage and languages, the particularities of cultural expressions are enormous, even within nation-states. The long-lasting effects of colonial conquest are still present. For one thing, mainstream national priorities – usually built around mestizo identities- are very different from indigenous ones that emphasize respect and support for rescuing and preserving their traditional cultural expressions and representations. Considerable variation also exists across regional cultural powers like Mexico, Brazil and Argentina and the rest of the region.

The aim of this article is to establish key trends in the evolution of the debate about cultural and trade policy tradeoffs in Latin America and of variation in policy approaches across the region. Using comparative analysis methodology, the research involves the identification of critical junctures in this debate, key actors and institutional learning and policy emulation across time. The article concentrates on those areas of cultural policy that have directly intersected with trade in Latin America, specifically: cultural industries and traditional knowledge (TK), including indigenous cultural expressions. The analysis starts in 1980 when the first wave of neoliberal reforms made these two policy spaces intersect (García Canclini 2000). The drastic call for getting the prices right and lifting all industrial protection measures affected all sectors of Latin American economies, including cultural industries.

The plan of the article is first, to offer an overview of the intersections between trade and cultural policies before and after liberalization started in Latin America. The second part dissects policies directly related to cultural industries and trade and the strategies states followed to address the trade-offs. Key cases will be analyzed in more detail. The third part is dedicated to Latin American indigenous peoples and their struggle for the inclusion of traditional knowledge, traditional culture and access to genetic resources within the WTO intellectual property rights debate and how Latin American national states embraced this fight at multilateral and bilateral trade negotiations. Finally, the conclusion will address the region's complex web of trade agreements and the effects it has had on cultural policy.

## The creative economy and trade, an overview

Culture and trade policy traditionally followed different paths in Latin America. However, trade liberalization -implemented as part of the package of neoliberal reforms that swept Latin America since the 1980s- directly impacted two key cultural policy areas: cultural industries and indigenous traditional knowledge, including cultural expressions.

States with significant cultural production in films, books and music like Mexico, Argentina and Brazil were the first to react. Nevertheless, marginalized groups like the indigenous communities of Latin America felt the blow even harder. Indigenous organizations learned the hard way how highly profitable business appropriations of their genetic resources for medical applications in international markets could be. This typically occurred without proper attribution of source and knowledge, much less appropriate sharing of benefits (Pastor and Ruiz 2008; Del Castillo 2004; World Intellectual Property Organization 2001). By the late 1990s, states with large indigenous populations like Guatemala and Panama, but especially Peru, Bolivia and Ecuador -in the Andean Region- dedicated significant efforts to fight for intellectual property protection for traditional knowledge.

It was clear that trade liberalization took policy makers and the cultural community by surprise and forced a defensive reaction that took time to garner momentum and adequate public policy responses (Lay Arellano 2011). There was considerable variation in the pace and manner that countries reacted to and accommodated liberalization.

At the dawn of this debate, the central issue was cultural industries. UNESCO (1982) identified cultural industries as being, 'when cultural goods and services are produced, reproduced, stored or distributed on industrial and commercial lines, that is to say on a large scale and in accordance with a strategy based on economic considerations rather than concern for cultural development' (p. 21). The definition was an adaptation of Theodor Adorno and Max Horkheimer's take on the corrosive effect on cultural industry – in the singular- of late industrial capitalism after the Second World War. During the early 1980s, UNESCO embraced and expanded its inquiry into cultural industries to include analysis of the tradeoffs between cultural industry and trade (UNESCO 1982, 15). Since 2005, UNESCO has embraced the concept of 'creative economy' as interchangeable with cultural industries. It includes publishing, music, cinema, crafts and design (UNESCO 2011, 2019).

Discussions at the multilateral level had a lot of influence in Latin America. Debates about cultural policy and globalization started as soon as Latin America embraced neoliberal reforms in the late 1980s. Nestor García-Canclini was among the first to propose a radical critique about the inroads cultural expressions had made into markets and how markets have changed the way culture and identity are reproduced, from mass cultural products to indigenous expressions and folklore. The crucial concept he introduces is hybridization. In his words:

> "It is a versatile concept to explain the mix of classic and modern, elite and mass characteristics of culture ... with the capacity to include the broad set of intercultural exchange beyond the rigid ethnic boundaries of miscegenation or the religious understanding of syncretism" (García Canclini 1997, 119 my translation).

García-Canclini's imprint on the future debate about culture and globalization cannot be underestimated. The concept of hybridization broke with the traditional view of cultural policy as the protection of a static and unique national cultural identity exemplified in the sole defense of patrimonial sites, objects and expressions. The direct implication was that 'in times of globalization, migration and transnational multiculturalism, what is needed is a cultural policy that resolves confrontational positions and contributes to making trade, communications and other forms of interaction viable' (García Canclini 2000, 67 my translation). A more fluid conception of culture, one that expands and blends geographically and socially, domestically and internationally, against homogeneity emerged as a result.

Hybridization as the expression of cultural fluidity became a cornerstone of debates about open trade in the region, with some viewing it as an opportunity and others a hindrance. The best expression of the regional debates taking place was a 1998 seminar on Economic Integration and Cultural Industries in Latin America and the Caribbean. Most participants from all corners of the region sought carve-outs for cultural industry and cultural expressions against liberalization and globalization pressures from the global north (García-Canclini and Moneta, 1999, 4–5). At this point, only Mexico had negotiated a free trade agreement – NAFTA- and only Chile had plans to join negotiations of this type. Regardless, academic and public debates about culture in the age of trade liberalization started to gain momentum. Undoubtedly, García-Canclini's ideas were a leading force as seen in the many conference proceedings that circulated in the region since the 1990s and the way in which liberalization was seen both as a hindrance but also as an opportunity for spreading Latin American culture across the globe.

While these intellectual debates helped to frame the discussions away from nationalistic views of identity and patrimonial heritage, states prioritized trade over cultural policies, with no exceptions. The size of cultural industries within the economy is quite small. Latin America's core cultural products simply did not represent a big enough share of total exports to justify defending some kind of protection. It represented 0.8% of the total in 1980, 3% in 2004, just to decline again to 1.2% by 2013 (UNESCO 1980, 2004, UNESCO 2014 respectively).

Cultural goods -as defined by UNESCO- are the core of the trade and culture policy debate (UNESCO 2014). They represent the most important aspects of the creative economy of a country engaged in commercial exchange. Most importantly, the trading patterns of core cultural goods demonstrate there is no direct relationship between trade liberalization and FTAs.[1] Countries with an aggressive stance on trade liberalization like Mexico, Colombia and Peru experience similar levels of growth in cultural exports as others with protectionist trade policies like Brazil or Bolivia. All in all, what seems to make a difference is not trade openness versus trade protectionism but the extent to which there are policies in place supporting the production of cultural goods and services in the form of low interest credit or annual prizes and grants to accomplished producers. The article will discuss some of these policy strategies in the following paragraphs.

Overall, the export performance of cultural goods varies dramatically across the region, as Table 1 shows. While most of the Central American countries experienced positive growth, other states went into whirlwinds of consistent decline like Venezuela, Uruguay and Argentina. The most remarkable case is Panama with an average 27% growth rate in the last 15 years. Again, most of Panama's gains were achieved in performing arts and audiovisual production for export, mainly video and cinema (UNCTAD 2015).

Venezuela experienced the most dramatic decline with −24% depression of its production capacity in the same period. While the downfall affected all cultural products, audiovisuals suffered the most with −59% collapse of television production in less than two decades. Until the 1990s, Venezuela was the second largest exporter of soap operas in Latin America after Mexico (Barrón Domínguez 2009, 10).

The items that boost the export totals are few, namely, music recording and audiovisual production, mainly soap operas and cinema. Therefore, these items were the first to suffer the effects of trade liberalization. Mexico is by far the largest producer of audiovisual content in the

**Table 1.** ranking main exporters of cultural goods in Latin America.

| Ranking | 2002 | 2007 | 2012 | 2015 | Growth rate |
|---|---|---|---|---|---|
| Mexico | 3703.68 | 4209.02 | 4446.12 | 5447.10 | 3% |
| Brazil | 628.17 | 1042.86 | 916.90 | 882.93 | 3% |
| Colombia | 291.26 | 636.24 | 452.10 | 452.00 | 2% |
| Chile | 170.36 | 354.44 | 380.77 | 207.22 | 2% |
| Argentina | 141.82 | 233.44 | 209.31 | 92.85 | −3% |
| Peru | 123.71 | 238.26 | 270.95 | 199.51 | 4% |
| Bolivia | 69.54 | 99.11 | 80.99 | 138.91 | 5% |
| Costa Rica | 62.07 | 82.26 | 106.38 | 69.75 | 1% |
| Uruguay | 37.51 | 35.29 | 24.04 | 14.97 | −7% |
| El Salvador | 28.35 | 79.76 | 125.44 | 133.77 | 13% |
| Ecuador | 25.70 | 24.09 | 33.62 | 30.02 | 1% |
| Guatemala | 23.07 | 98.97 | 150.51 | 146.38 | 15% |
| Venezuela | 17.95 | 0.00 | 0.42 | 0.00 | −24% |
| Honduras | 10.13 | 22.46 | 26.07 | 0.00 | 10% |
| Panama | 8.94 | 590.87 | 8.55 | 6.08 | 27% |
| Nicaragua | 5.61 | 2.33 | 4.69 | 10.32 | 5% |
| Paraguay | 3.59 | 5.78 | 6.88 | 19.17 | 14% |

UNCTAD, Creative economy database 2018

continent and one of the five most important worldwide. The next most important soap opera exporters in the region: Brazil, Argentina, Colombia, Chile and Venezuela distantly trail Mexico as the table shows. Notwithstanding the importance of its cultural industry, it has not carved out defensive approaches or red lines during trade negotiations. In fact, Chile is the only country that negotiated a 'cultural reserve' in its FTA with the United States. The purpose of the reservation was mainly to create a free space for implementing public policies that preserved national unity and heritage and guaranteed national content in domestic consumption.

Surprisingly, no other Latin American country used the same strategy to carve out culture – or at least some aspect of it- during FTA negotiations. Not even small countries in Central America with less experience in trade negotiations but significant production of music and television like Guatemala, Dominican Republic and Panama followed any specific strategy to carve out cultural exceptions. This approach did not differ when different partners sat at the negotiating table, whether it was the United States or the European Union.

Latin American countries have traditionally preferred to resort to multilateral and regional organizations for advancing cultural policies and programs for cultural industry promotion and exchange. The two-level game had substantial benefits for the region. For one thing, it eased tension at high-stakes negotiations, usually with asymmetric powers like the United States and Europe. On the other hand, culture was always one of the few issues that received united support within the different integration schemes that Latin American countries embraced and, therefore, could advance smoothly at international and regional organizations.

For the most part, Latin American countries have always moved at different speeds creating, adjusting and reforming cultural policies (García-Canclini 2008). The type of incentives vary from country to country but mainly the instruments are similar: film and publishing funds, tax credits, subsidized credit, grants and national prizes, annual bids and state promotion abroad. The causes of variation are complex and have layered over the decades, but the most important variable has been the timing and strength of policy incentives to produce cultural goods. Mexico is a crucial case that proves this point. It was not only the fact that cinema and television production received the full package of incentives available during the Import-Substitution Industrialization era. It was also the fact that this policy treatment started early on and gave the industry the time to compete in international markets. Other cultural industry power hubs – Colombia, Argentina, Chile and most recently Brazil- did not have policy incentives as strong as the Mexicans during the ISI phase. And when they did, their respective industries (usually cinema and television production) exceled at exporting cultural goods. Export capacity tended to wane once governments either lowered or removed those incentives. To explain this variance, the following section will review the policy trajectory of major cultural industry players in Latin America, starting with Mexico.

## Mexico, the outlier and other policy variations

Mexico is the only Latin American country among the 10 world's largest exporters of cultural goods and services (UNESCO 2019). Moreover, Mexico exports eight times as much as the next country on the ranking of the most successful exporters of cultural goods in Latin America (Table 1). It is not surprising that Mexico still has the stronger public incentives to keep its creative industry increasing its trade flows worldwide compared to any other Latin American country. Even though Mexico achieved only modest gains after liberalization, the initial comparative advantage made Mexico an unbeatable powerhouse of cultural production for export among other Latin American economies. This is true not only in audiovisuals and TV production – the most important sector in the region- but also in areas like arts and crafts, design, publishing and new media (UNCTAD 2015).

To explain Mexico's resilience as a major exporter of cultural goods and services, it is necessary to go back in time. Mexico was a pioneer of cultural promotion policies in the region under the leadership of the influential intellectual José Vasconcelos. As early as 1921, the then Secretary of Public Education promoted editorial production with exporting objectives, the creation of libraries across the country and most importantly for future trade purposes, the establishment of programs of Mexican cultural promotion throughout Spanish America. During his tenure, *Fondo de Cultura Economica*, the largest editorial publisher in Latin America was founded (Martinez 1977, 11). Nonetheless, cinematography superseded editorial publishing as the center of cultural policy preoccupations in the following decades. The first law to promote the Mexican cinematographic industry was passed in 1949. The law established not only economic incentives, including prizes, grants and public contributions exclusively to national productions but also set a maximum of 50% screen time for foreign films or less, if the industry offer exceeded capacity in a specific year (Diario Oficial 1949, 3–4).

The film industry law of 1949 and its subsequent iterations became the cornerstone to explain the intersection of cultural and trade policy, since it assimilated cultural production to the Import-Substitution Industrialization effort. When the radio and television broadcasting law passed in 1960, it followed the same pattern. It matched the subsidies, benefits and protection already in place for the film industry to television as well, even asserting that the majority of airtime for speakers should be assigned to Mexicans only (Justia 2006). Previous to the 1980s, broadcasting of foreign films and TV was the exception, not the rule.

By the early 1990s, film industry protection and subsidies were so significant that president Felipe Salinas de Gortari sped up their overhaul in the middle of NAFTA negotiations in 1992. Salinas' rationale was to remove all protectionist distortions, like strict quotas of foreign production or direct subsidies to the industry, to clear the negotiation table for liberalization. Thus, he lifted without much discussion all subsidies and special treatment to national production established by the 1949 law (Justia 2006). Fiscal constraints and drastic cuts in the size of the state helped Salinas moved the reforms even faster. At the end, NAFTA did not carve out a cultural exception for Mexico as it did for Canada. The most important achievements of Mexican negotiators during NAFTA were the recovery of copyright royalties for films that were already in the public domain in the United States and the right to regulate dubbing in the film industry (Reina, Gamboa, and Guerra 2004). The recently negotiated USMCA -that will replace NAFTA- walked back straightforward liberalization of cultural industries. Mexico did insert cultural industries among the exceptions. Most importantly, Annex 15-E of Chapter 15 about cross-border trade in services makes clear that cultural industries are exempted from MFN and national treatment obligations. The exceptions are stipulated for television and radio broadcasting, newspapers and magazines, film and audiovisual services. In addition, similar wording is repeated in the General Exceptions chapter. Since Canada carved out the exception for its cultural industry, Mexico and the US benefit from it by being able to adopt or maintain measures to promote, protect and support cultural industries in a reciprocal fashion along their Canadian counterpart, including excluding cultural industries from national treatment and market access regulations (USMCA, §15 Annex 15-E; §32 Art. 32.6, 2018).

Cultural policy was indeed redefined because of NAFTA. It took a decade for the Mexican cinematographic industry to react and assess the effects of liberalization in their once famous entertainment industry. Social organizations, among them the union of actors, cinematographers and producers, effectively lobbied for counter measures. The reforms of 2001 and 2006 restored public funding and equal protection measures to the Mexican film industry. After liberalization, fewer policy instruments were available. One of the instruments of choice to protect national identity and cultural production was the prohibition of dubbing of foreign films, with the exception of children's movies, and the reintroduction of a quota for Mexican cinema at a minimum of 10% (Lay Arellano 2011). The reform was careful to avoid any conflict with international treaties and trade agreements already in force.

The overall results of the trade liberalization and the defensive policy reform that followed are mixed. On the one hand, the Mexican film and television industry benefited from increasing foreign direct investments and international connections with major film distributors in the United States and Spanish speaking countries, while increasing its overall quality. On the other, the overwhelming power of US cinema had diminished the audience and consumption of national cinema in its own territory. Moreover, theatre attendance did not recover the peak levels reached during the 1970s and 1980s during the time of subsidized ticket prices (de la Garza 2016, 767).

There is no question that trade liberalization policies slowed down Mexican cultural industry and export capacity in the last two decades (Lozano 2006). However, the initial boost of policy incentives during the first half of the 20th Century created positive feedbacks for the industry for the years to come. It is still the largest exporter of cultural goods in the region (Piedras 2004).

It proved very difficult for any other Latin American country to catch up to Mexican prowess. Not even Brazil, the largest economy in the region, had a comparable set of incentives. To be sure, Brazil did implement a national policy since the 1930s, but it mainly consisted of creating the first museums, libraries and academies of art in the largest cities, along with a national service to account for the historical and artistic patrimony of the country. Getulio Vargas' administration's central goal was to institutionalize a public system that provided cultural services for the masses (Calabre 2009, 16). The policy did not aim to create cultural industries for export; it was rather an effort to build a national sense of patrimonial heritage, similar to almost all cultural policies in Latin America at the time. The same system remained in place until 1985 when José Sarney created the Ministry of Culture. However, the downturn of the economy led to drastic cuts in public support for cultural products and the cultural industry into the end of the century (Dias Da Silva 2014).

The situation radically changed with the arrival of president Luiz Inacio 'Lula' Da Silva. Brazil was starting to benefit from the windfall of resources during the commodities boom of the early 2000s. Under his administration, cultural policy received not only more resources but also more attention. Gilberto Gil, one of the most respected musicians in the country, led the reforms to increase and diversify Brazilian cultural capital (Rubim 2010). Most importantly, the internationalization of Brazilian cultural industry was for the first time included explicitly as part of public policy. Domestically, this movement implied necessarily to support the private sector that was producing it. The outcome was the creation of an International Centre of Creative Industries in the city of Bahia. Internationally, it implied a proactive shift to provide cultural and trade promotion of Brazilian products as well as defense of intellectual property and copyrights of new creations, at international fora like the World Trade Organization, the World Intellectual Property Organization and different United Nations organizations like UNESCO and UNCTAD (Novais and Brizuela 2010, 222–223). Notably, Brazil only became a significant exporter of cultural products after the year 2000, when its exports reached more than 600 million dollars the first five years and peaked under Lula Da Silva in 2007 with a billion dollars in sales abroad. As incentives slowed down, exports also decreased, as Table 1 shows.

Besides Mexico and Brazil, only Chile and Colombia have successfully weathered the storms of trade liberalization. Albeit, on different terms. Chile was the first country in Latin America to effectively negotiate a 'cultural reserve' in its free trade agreement with the United States. The cultural reserve carved out public policy dominions in the areas of publishing, audiovisual production, regional broadcasting and arts for the Chilean state (Reina, Gamboa, and Guerra 2004). What is more, Chile established an important mid-way solution between Canada's 'cultural exemption' demands and fully-fledged liberalization. Chile preserved its control of policies that directly affect Chilean cultural heritage and its cultural industry while opening the door for progressive liberalization of cultural goods, but not services. The result was a sustained moderate rate of growth across its creative economy with the exception of publishing and visual arts. Chile has become the fourth largest exporter of cultural goods in the region, despite the many FTAs it has signed in the last two decades (UNCTAD 2018).

Colombia has a different edge. It is the second largest producer and exporter of books and other publishing material after Mexico. If design and visual arts are included, Colombia outperforms Argentina by far. The anchor policy was its famous international book fair established by the first national plan for culture in 1974 (Bravo 2008, 134). However, comparative advantages were not on their side. The country was not a strong producer of paper pulp and other basic raw materials but managed to keep the sector booming through the extended common market of the Andean Region. During the 2000s FTA negotiations with the US and the European Union, Colombia focused on lowering tariffs for raw materials most needed by the publishing sector (Reina, Gamboa, and Guerra 2004).

Nevertheless, the most important aspect of Colombia's cultural development in the wake of trade liberalization is audiovisual production. Colombian success in producing and exporting soap operas during the 2000s took everybody by surprise. What is little known outside Colombia is that it was the consequence of radical shifts in public policy. Until 1999, the National Television Commission (CNTV) held all the control not only of airtime but also of programming and TV production. The complete deregulation of TV production meant a swift privatization process with the two largest groups of the country taking control of the sector (TV Mas, September 2009). Besides tapping into the Colombian tradition of creativity in performing arts, producers could also count on a regular source of public finance and matching funds from a public-private fund created by the state to support film and television production (Getino 2012; Medina and Barrón 2010). By 2001, the most important achievement of Latin American TV production was on air and exporting aggressively to the world: *Betty, the Ugly*. This soap opera opened the door for huge gains for the country's audiovisual exports. Colombia went from exporting 8% of all Latin American production in 2004 to 12% by 2009 (Barrón Domínguez 2009, 2, 8). It was clear that trade policy was consistently coordinated with a cultural policy focused on increasing creativity gains by contributing funds and intellectual property rights support in the bid for increasing exports and royalties from the copyrights they were selling.

By contrast, Venezuela was in a downward spiral of losing revenues and market share following opposite policies. First, in 2006 a law that sanctioned the contents of what soap operas could show to the public created an atmosphere of self-censorship. Then, in 2006 the state proceeded to nationalize and take control of one of the main broadcasters and TV producers in the country, RCTV, one of the two main exporters of soap operas (Oliva 2017). However, the most important reason for the precipitous downfall was political. President Hugo Chavez's attacks on the credibility of the two main media conglomerates and soap opera production companies -Venevision and RCTV- consistently cut sources of revenue that curtailed future investments. By 2009, Venezuela just retained 8% of its international markets and by 2014 both companies abandoned the market of soap operas all together (Serafini 2018). The Venezuelan case highlights the extent to which cultural production for export heavily depends not only on positive government policies, or at least neutral ones. Venezuela did not have a policy in place to subsidize TV production or even provide consistent stimulus to its main exports. President Chavez' persistent undermining of these companies' credibility was enough to cause the downfall of its production capacity and its ability to export and maintain its niche in international markets.

This short review of the most prominent cultural exporters in the last three decades shows significant variation in cultural policy options in relation to trade. For one thing, the Mexican and Brazilian cases demonstrate that the size of the economy is not necessarily correlated with strong cultural policies. While Mexico demonstrated a consistent effort to coordinate trade and cultural policies for export even after trade liberalization and NAFTA, Brazilian policies remained modest for much of the 20th century. It was only the windfall fiscal benefits of the commodity boom of the 2000s and the leadership of a prominent composer and cultural icon that moved policy in a different direction during the early Workers Party years in power. In the case of Mexico, the initial vision of a strong cultural policy for export provided positive feedbacks along the line and kept the industry's export drive, even in the face of liberalization and drastic cuts to subsidies and protection for the sector (Sánchez Ruiz 2004).

What is clear is that cultural policy evolved over time, albeit reluctantly. The evolution was a direct response to liberalization pressures but also to commodity booms that increased public funding available for the arts. But even when there were strong examples of policy coordination and learning between trade and cultural policies like the case of Colombia, there was not always collaboration. The smaller the country, the less likely it was that policy coordination could occur. In turn, FTAs forced moves to defend culture and cultural production.

Moreover, options about trade liberalization also marked a distinct difference in the way countries approach cultural policy. The Pacific Rim – with the exception of Ecuador- all opted for a rapid pace of liberalization through negotiation of multiple free trade agreements. On the contrary, Mercosur countries – Brazil, Argentina, Uruguay and Paraguay- plus Venezuela and Bolivia did not embrace trade liberalization through FTAs and thus, chose a different route to defend and expand cultural industries and defend cultural expressions.

For the most part, Latin American governments preferred to wage the cultural battle through regional and multilateral agreements rather than defend culture and indigenous patrimony during free trade negotiations. UNESCO, the World Trade Organization, the World Intellectual Property Organization, and regional bodies like the Central American Union, Mercosur and the Andean Community became the loci for defending Latin American cultural industries and preventing cultural misappropriations (Oyamburu 2000).

Mercosur is a case in point. It is certainly the only regional integration project that saw culture as an integral part of its project from the start. The regional integration agreement came into force in 1991 and by 1996 the member countries were already signing the Protocol for the Cultural Integration of Mercosur (Harvey 2001). They called it *Mercosur Cultural*. The protocol sets the table for a commitment to work together in areas like generating a regional system of information about cultural heritage, cultural industries and cultural trade inside and outside the common market. Moreover, it mandates regular meetings among Ministers of Culture to improve strategic coordination and to create regional programs and incentives for cultural industries. However, what is more remarkable about *Mercosur Cultural* is that its central promise is to promote increasing cultural exchange and trade among its members, by facilitating trade in cultural products and providing finance for cultural ventures (p. 13).

The initial enthusiasm soon faded. Although there are strategic gains in terms of better knowledge of cultural industries in the region and a constant flow of information between the member countries, cultural exchange has barely improved. Brazil consumes a very small percentage of cultural goods produced by the other three countries. However, Brazil is still the main source of exports for music and soap opera production in Mercosur without similar gains for the rest of the partners (Getino 2012). More importantly, regional financing for cultural goods ranges from limited to non-existent. National councils of arts and cinema are still the most important source of funding for Brazil and Argentina but they are also limited by fiscal constraints, always depending on the booms and busts of commodity exports (Simis 2007; Serafini 2018). The Andean Community had a rather small cultural program that was excessively dependent on foreign aid. The program strength has suffered accordingly (Karla Paez, personal interview, April 2015).

## Protection of indigenous cultural heritage

While cultural industries are generally the central focus of cultural and trade policy debates, indigenous knowledge is certainly the most successful story in Latin America at the intersection of cultural and trade policies. This debate also started in the early 1990s when the most important social mobilization of indigenous peoples across Latin America took place. In 1992, the indigenous leader Rigoberta Menchú won the Nobel Peace Prize for her struggle to achieve social justice for the Mayan communities, after thirty years of civil war in Guatemala (The Nobel Prize, 1992). Indigenous uprisings and social mobilization of indigenous peoples made news in Ecuador, Peru, Bolivia and Panama as well. The demands went beyond economic issues like basic needs, economic opportunities and land reform. The new movements called for respect and recognition of their cultural heritage, traditional knowledge and ethnic cultural expressions, believed to be under constant threat due to globalization (World Intellectual Property Organization 2001).

Indigenous communities in the Andean Region made the first forceful move to change the terms of the conversation regarding access to genetic resources and benefit-sharing from the commercialization of indigenous knowledge by multinational corporations, especially pharmaceuticals in 1992. The coalition, organized around COICA (Coordinator of Indigenous Organization of the Amazon Basin) actively lobbied the Andean governments to change the way mainstream Intellectual Property Rights (IPR) functioned. COICA's main claim was that IPR safeguards guaranteed patent rights to new pharmaceutical developments, oblivious to the fact that indigenous traditional knowledge is involved. Usually neither attribution of the source nor benefit-sharing contributions to the communities are involved (de la Cruz 2006).

Two cases of misappropriation of traditional knowledge raised awareness among the Andean Community country members. The first notorious case was *croton lechleri*, commonly known as *sangre de drago*[2] in the Amazon basin. Then, there was a second claim of commercial profit from the botanical specie *uncaria tomentosa*, commonly known as cat's claw among Amazon communities in Peru and Ecuador. A damaging article by Vicky Reyes (1996) exposed how an international corporation tried to trick Amazon communities into sharing their knowledge in exchange for 'benefits'. The Quichua community of Jatun Molino was promised a better airport, basic medicines and a salary in exchange for the shaman knowledge about the medicinal properties of the plant and wages for 30 locals that worked collecting plants (p.83). Needless to say, the offerings never materialized.

In spite of promises of long-term benefits and shared ownership of the knowledge acquired, the community was never mentioned in the patent applications or in further communications about their work with the community. What is more, pharmaceutical companies pitted communities against one another by partnering with only one, since knowledge about the healing properties of *sangre de drago* were collective knowledge held by all the communities in the territory (p. 85). Later on, similar claims were advanced about *ayahuasca*, an Amazon herb used as an opioid and purportedly capable of treating pain. Cases like these empowered state officials, civil society organizations and political leaders to use different channels and strategies in multiple international fora to raise awareness and guarantee protection under international law.

The most receptive battleground for indigenous concerns regarding property rights and appropriation of their traditional knowledge is the Andean Community (CAN for its acronym in Spanish). CAN is the oldest regional integration project in the Americas and the only one that has created regional jurisprudence to encompass trade and trade-related legislation across the region since 1969. Thus, regional decisions adopted by consensus by the then five member countries became automatically incorporated into their national legal systems of laws. COICA and other indigenous organizations worked with the support of Ministries of Environment of the region to seize the opportunity the regional legal system provided.

The result was Decision 391, which regulated access to biodiversity and benefit-sharing (ABS). It was approved unanimously in July 1996 (Comunidad Andina 1996). Decision 391 took years of negotiation and intense lobbying between the agencies in charge of intellectual property rights, the ministries of trade and the ministries or agencies in charge of the environment that led the negotiation efforts in favor of indigenous rights before it entered into force in the five national jurisdictions (Ruiz 2010). However, the strategy has been working well. Decision 391 became the cornerstone to negotiate and approve Decision 486, the regional act that regulates intellectual property rights in the Andean Region since 2000 (Comunidad Andina 2000). It would later become the baseline legal document with which Colombia, Peru and Ecuador started FTA negotiations with the United States in 2002 (M.A. Alban, personal communication, June 16 2018).

At the same time, Peru was leading the negotiation effort for The Nagoya Protocol on Access and Benefit-sharing and Traditional Knowledge, part of the Convention on Biological Diversity. The Nagoya Protocol became for the Andean Region an important milestone in a broader negotiation strategy to introduce traditional knowledge (TK), Traditional Cultural Expressions (TCE) and access to genetic resources (GR) into TRIPS at the WTO (Ruiz 2003). This move was done while negotiating important FTAs with the United States and the European Union, which helped them advance their own negotiating positions while setting a precedent for future negotiations. The strategy served the Andean Region well and, to be sure, its litmus test was going to be FTA negotiations with the United States.

Indeed, Peru and Colombia stood their ground when it came to negotiating traditional knowledge and benefit-sharing schemes. The strategy of promoting the issue of indigenous traditional knowledge and their right to share the benefits from the commercial use of their collective knowledge at different multilateral conventions, not only the trade-related ones, proved effective. The FTA with the United States respected the position defended by Peru and Colombia. The unexpected result is that Peru included in the law that introduced all reforms required to comply with its FTA with the United States, provisions that defend the non-patentability of traditional knowledge. For instance, Article 25 banned the possibility to demand a patent for any living being, including animals or plants, biological material in whole or in parts, and most importantly, national biological processes (Ley 29316 2009; Art 25 Lit, b, c, d). Moreover, Article 120 specifically inserted sanctions against requests for patents that surreptitiously involve traditional knowledge (Ley 27811 2002). The law was in line with a specific law passed about the issue in 2002 (Ley 27811 2002). Colombia had already modified its national intellectual property rights legislation to reflect Decisions 391 and 486. In turn, these provisions became a precedent for the next FTA negotiations with the European Union. The EU also favored provisions that defended and upheld indigenous rights to ABS.

Still, there are increasingly critical views about ABS achievements so far. To be sure, international treaties like the CBD, the Nagoya Protocol and the Andean Decisions created a strong barrier of protection against genetic piracy and cultural appropriation that were upheld during FTA negotiations. The Trans-Pacific Partnership, the latest comprehensive trade deal of this trend, guarantees the respect for TK and cultural appropriations in its General Provisions. Moreover, the parties made the compromise to cooperate between them and establish appropriate measures to respect, preserve and promote TK and traditional cultural expressions (CP-TPP, Art. 28.9 2018). However, the strong barrier of legal protection did not generate the expected results on the ground. Access and benefit-sharing contracts had barely become a reality for indigenous communities on the ground. More cases of genetic piracy and cultural appropriation happened in Peru, like the case of commercialization of Maca by an international company without attribution of rights or benefit-sharing involved (Del Castillo 2004, 28). In the Andean Region, there is increasing concern that pharmaceutical companies still prefer to circumvent the system rather than to engage in grueling negotiations with communities and indigenous peoples. New technologies like the human genome had made the effort even less necessary, since they can replicate DNA from plants and animals with just traces of cells, thus making recurrent exploration unnecessary (Ruiz, Vogel, and Zamudio 2010).

The options of misappropriation do not end with the genetic resources and medicinal traditions of indigenous peoples. Guatemalan indigenous peoples have also fought to prevent their design, arts and crafts, textiles and other cultural expressions from massive commercialization without attribution. They have demanded that multinational companies refrain from using their designs and symbols but so far, their demands have gone unheard (Bastos and Camus 2004).

## Conclusions

On the whole, culture is at a crossroads with trade policy in Latin America. Trade liberalization, especially free trade agreements, put cultural industries and cultural policy on the defensive. Even Mexico, the stronger cultural exporter of the region struggled to coordinate cultural and trade policy after NAFTA entered into force in 1994, despite being the only country that designed cultural policies with the intention of creating a strong cultural industry for export as early as 1921. The relationship between culture and trade is especially understood through the prism of cultural industries for export. The way that trade agreements and other negotiations could advance (or not) market advantages for the main exports of the creative economy is emphasized. However, indigenous knowledge and cultural expressions are also objects of defensive policies across the region. This is especially true in the Andean Region where bio-piracy and cultural misappropriations of traditional knowledge moved governments to advance an aggressive defense of this knowledge in multiple international fora and during free trade negotiations.

The central cultural industry sensitive to trade liberalization in Latin America is music recording and television production of soap operas. Mexico is by far the largest producer of audiovisual content in the continent and one of the five most important worldwide (WIPO 2014). Its export capacity considerably exceeds the next most important soap opera exporters in the region: Brazil, Argentina, Colombia, Chile and Venezuela. Notwithstanding the importance of this cultural industry, it has not carved out defensive approaches or red lines during trade negotiations. In fact, Chile is the only country that negotiated a 'cultural reserve' in its FTA with the United States. The purpose of the reservation was mainly to create a free space for implementing public policies that preserve national unity and heritage and guarantee national content in domestic consumption. Surprisingly, no other Latin American country used the same strategy to carve out culture – or at least some aspect of it – from FTA negotiations (Umaña 2005).

Smaller countries with less trade negotiation experience, like Central American countries, did not have any specific strategy to defend culture or carve it out from trade negotiations. This approach does not differ when different partners sit at the negotiating table. Latin American countries have traditionally slated regional organizations as the loci of choice for advancing cultural policies and programs and cultural industry promotion and exchange.

## Notes

1. The list includes heritage and patrimonial goods, including collectors pieces and pieces over a 100 years old in addition to books, newspapers and periodicals and other printed material; recorded and audiovisual material as well as products out of the visual arts like paintings, sculpture and lithography. The measure includes audiovisual and related services and copyright royalties and fees (UNESCO 2004, 15).
2. *Sangre de drago* is a natural extract coming from the tree called *Drago* that is a natural healer of scars and minor cuts. In addition, it is an effective cure for gastritis and hemorrhoids.

## Disclosure statement

No potential conflict of interest was reported by the author.

## Funding

This work was supported by the Social Sciences and Humanities Research Council of Canada [756-2015-0717];

## ORCID

Grace Jaramillo http://orcid.org/0000-0001-7730-5046

## References

Barbalho, A., and A. A. C. Rubim. 2007. *Políticas Culturais No Brasil*, 133–155. Vol. 1. Salvador: Edufba.

Barrón Domínguez, L. 2009. "La Comercialización De La Telenovela Mexicana En El Extranjero." *Razón Y Palabra* 14 (70): 3–18.

Bastos, S., and M. Camus. 2004. "Multiculturalismo Y Pueblos Indígenas: Reflexiones a Partir Del Caso De Guatemala." *Revista Centroamericana De Ciencias Sociales* 1 (1): 8.

Bravo, M. E. 2008. "Políticas Culturales en Colombia." In *Políticas Culturais na Ibero-América*, edited by A. C. Rubim, and R. Bayardo, 119–158. Salvador: EDUFBA.

Calabre, L. 2009. *Políticas Culturais No Brasil: Dos Anos 1930 Ao Século XXI*. Rio de Janeiro, Brazil: Editora FGV.

Comprehensive and Progressive Transpacific Partnership. 2018. art. 29.8, Nov. 1, 2018, Ch.29 E.G.P. 29-8.

Comunidad Andina. 1996, July 2. "Decision 351: Regimen Sobre Propiedad Intelectual." http://www.wipo.int/edocs/lexdocs/laws/es/can/can011es.pdf

Comunidad Andina. 2000, September 14. "Decision 486: Regimen Sobre Propiedad Intelectual." http://www.wipo.int/edocs/lexdocs/laws/es/can/can012es.pdf

de la Cruz, R. 2006, November 30. *Perspectivas, Experiencias Y Prácticas En La Protección De Los Conocimientos Tradicionales Y Expresiones Culturales De Las Comunidades Indígenas. Estudio Regional En Los Países Andinos*. Geneva: UICN. http://www.wipo.int/meetings/en/doc_details.jsp?doc_id=131340

de la Garza, A. 2016. "Film Policy under Globalization: The Case of Mexico." *International Journal of Cultural Policy* 22 (5): 758–769. doi:10.1080/10286632.2016.1223639.

Del Castillo, L. 2004. "Diversidad Biológica y Biopiratería: El Caso de la Maca." *Debate Agrario*, 37: 23–38.

Diario Oficial. 1949. "Organo del Gobierno Constitucional de los Estados Unidos Mexicanos.„ Ley General de Cinematografía. 31 de diciembre de 1949, Tomo 178, Número 53.

Dias Da Silva, R. M. 2014. "As Políticas Culturais Brasileiras Na Contemporaneidade: Mudanças Institucionais E Modelos De Agenciamento." *Sociedade E Estado* 29 (1): 199–224. doi:10.1590/S0102-69922014000100011.

García Canclini, N. 1997. "Culturas Híbridas Y Estrategias Comunicacionales." *Estudios Sobre Las Culturas Contemporáneas* 3 (5): 109–128.

García Canclini, N. 2000. Políticas culturales: de las identidades nacionales al espacio latinoamericano.

García Canclini, N. 2008. *Las Industrias Culturales Y El Desarrollo De México*. México: Siglo XXI.

García-Canclini, M., and C. J. Moneta. 1999. "Las industrias culturales en la integración latinoamericana.„

Getino, O. 2012. "Economía Y Desarrollo En Las Industrias Culturales De Los Países Del MERCOSUR." *Revista De Estudios Para El Desarrollo Social De La Comunicación* 1 (1), 97–116.

Harvey, E. R. 2001. *MERCOSUL/MERCOSUR: The Market & Beyond*. Austin, TX: University of Texas.

Justia, M. 2006. "Ley Federal De Cinematografía." https://mexico.justia.com/federales/leyes/ley-federal-de-cinematografia/gdoc/
Lay Arellano, T. 2011. "La ley federal de cinematografía a 13 años de su reforma."
Ley 27811. 2002, July 24. "Ley Que Establece El Régimen De Protección De Los Conocimientos Colectivos De Los Pueblso Indígenas Vinculados a Los Recursos Biológicos." https://www.indecopi.gob.pe/documents/20791/199826/Ley27811-spanish.pdf/ebf10223-52ba-4a15-b790-90caf0a059a1
Ley 29316. 2009, January 13. "Ley Que Modifica, Incorpora Y Regula Diversas Disposiciones a Fin De Implementar El Acuerdo De Promoción Comercial Suscrito Entre El Perú Y Los EUA." https://peru.justia.com/federales/leyes/29316-jan-13-2009/gdoc/
Lozano, J. C. 2006. "Diversidad Cultural Y Televisión En México." *Comunicación Y Sociedad* 5: 137–156.
Martínez, E. 1977. "Política Cultural de México.„ *Políticas Culturas: Estudios y Documentos.*
Medina, M., and L. Barrón 2010. "La Telenovela En El Mundo." https://dadun.unav.edu/handle/10171/13613
Novais, B. D. V., and J. Brizuela. 2010. "Políticas Internacionais." In *Políticas Culturais No Governo Lula*, edited by A. Rubim, 219–240. Salvador: Edufba.
Oliva, C. January, 2017. "¿Por Qué Se Fue a Pique El Imperio De Las Telenovelas Venezolanas?" *La Hora.*" http://www.lahora.cl/2017/01/se-fue-pique-imperio-las-telenovelas-venezolanas/
Oyamburu, J. 2000. *"Visiones Del Sector Cultural En Centroamérica."* http://www.cervantesvirtual.com/obra/visiones-del-sector-cultural-en-centroamerica/
Pastor, S., and M. Ruiz. May 2008. "El Desarrollo De Un Régimen Internacional De Acceso a Los Recursos Genéticos Y Distribución De Beneficios Equitativo Y Eficiente En El Contexto De Nuevos Desarrollos Tecnológicos. Documento De Investigación." *Iniciativa Para La Prevención De La Biopiratería* 3 (9). Lima, Perú. http://www.spda.org.pe
Piedras, E. 2004. *¿ Cuánto Vale La Cultura? Contribución Económica De Las Industrias Protegidas Por El Derecho De Autor En México.* México: CONACULTA.
Reina, M., C. Gamboa, and M. L. Guerra. 2004. *La Cultura En Las Negociaciones Comerciales Regionales.* Fedesarrollo: Mimeo.
Reyes, V. 1996. "Sangre De Drago: La Comercialización De Una Obra Maestra De La Naturaleza." *Ecología Política* 11: 79–88.
Rubim, A. A. C. 2010. *Políticas Culturais No Governo Lula.* Salvador, Brazil: Edufba.
Ruiz, M. 2003. "¿Es Necesario Un Nuevo Marco Jurídico Para La Bioprospección En La Región Andina? Breve Revisión Crítica De La Decisión 391." *Serie De Política Y Derecho Ambiental SPDA* 14: 1–8.
Ruiz, M. 2010. *Valoración Y Protección De Los Conocimientos Tradicionales En La Amazonía Del Perú: Sistematización De Una Experiencia.* Lima: SPDA.
Ruiz, M., J. H. Vogel, and T. Zamudio. March 2010. "La Lógica Debe Prevalecer: Un Nuevo Marco Lógico Y Normative Para Un Nuevo Regimen De Acceso a Los Recursos Genéticos Y Distribución Justa Y Equitativa De Beneficios." *Documentos De Investigación* 4 (13). https://spda.org.pe/wpfb-file/20100316110126_-pdf/
Sánchez Ruiz, E. E. 2004. "El Empequeñecido Cine Latinoamericano Y La Integración Audiovisual ... ¿ Panamericana?:¿ Fatalidad De Mercado O Alternativa Política?." *Comunicación Y Sociedad*, no. 2. http://comunicacionysociedad.cucsh.udg.mx/index.php/comsoc/article/view/4218/3974
Serafini, D. 2018, May 11. "Los Altibajos Del Mercado De TV De Exportación En América Latina." *The Daily Television.* http://www.thedailytelevision.com/articulo/mas/players/los-altibajos-del-mercado-de-tv-de-exportacion-de-america-latina
Simis, A. 2007. "A política cultural como política pública." *Políticas culturais no Brasil. Salvador: EDUFBA* 1: 133–155.
TV Mas. September 2009. "Informes Regionales: Colombia, Una Década Movida." http://tvmasnovela.tv/paginas_edicionActual/may-june09/informes2.html
Umaña, G. 2005. "Aspectos No Comerciales De La Negociación Del TLC." *En: Temas no comerciales en la negociación comercial entre Colombia y Estados Unidos-LC/L. 2278-P-2005-p. 7-16.*
UNCTAD. 2015. Creative Economy Outlook and Country Profiles: Trends in International Trade in Creative Industries.
UNESCO. 1980. "Cultural Industries: A Challenge for the Future of Culture. In *Proceedings of Meeting on the Place and Role of Cultural Industries in the Cultural Development of Societies, Montreal.* Paris: UNESCO.
UNESCO. 1982. *Cultural Industries: A Challenge for the Future of Culture.* Paris, FR: UNESCO. https://unesdoc.unesco.org/ark:/48223/pf0000049972?posInSet=3&queryId=20def547-0c50-49e7-805e-6ca3743bb567
UNESCO. 2004. *International Flows of Selected Cultural Goods.* United Nations Organization for Education, Science and Culture.
UNESCO. 2011. "What Do We Mean by the Cultural and Creative Industries?" UNESCO: Document, 11. https://en.unesco.org/creativity/.../What%20Do%20We%20Mean%20by%20CCI.PDF
UNESCO. 2014. "International Flows of Selected Cultural Goods." unesdoc.unesco.org/images/0014/001428/142812e.pdf
UNESCO. 2019. "Creative Industries." http://www.unesco.org/new/en/culture/themes/creativity/creative-industries/
United States-Canada-Mexico Agreement, Annex. Nov. 30, 2018. 15-E, Ch.15 E.G.P 24-26; art. 32.6, Ch.32 E.G.P. 32-8,9
World Intellectual Property Organization. 2001. *Intellectual Property Needs and Expectations of Traditional Knowledge Holders: WIPO Report on Fact-finding Missions on Intellectual Property and Traditional Knowledge (1998-1999)* (No. 768). WIPO.

# Cultural politics in the South Korean cultural industries: confrontations between state-developmentalism and neoliberalism

Woongjae Ryoo and Dal Yong Jin

**ABSTRACT**
This paper examines Korea's cultural policy in tandem with the Korean Wave. It maps out the vital role of the Korean government in the Korean Wave phenomenon in the midst of the confrontations between neoliberal globalization and developmentalism. It investigates the ways in which Korea has developed the Korean Wave by analysing whether or not neoliberal ideologies have completely altered state developmentalism. More specifically, it studies the major characteristics of each administration between 1993 and 2016 in cultural policy, leading to the theorization of the nation-state in the context of the Korean Wave. Since studies of cultural policy assume that a wide range of policy tools are available to a government in promoting its cultural industries, it examines not only major cultural policy directions driven by each president, but also governmental practices executed at the level of the executive branch, in particular, the Ministry of Culture, Sports, and Tourism.

## Introduction

Since the late 1990s, South Korea (hereafter Korea) has rapidly developed its cultural industries and emerged as one of the major hubs of transnational popular culture. The Korean cultural industries have developed several cultural products, such as television programmes, music and films, as well as digital technologies and culture, and Korea has substantially expanded the export of these products to Asia, later to the Western markets. These local cultural products have made global sensations as both Western fans and Asian audiences are enjoying Korean cultural products. Consequently, the Korean Wave (Hallyu in Korean), which is the rise of Korea's cultural industries and the parallel growth of Korean popular culture in the global markets, has become a symbol of local-based transnational cultural industries and popular culture (Jin, 2016).

More recently, with the rapid growth of social media, such as YouTube and Facebook, as well as smartphones, K-pop has become one of the most important cultural forms.[1] Meanwhile, Korean game industries have continued to be the leader in the global trade as the largest exporter among local cultural industries. The contemporary Korean Wave has greatly expanded its influences as several new cultural forms, including animation, characters, and mobile games in addition to television dramas, films, and music, have rapidly penetrated the global cultural markets. With the increasing popularity of these local cultures, Korea has rapidly advanced its export of cultural products, from $188.9 million in 1998 to $4,679.3 million in 2015 (Korean Creative Content Agency 2016; MCST 2016). As the Korean Wave has continued to grow in terms of foreign export, the Korean government attempts to utilize Hallyu to enhance national images. For example, several recent presidents, including Lee Myung-bak and Park Geun-hye sought to connect the Korean Wave and soft power referring to 'the ability to get what you want through attraction rather than coercion or payments' via culture, values and foreign policies (Nye 2004, 256). Therefore, these presidents continued to emphasize the significance of traditional popular culture, including television programmes, films, and music for expanding cultural export and enhancing the country's brand power (Lee 2013, 191) as they represent the Korean Wave, although video games are bigger than these cultural areas in foreign trade.

There have been several dimensions that have played primary roles for the growth of Korean culture in the global markets, such as the 1997 economic crisis,[2] the emergence of East Asian economy, the surge of cultural industries corporations, and competition among them. In this process, the diverse images, texts and styles circulating within Asia and beyond were providing new opportunities to construct an alternative consciousness and identity formation through the sharing of culture, as exemplified in the case of Korean television dramas and K-pop (Ryoo 2009, 144). Most of all, the role of the Korean government as a provider of legal, policy, and financial resources to the cultural industries has become one of the major elements.

This essay is to investigate the state cultural policy, focusing on the shifting role of the Korean government in the local cultural industries by analysing key confrontations between neoliberal globalization and developmentalism. It exemplifies the major characteristics of each administration between 1993 and 2016 in cultural policy, leading to the theorization of the role of the government in the realm of culture. Since studies of cultural policy assume that a wide range of policy tools are available to a government in promoting its cultural industries (Hesmondhalgh and Pratt 2005; Kwon and Kim 2014), it maps out not only major cultural policy directions driven by each president, but also governmental practices executed at the level of the executive branch, in particular, the Ministry of Culture, Sports, and Tourism.

This essay employs the political economy approach, in particular a historical analysis because it is useful to find out the causes behind the shifting process of the Korean cultural industries. It formulates three major time periods to clarify the relationship between developmentalism and neoliberalism based on the major characteristics of the cultural politics of the Korean administrations: (1) the neoliberal developmentalism era between 1993 and 1998, (2) the neoliberal cultural reform era between 1998 and 2008, and (3) the developmental neoliberal era between 2008 and present. It utilizes several major source materials, such as presidential addresses on the cultural industries and the Korean Wave, secretarial addresses and documents from the Ministry of Culture, Sports and Tourism and other pertinent cultural agencies, including the Korea Creative Content Agency (KOCCA) and the Korean Film Council (KOFIC). The value in these documents lays in the detailed information and data they provide on the cultural industries and corporate activities.

## The shifting roles of the nation-state amid neoliberal globalization

The Korean cultural industries have grown in the midst of the conflicts between state-led developmentalism and neoliberal globalization, which parallel with the major arguments in the national economy. To begin with, starting in the 1960s, Korea has developed one of the strongest state-led developmental models, which pursue a top-down and export-led economy. In Korea, 'developmentalism' entails government intervention to promote economic development in partnership with *chaebol* – a family owned conglomerate. Therefore, developmentalism in the Korean context has been 'a state-driven political doctrine coined by the state to combat harsh domestic economic conditions' (Lee and Kim 2010, 315). In particular, Korea's developmentalism was rooted in a 'compressed development model' that Park Chung-hee formulated. In order to expedite the growth of national economy within a short period of time, the Park regime developed several Five-Year Economic Plan starting in 1962, and these plans focused on the shift of Korean economy from war-torn agricultural industries to heavy and chemical industries, and later to information and communication technologies-driven industries.

In the realm of the Korean cultural industries, the practice of developmentalism had been actualized mostly in the form of regulation. The cultural industries were marginal in terms of their contribution to global trade,[3] therefore, the Korean government mainly focused on the role of culture in nation-building,[4] while regulating cultural content through heavy censorship. The consecutive military governments until 1988 had also blocked foreign popular culture through both the screen quota system in the field of film and the programme quota system in the realm of broadcasting. In other words, during the developmental era until the late 1980s, the Korean government controlled the cultural industries with several measures, such as the public ownership of broadcasting, protection of the domestic cultural market from foreign penetration, and strong censorship on cultural content, with some promotional cultural policies.

The situation surrounding the cultural industries significantly changed as the Korean government starting in the late 1980s, and continuing through the mid-1990s, adopted neoliberal economic reforms, and consequently neoliberal cultural policies, emphasizing the minimal role of the government. The ideals of neoliberalism, which emphasize the supremacy of market forces, the need for deregulation and liberalization, and the necessity of limiting government intervention in economic activity, contrast sharply with the emphasis on the potential benefits of state intervention in economic activity (Cherry 2005, 329). As is well documented (Friedman 1982; Harvey 2005), the notion of neoliberalism originated in the 1930s, and it is especially associated with the primacy of the market, the privatization of state enterprises, maximized competition through liberalization and deregulation of the economy towards monetary policies favouring businesses and corporations. As such, neoliberalism is grounded in the assumption that 'governments cannot create economic growth or provide social welfare. Instead, private companies, and, most importantly, unhindered markets are best able to generate economic growth and social welfare' (Bockman 2013, 14). Some scholars (Pang 2000; Lim and Jang 2006; Kang 2012) contended that the Korean economy had made a transition towards a neoliberal market economic system, in particular in tandem with the 1997 economic crisis, and the government is no longer capable of carrying out the same developmental policies as in the 1980s.

Some shifts in local cultural policies are embedded in changing scenes and politics of a series of global finance and economic development. For instance, in the realm of culture, as the most powerful force, the U.S. government, alongside several transnational media corporations, has forced other governments to take on neoliberal reforms, including the liberalization of the cultural market. As these demands took root, many countries have been compelled to adopt neoliberal globalization to survive and nurture their own cultural industries as part of globalizing cultural markets. Therefore, several scholars (Strange 1996; Sinclair 2007) argue that the nation-state as a meaningful unit in the global culture is in decline, as diverse globalizing processes, in particular the liberalization of the local cultural markets, undermine it. Castells (2009) also argues that globalization, in its different dimensions, destabilizes the autonomy and decision-making power of the government. In cultural trade, Harvey (2006) especially points out that the nation-state has been challenged, although the pivotal role of the nation-state is worthy of careful attention. Meanwhile, Hjarvard (2003) emphasizes that the weakening role of the nation-state has subsequently resulted in the decreasing role of local culture and cultural identity in many non-Western countries.

Within this context, many globalization theorists forecast the end of national boundaries, national corporations, national industries, and the end of national economies, including the media and cultural industries sectors, where all will merge into corresponding transnational organizations outside the reach of national regulations and actions. These views rest on the shared assumption that economics increasingly controls politics, where economic globalization transforms the political and the social affairs of interconnected human communities throughout the world (Kim 2000). Contrary to these continuing predicates of globalization theory, our central claim is to argue against the normative body of works that see globalization as an enduring and inevitable process that offers the promise of widespread and potentially unparalleled prosperity for the planet (Ryoo 2008, 873, 874).

Instead, our contention is that globalization is a historically contingent and complex dialectical process that exists in tension and in oscillation with the different path of modernization and developmentalism. The movement between these two orientations toward cultural policies corresponds with the South Korean case. We argue that neither neoliberalism nor developmentalism is a stabilized ideology of state involvement (or disinvolvement) with its cultural, as well as economic policies, but a specific mode of state involvement in the guise of laissez-faire. Although cultural policies may still not be at the top of policy-makers' agendas, the importance of their influence on international and national politics is undeniable. Two broad forces, one rooted in political economy of globalization and the other in the latter's cultural politics may be identified (Singh 2010, 9).

As the global cultural industries since the early 1990s have become some of the major sectors in the global economy (Herman and McChesney 1997), the role of nation-states on cultural industries policies and cultural flows has been more complicated and nuanced because nation-states still play a major role in the growth of domestic cultural industries (Fulcher 2000; Liow 2011; Hundt 2015). In fact, several scholars (Wong 2004; Cherry 2005; Hundt 2005; Kim, Han, and Jang 2008; Suh and Kwon 2014) argued that government intervention has persisted in many countries, including Korea 'despite market-oriented reforms and neoliberal globalization' (Suh and Kwon 2014, 680), and the Korean government has indeed retained its strong control as a developmental state in the national economy and the cultural sector.

In the cultural industries, several media critics also argued for the consistent and even intensifying role of the government. Pieterse (2004, 46) claims, while 'neoliberal ideology pleads for small government,' some nation-states are still strong and regulate by deregulating. Some critical media scholars (Fulcher 2000; Sánchez Ruiz 2001; Stuart 2001; Wu and Chan 2007) also argue that the role of the government and cultural trade is more complex than many globalists who claim the decreasing role of the government, because many countries have continued to protect their own popular culture, effectively staging confrontations with globalization. Taking the Canadian cultural market as an example, Stuart (2001, 431) argued that 'the mass culture often originating in, but no longer wholly associated with the United States, has not produced the death of Canada as a nation-state, nor is it likely to do so.'

As such, over the past two decades, the national cultural industries and consequently the Korean Wave have grown amid the conflicts between state-developmentalism and neoliberal globalization. In particular, 'with the popularity of Korean popular culture in many parts of the world, Korea, which was once a representative Asian developmental state, has been a pivotal subject of research in the debates over the characteristics of post-developmental states,' as it has rapidly adopted neoliberal reforms (Heo 2015, 351). The Korean government since the mid-1980s has deregulated and liberalized the cultural industries based on its neoliberal tendencies; however, the Korean state has developed its unique cultural policy to support and/or initiate the growth of the cultural sector.[5]

More specifically, while the Korean government has executed neoliberal reform in other fields, many administrations have adopted a state-led development approach in the realm of popular culture, while some administrations took neoliberal cultural tendencies. Therefore, the development of the Korean cultural industries has been a showcase and the remarkable growth cannot be understood without considering the role of the government in supporting the advancement of the industries with both legal and financial arms. As Lee (2013, 186) aptly puts it, 'the cultural policy's full embrace of the phenomenon to the degree where the Korean Wave itself becomes a policy paradigm will be reflected in the historical transformation of the relationship between the state and the popular culture.'

Within the Korean administrations, neoliberal cultural policies between liberal and conservative governments have substantially changed according to their political agendas. Therefore, the execution of developmental paradigm of nation-state against neoliberal globalization for the Korean Wave cultural policies and tradition needs to be fully analysed. The nuanced analysis of the conflicts between liberal administrations emphasizing neoliberal developmentalism – primarily utilizing neoliberalism to develop cultural industries – and conservative administrations mainly appropriating developmentalism will shed light on the current debates on the role of the government in the Korean Wave phenomenon in the global markets.

## The emergence of neoliberal developmentalism in the pre-Hallyu era

While there are several sociocultural elements in developing the local cultural industries, one of the most significant characteristics is cultural policy that has greatly influenced the Korean Wave. The acceptance of Korean cultural products in the global markets has markedly shifted as cultural policy has evolved. Historicizing Korea's cultural policy until the early 1980s, two major approaches had been developed by the government. One is the emphasis on cultural identity through culture and art. Back then, the essential cultural policy objective focused on arts, such as national music, painting and calligraphy, and tried to establish cultural identity while promoting the vitalization of the arts, which implies that cultural policy under the military regime was primarily synonymous with arts policy (Yim 2003, 99–101). For the military regimes, cultural policy was not for the cultural industries, because they did not consider culture as part of the industries that they supported. Therefore, cultural policy was limited to traditional music and arts, instead of popular culture. The other is cultural policy as control of the cultural industries through censorship. The ultimate goal of the Park Chung-hee (1962–1980) regime was to achieve a high level of economic development to provide legitimacy for their military government. All other social, political and cultural domains of the nation were mobilized by the Park regime to achieve the political and economic goals (Kwon and Kim 2014). The cultural industries were heavily censored and controlled by the governments, so they were very underdeveloped.

Starting in the early 1990s, changes in the political, economic and social environment led to a shift in the government's perception of the cultural industries, which means that the governments after 1993 came to acknowledge the economic importance of culture, not as an art but as a commodity (Jin 2011a; Kwon and Kim 2014). After the 1990s, when the neoliberal vision became a global norm, the Korean government put abundant stress on unlimited competition with other countries on a global scale. The Kim Young-sam government (1993–1998) designated 1994 as the year for enhancing national competitiveness and pushed to make Korea a member country of the OECD (Organization for Economic Co-operation and Development).

The Kim government consequently brought the concept of the cultural industries to cultural policy, shifted the focus of cultural policy from arts to commercial cultural industries, and intensified the commodification of local popular culture. This means that the Korean government has allowed the cultural sector to operate in accordance with the logic of neoliberalism (Jin 2016). As Adorno and Horkheimer (1972) argued, cultural goods and services began to be commercially produced, reproduced and distributed as a part of a strategy directed towards economic growth in Korea.

However, the Kim government continued state-led developmentalism in that it 'set up the Cultural Industries Directorate in 1994 within the cultural ministry whose policy priorities included the industrialization of culture and the internationalization of Korean culture' (Lee 2013, 189). The Kim government understood the significance of export – the internationalization of Korean culture – for the Korean economy as the country has achieved its economic growth based on an 'export-led economic model' (Amsden 1989). The Kim government started to support the audio-visual sector, which became a basis for the growth of the Korean Wave afterwards. The government, for example, initiated the growth of the film industry by enacting the Motion Picture Promotion Law in 1995 (Shin 2005). The new law included diverse incentives, including tax breaks for film studios to welcome *chaebol* (family-owned conglomerates, such as Samsung, Hyundai, and LG) capital into the film industry (Paquet 2005). The Korean government back then, therefore, advanced neoliberal developmentalism, which means that it started to adopt neoliberal globalization strategies while continuously utilizing governmental intervention in the realm of culture. As such, the conflicts between neoliberal reform and developmentalism starting in the Kim Young Sam government has become a unique nature of Korea's cultural policy, which has eventually advanced the growth of domestic cultural industries.

## Neoliberal cultural industries policy in the liberal governments

Since the late 1990s, the Korean government has taken significantly different positions towards the cultural industries and the Korean Wave in terms of political ideologies and the nature of government intervention. Both the Kim Dae-jung and Roh Moo-hyun administrations were liberal and initiated several supports to the cultural industries; however, they mainly pursued neoliberal reforms, characterizing a small government. For example, the major neoliberal cultural policies that the liberal governments pursued came in the form of changes in the screen quota system and indirect promotion policies for the Korean Wave phenomenon (Jin 2016).

Most of all, the Kim Dae-jung government (1998–2003) emphasized neoliberal globalization, stressing the need to understand the rules for unfettered competition on a global scale. After the 1997 financial crisis, which was the worst economic crisis in Korea's modern history, resulting in the International Monetary Fund (IMF) bailout programme, the Kim Dae-jung government had no choice but to develop neoliberal reforms under the IMF programme. The Kim government tried not to hinder Korean cultural penetration just started in many Asian countries by employing indirect promotion policies, avoiding the appearance of initiating Korea's cultural invasion into other Asian countries (Jin 2011b). For example, the Kim government has relatively less supportive broadcasting policies for local media industries than the previous administrations. In 2001, three major networks, such as KBS, MBC, and SBS dominated television programme production and accounted for 90.6% of television programme exports (Korea Press Foundation 2003, 302). However, the Broadcasting Act Enforcement Ordinance under the Kim government demanded network broadcasters must air up to 40% of programmes produced by independent producers to develop domestic audiovisual industries; therefore, the number of small producers increased (Jin 2011a). The Kim government's plan to develop domestic audiovisual industries by increasing television programmes produced by independent producers certainly showed the decreasing role in major networks, representing the broadcasting industry, which can be considered as one of the major neoliberal cultural policies.

In fact, as clearly indicated in the New Culture and Tourism Policy announced in 1998, the Kim government pursued a small but efficient government under the IMF bailout programme. The cultural sector was not exceptional. Although the Kim government developed several financial and legal measures, including the expansion of culture within the government budget to 1%, to funding cultural industries, its supports to the cultural industries, again, aimed to avoid any direct intervention (Ministry of Culture and Tourism 2001, 28). The Kim government strategically pursued indirect, instead of direct and active, policies. During the process, the Kim government executed to break up the government and big corporations, in this case, major networks, which was neoliberal in nature.

The indirect and inactive cultural policy continued to the end of the Roh Moo-hyun government, although the degrees were different, primarily because of Roh's political decision to get a Korea-U.S. FTA (free trade agreement). During his initial stage of presidency, Roh, as the most liberal politician, clearly expressed his intention to support the cultural industries and created several supporting mechanisms; however, President Roh changed his economic and cultural policy directions. In other words, President Roh originally emphasized creativity, diversity, and dynamism in the cultural sector of the inaugural stage of the government; however, Roh suddenly pursued growth of the national economy by working with large conglomerates and foreign forces, which greatly influenced his cultural policy (Choi 2013; Jin 2016).

During his inauguration speech, indeed Roh (2003) talked about his intention to support the cultural industries by saying, 'I will promote culture and extend active support for the progress of culture industries.' Just before starting the FTA drive, during his congressional speech in October 2004, he stated that

> cultural creativity and diversity are great assets to open Korea's possibility and future. In recent years, Korean movies had received several awards in global film festivals, and drams embedded in local mentalities and cultures generated the Korean Wave boom in several Asian countries. I will actively develop the cultural industries as a future driving force.

Ultimately, he kept his promise, at least for a while.

The Ministry of Culture and Tourism also developed its supportive policy measures. One of the most significant directions could be found in C-Korea 2010 Vision. The Ministry of Culture and Tourism developed the C-Korea 2010 blueprint designed to meet three policy objectives to turn Korea into a top five culture industry country in the globe;

> The ministry's blueprint initiatives are based on three C's: content, creativity and culture. In order to spread the word about Hallyu around the world, the blueprint envisions Korean Plazas in 15 cities in Asia, Central and South America and Western and Eastern Europe. These tourism and commodity-related pavilions are expected to attract widespread interest in Korea and its culture and to create demand for Korean cultural industry exports. C-Korea 2010 puts private sector creativity in the driver's seat with the goal of becoming a key supporter of the nation's drive to achieve a US$30,000 per capita gross national income (GNI). In this respect, it envisions culture industry incubators with a focus on a market-friendly structure, the establishment of a special fund and the encouragement of build-transfer-lease (BTL) projects. (C-Korea 2010)

However, once Roh desired to advance national economy, Korea's cultural policy dramatically shifted. President Roh's primary economic objective was reaching a per capita income level of U.S. $20,000. According to The Proposed South Korea-U.S. Free Trade Agreement (KORUS FTA) (2007), Roh made an FTA the top economic priority during his tenure. Soon after his election in 2002, Roh committed himself to raising Korea's per capita gross domestic product (GDP) to $20,000 by the end of the decade and to transforming Korea into a major economic hub in Northeast Asia by expanding the economic reforms.

President Roh's political direction, again, fundamentally changed before and after his drive towards the Korea-U.S. FTA. In his speech on The Export Day in October 2006, he stated that 'I continue to try to enhance national images in conjunction with the diffusion of Hallyu.' However, he dedicated much time to support his new policy priority, which is the FTA by saying,

> The Korea-U.S. FTA is a new opportunity for Korea to jump to developed economy. The FTA will intensify Korea's stance in the largest global market and positively influence foreign direct investments .... I will do my best to settle by all means the Korea-U.S. FTA. (Roh 2006)

Once Roh shifted his political economic agenda, the government, including the Ministry of Culture and Tourism, had to change its policy priorities. Chang-dong Lee – the Minister of Culture and Tourism – for example, changed his stance. Lee was himself a movie director who fiercely opposed the reduction of the screen quota yet had to change his position when President Roh strongly pursed the Korea-U.S. FTA (Kim 2011).

Consequently, the Korean government scapegoated the screen quota system, which had contributed to the growth of Korean cinema since its introduction in 1967. In 2006 the Roh government deregulated this pivotal policy for Korean cinema under pressure from the U.S. as a precondition for starting talks for the Korea-U.S. FTA, which means that the role of the government in the film sector substantially decreased (Kim 2011). The government has reduced the screen quota, from 146 days per year to 73 days a year, from July 2006 onwards, which has severely influenced Korean cinema for several years.[6] The Roh government also significantly changed foreign ownership within the broadcasting sector. Korea has made the commitment to phase in 100% foreign ownership of programme providers (channel operators), other than those offering multi-genre, news or home-shopping programming, for firms that establish a local subsidiary. It also allowed U.S. investment in IPTV, which opened substantial new opportunities for U.S. interests in the Korean broadcasting marketplace (The United States-Korea Free Trade Agreement 2007). The Roh government also cut the budget for the cultural industries. In particular, the Roh government abrogated the Cultural Industry Promotion Fund in 2007, which was established in 1999 to support corporations operating in the cultural industries, resulting in the plummeting of financial support to the cultural industries (Park 2012; MCST 2013, 41).

Meanwhile, in 2007 the Ministry of Culture and Tourism changed the fundamental notion of C Korea 2010; emphasizing contents, culture and creativity, to culture, competitiveness, and creativity. During his speech at the Global Culture Forum 2007 Seoul, Myung Gon Kim (2007) – the Minister of Culture and Tourism – stated that

> we need to enhance competitiveness. In a culture where competitiveness is considered to be the most important value, only those cultures that survived in competition will most likely be regarded as strong and good ones. This will severely damage cultural diversity.

In this respect, he continued to state that 'we need to abandon the attitude of giving our priority only to the economy and see creativity, diversity, and identity as a whole to judge competitiveness.' However, he also mentioned that 'there is a strong demand for appropriate policies to sharpen the competitive edge of our culture-related industries, including the cultural industry, which can yield high added value.' While emphasizing the significance of cultural diversity and creativity, he addressed the notion of competitiveness as one of the most significant agendas for the cultural industry, which clearly proves the nuanced and sophisticated government policy in the Roh government. It implies that, although the Roh government's cultural policies sought to appropriate the logics of neoliberal reforms, we also need to understand that this might be a more of strategic manoeuvring of cultural policies in a flexible fashion to fit to local conditions and context, in the midst of globalization. In other words, indicating its overall sociocultural concerns for cultural policy, the Roh Moo-hyun government (2003–2008) expected the Korean Wave to serve as a potential catalyst for transnational cultural dialogue, the development of Northeast Asian culture and increased cultural collaboration within the Asian region (Ministry of Culture and Tourism 2004; Lee 2013, 191).

As proved in many other countries, including the U.S., popular culture is a distinctive area that the government supports in terms of planning and infrastructure (Lee 2007), not only because of its potential as cultural industries creating economic values, but because of its crucial role of nation-building. As such, the growth of local popular culture and its export to the global markets deeply influence both people's cultural activities and national images, which justify the active role of the government. However, the liberal governments in Korea were primarily negligent because these governments weighed the country's economic growth over the cultural industries in responding to both global and local political-economic milieu surrounding their administrations.

## Developmental neoliberal cultural industries policy in the conservative governments

Cultural industries policy has changed once again since 2008. The conservative governments, both the Lee Myung-bak and Park Geun-hye administrations developed new policy measures to advance the export of cultural products. Favourable cultural policy for the cultural industries by the conservative governments has been well articulated in presidential speeches. The two previous liberal governments focused on the national economy by sacrificing the cultural industries in terms of the government funding and legal measures, moves which were triggered by the 1997 economic crisis and the subsequent IMF bail-out package. However, the two conservative administrations considered the cultural industries as one of the most significant areas that the government must support to foster growth. During his inauguration speech, Lee (2008) stated;

> The Korean Wave that is now well placed around the globe testifies to the advantage of skillful replications of such a long tradition. Modernization of traditional culture is useful for facilitating arts and culture and such attempts surely dignify the country's economic prosperity. Now, culture has become an industry. We must develop our competitiveness in our content industries, thereby laying the foundation to become a nation strong in cultural activities. The new Administration will do its best to bring the power of our culture into a full blossom in this globalized setting of the 21st century.

The policy changes from hands-off, which is indirect and passive, to hands-on, which is direct and active, approaches in the cultural industries were faithfully executed by the executive branch, in particular the Ministry of Culture and Tourism.

On the one hand, the Lee government newly established the Ministry of Culture, Sports and Tourism (MCST) in 2008 by converging the existing Ministry of Culture and Tourism (MCT) and the Ministry of Information and Communication (MIC). The MCST developed the notion of the content industries in the Lee government and creative industries in the Park Geun-hye government and placed their importance as primary driving forces within the wider national economy. This means that both the Lee and Park governments intended to develop popular culture as cultural commodities for the Korean economy.

Instead of developing new creative mechanisms to advance cultural identity and sovereignty in the cultural industries, by furthermore commercializing and marketizing cultural content, they jumped on the band wagon that was already operating at increasing speed and scope.

On the other hand, the Lee government supported the cultural industries with both financial and legal arms. In 2011, the Korean government established the Contents Industries Promotion Committee, chaired by Prime Minister. The Committee developed on annual action plans consisting of several strategies to strengthen the competiveness of Korea's creative industries. For example, based on the discussions and actions plans decided by the Committee, the Korean government decided to spend a total of 452.2 billion won in 2015. The government therefore supported Korean film festivals and helped broadcast Korean TV soap operas abroad in a bid to promote cultural exchange and to improve Korea's national images (Contents Industry Promotion Committee 2011; Limb 2014).

While several reasons explain why the Lee government pursued these cultural policies, the Lee government, followed by the Park Geun-hye government, especially sought to connect the Korean Wave and soft power. Again, as Nye (2004, 256) argued, soft power means 'the ability to get what you want through attraction rather than coercion or payments' via culture, values and foreign policies. The Lee government continuously emphasized that the government planned to build up national power with culture. During the first year of Lee's administration, the government highlighted culture as a criterion of national competitiveness and a sine qua non for improving the national brand, thereby strengthening the ability of public diplomacy and giving positive impressions to foreign people, and improving enterprises' images overseas (MCST 2009, Kim and Jin 2016). In this regard, the Lee government expanded the scope of the Korean Wave to food, sports, and tourism. It is certain that

> the Lee government fundamentally developed the cultural industries with the name of contents industries, emphasizing the production and the export of cultural contents; as if he is the CEO of a corporation, the Lee government was known as corporate state. (Choi 2013, 257)

The Lee government was

> the most neoliberal of all Korean governments. It sought to promote the growth of the economy through pro-business policies such as low corporate taxes and low interest rates. Even under Lee, however, the government retained its capacity to intervene in the economy

as well as in the cultural industries (Suh and Kwon 2014, 689). In this regard, the Lee government's cultural industries policies can be identified as developmental neoliberalism, because it mainly developed the nexus of the government and big corporations, including mega media and cultural firms. The priority of the Lee government in the cultural sector was the growth of cultural contents developed by major cultural industries corporations, including CJ and Lotte, and it continued to deregulate and liberalize the cultural markets.

Meanwhile, as one of the key presidential election promises was continued support for Korea's creative economy and its cultural industries, the Park Geun-hye government (2013–2017)[7] pursued and even intensified its supportive cultural policy in the cultural industries (Kwon and Kim 2014; Jin 2016). Park planned to implement more funds and policies for the culture sector when she stepped into power in February 2013 (Lee 2012). During her inaugural speech on 25 February 2013, Park emphasized the significance of the Korean Wave and her intention to support it:

> In the 21st century, culture is power. It is an era where an individual's imagination becomes creative contents. Across the world, the Korean Wave is welcomed with great affection that not only triggers happiness and joy but one that instills abiding pride in all Koreans .... The new administration will elevate the sanctity of our spiritual ethos so that they can permeate every facet of society and in so doing, enable all of our citizens to enjoy life enriched by culture. Creative activities across wide-ranging genres will be supported, while the contents industry which merges culture with advanced technology will be nurtured. In so doing, we will ignite the engine of a creative economy and create new jobs. (Park 2013)

As President Park planned, the MCST (2013) immediately announced that it would substantially improve its supporting mechanism to the cultural industries. During the annual report to the president in March 2013, the ministry stated that it especially fosters five major contents areas which are globally competitive, consisting of digital games, K-pop, animation/character, music, and musical. For example, it planned to construct a K-pop performance centre near Seoul, while expanding its financial subsidies to the animation/character sector, from 92 million Korean won in 2013 to 200 million won in 2017. Unlike previous governments, the conservative governments also announced that they planned to develop fashion and webtoon as new areas of the Korean Wave (MCST 2013, 20, 21).

The government budget also demonstrates the increasing role of the conservative government in the cultural industries. Unlike the liberal governments, in particular, the Roh Moo-hyun government which decreased the budget towards the cultural industries of the Ministry of Culture, Sports and Tourism, from 12.7% in 2003 to 9% in 2007, the conservative governments have increased the same budget, from 9.9% in 2008 to 15.6% in 2015 (MCST 2013, 41, 2015; Jin 2016). The Park government's main agenda indeed was to increase the allotted budget for the culture ministry to 2% by the end of her term in 2017. As of 2012, it was 1.14% as being far from the average of 1.9% for other OECD countries (Lee 2012).

Of course, as in the Lee government, the Park administration's cultural politics was complicated as her administration made several negative political decisions in the realm of the cultural sector, including its budget cut to the Pusan Film Festival and the creations of the blacklist of artists encompassing more than 1000 anti-government cultural producers, media scholars, and practitioners. Officially, Park has made promoting movies and other cultural products one of her key priorities. But secretly, her government has blackballed artists, reviving a practice of past military dictators like her father, Park Chung-hee, and in so doing has "seriously undermined the freedom of thought and expression" (Hun 2017). The Park administration certainly executes its role as a developmental state, either supporting the cultural sector through government budgets or severely regulating the cultural sector through budget cuts and/or censorship.

In the Korean context, the developmental state is still running strong although the major characteristic is being changed as sociopolitical milieus are played out. Neoliberal globalization enforces certain restrictions on particular levels of cultural policy; however, the character of the Korean state has continued supporting cultural industries. As the cultural industries have become one of the most significant parts of the national economy in terms of exports, the Korean governments, in particular, the conservative governments have prioritized the cultural sector. The government sometimes emphasized its role as the regulator through financial and legal mechanism.

As such, cultural industries policy in the conservative governments emphasizes the commercial role of Korean popular culture in the global cultural markets and develops mechanisms to support cultural exportation. For the Lee and Park governments, the cultural flows of local popular culture were essential because, again, the Korean Wave has played a major role for both the national economy and soft power. Although transnational flows of culture have increased and made it far more difficult for the nation-state to control, there are great variations in the capacity of states to control (Holton 1998, cited in Fulcher 2000). The Korean government has reconstructed its authority in the middle of the confrontation between neoliberal reforms and state-developmentalism. The Korean government since 2008 has advanced a developmental neoliberal cultural policy, which means that the government, instead of only adopting neoliberal reforms, has acted as a key supporter of the Korean Wave in the tradition of its state-led interventionism. Given that the nature of the support, emphasizing competitiveness and global flows of local popular culture, is neoliberal, it is certain that neoliberalism has been embedded in the process; however, neoliberalism cannot eradicate the significance of the nation-state in the Korean context.

## Discussion and conclusion

This essay has analysed the role of the nation-state with the case of the cultural industries. During the growth of the local cultural industries and consequently the Korean Wave over the past twenty years, cultural policy has been considered one of the most significant driving forces. What is interesting is that the Korean government has fundamentally changed its cultural policy toward the cultural industries amid conflicts between neoliberal and developmental perspectives. In other words, the local cultural industries have been advanced sometimes by emphasizinq developmentalism and at other times focusing on neoliberal cultural policies.

The Korean Wave phenomenon has begun with some television programmes mainly since 1997, therefore, it started to analyse the increasing role of the Kim Young-sam government, which paved the road for the growth of cultural industries. The Kim government extensively adopted neoliberal reforms; however, unlike other countries, such as Mexico, Brazil and Chile, it strategically emphasized the significance of the cultural industries and the export of cultural products. As his concept of globalization did not only open the domestic market to foreign forces, but also ask domestic corporations to penetrate the global markets, the government pursed several supportive cultural policies to enhance the national economy. In this context, the Kim government can be characterized by 'neoliberal developmentalism,' by which neoliberalism is utilized as a tool to fulfil government's developmental purposes (Yoon 2009).

The two following liberal governments – Kim Dae-jung and Roh Moo-hyun – continued developing neoliberal economic policy. It was indispensable for the Kim Dae-jung government primarily because of the 1997 economic crisis. The Kim Dae-jung government had no choice but to develop neoliberal reforms in return for the IMF bailout programmes. In the case of the Roh Moo-hyun government, Roh championed neoliberal globalization as evidenced in the case of the U.S.-Korea FTA. During the process, although the government offered limited support to the cultural industries, these areas were not a main concern for liberal administrations. The liberal governments had continued to adopt an increasingly neoliberal approach that is less supportive of government intervention in the cultural industry.

The role of the Korean government in tandem with the cultural industries much changed when Lee Myung-bak took political power in 2008. The conservative governments until the Park Geun-hye administration have developed their cultural policies, renamed the cultural contents and the creative industries. As expected, they have taken the core of a neo-liberalized regime; however, they undertake active and direct cultural policy measures. While the relationship between the nation-state and the cultural industries has undergone a vibrant transformation since the early 1990s, the conservative governments have acted as the supporters of the growth of the Korean cultural industries.

> Neoliberal and consumerist orientation in cultural policy did not outdate its long-standing development approach: governmental planning and investment have intensified in order to address the policy goal of helping Korean cultural industries fit in the increasingly globalized economy and expanding their overseas markets. (Lee 2013, 186)

The conservative governments had taken developmental neoliberal policy, which emphasized the role of the nation state in the cultural sector, while continuing their expansion of neoliberal reforms. As Pieterse (2004) points out, one of the fundamental contradictions of neoliberal globalization concerns the role of government which arguably opened up in the Korean cultural industries and the Korean Wave.

In general, under neoliberal reform, the primary role of the Korean government has been somewhat decreased; however, the nation-state remains and unexpectedly intensifies its role in popular culture. 'The nation-state changes, as does the context within which it operates, but there is no sign of its demise or withering away' (Fulcher 2000, 541), and in countries like Korea, it is not likely to witness the decreasing role of the nation-state with some exception. While implementing its commercial identities, the government plays a significant role. It illustrates that neoliberalism does not necessarily weaken nation-states in the realm of popular culture. Instead, In some circumstances, the government has reinforced and even intensified its centrality to cultural life. The Korean cultural industries and the Korean Wave have grown in the middle of a coexistence of neoliberalism and developmentalism. Neoliberalism has not completely altered the Korean state-interventionism in the cultural industries, while state-led developmentalism only cannot be a sole mechanism in the growth of the local cultural industries.

In this respect, it is not dangerous or controversial to argue that the Korean governments have advanced the logic of neoliberal agendas, while structurally developing state-led developmental principles, which make the Korean cultural industries and the Korean Wave unique in terms of the role of the nation-state. In the realm of popular culture, the Korean government has developed a style of neoliberalism with Korean individualities rooted in developmental paradigm. There is no doubt that

Korea began the transition to a neoliberal state in the late 1980s, but the fundamental stance of the government remained that of a developmental state throughout, and that the capacity of government to exercise strong intervention in the cultural industries has been retained in a different degree and attitude according to each administration's agenda and ideology. In other words, this coexistence of cultural policies was a deliberate choice of the government, which deployed a flexible policy mix in responding to changes in the environment and hence contributed to continuing growth and development over the past two decades (Suh and Kwon 2014).

Of course, it is certain that the Korean government, whether they execute neoliberal developmental, neoliberal, or developmental neoliberal mechanisms, commonly develops cultural policy emphasizing market-based aspects of the creative industries. In other words, all successive governments have developed their cultural policies in the name of economic imperatives. Since the Kim Young-sam administration introduced globalization, the Korean state has emphasized the market and supported cultural industries corporations, many of them being mega corporations. Korea's cultural policy has not been purely formed by the notion of cultural identity, and these administrations have not been actively initiated in developing national culture, but cultural economy embedded in the Korean Wave.

To conclude, both liberal and conservative administrations have promoted the competitiveness of Korean national economy and image through the growth of cultural industries and the Korean Wave; however, the scale and scope of each administration toward their cultural policies were not identical in their emphasis on developmentalism and/or neoliberalism. This kind of difference in its agenda and ideology of each administration has resulted in considerable structural transformations in national mediascape, as well as global cultural scene.

## Notes

1. K-pop was relatively unknown to the global music markets until early 2001 when SM Entertainment began to promote a teenage-girl singer named BoA who precisely targeted the Japanese market (Jung 2013). In the music industry, the foreign export includes recorded music (sales of music CDs), digital music (online sales), and music events, including music concerts. However, given rampant illegal downloads of music, the popularity of K-pop in the 2010s could be much bigger than the money value mentioned above (MCST 2012).
2. For example, the Korean cultural industries, such as broadcasting and film, had to develop their own local cultural products because many cable program providers had not enough budget to import foreign programs in the post 1997 economic crisis and also they were mandated to do so according to their government-issued licences and programing guidelines.
3. Then, the cultural industries were not the main part of the national economy and popular culture was not a tangible commodity for the governments who pursued export-led economic policies.
4. Admitting diverse approaches and interpretations, this essay mainly interprets the nation-building process from a political economy approach because the Korean government mainly utilized the notion of nation-building for the development of the national economy. As Mosco (1996, 200) argued, 'processes of nation-building are viewed as occupying a political space either supporting or resisting the economic imperative,' and therefore nation-building is a political economy process. Of course,

   > nation building is more than a political or a cultural question led by governments, because it is also 'an economic strategy for determining the most appropriate way of consolidating an economic system based on industry, commercial relations and professional know-how.' This means that we must accept that 'national identity, as a collective identity, is defined not only by the producers' proposal.

   At the same time, "it must be known how the production process works, how television programs and films define the nation, 'on which terms cultural policy is involved in the process, and which economic and political factors must be taken into account" (Enric 2007, 50).
5. In the realm of culture, the direct distribution rights of Hollywood studios started in 1988, which was forced by the U.S. government and Hollywood studios cleared indicated that the Korean government started to develop neoliberal reforms by deregulating and liberalizing the cultural markets.
6. The exports of domestic films plummeted, from $76 million in 2004 to only $13.6 million in 2010, with a slight recovery in recent years (e.g. $29.3 million in 2015) (Korean Film Council 2016).
7. President Park Geun-hye was removed from office on 10 March 2017, as the Korean Constitutional Court unanimously upheld a parliamentary vote to impeach her for her role in a corruption and influence-peddling scandal. The impeachment marks a historic moment in Korea that adopted democracy only 30 years ago. In sharp

contrast with Korea's history of military coups, peaceful protests this time led to the removal of an elected leader (Fifield 2017). President Park became Korea's first president to be impeached, and this resulted in quick elections for a new president to be held within 60 days, that was held in 9 May 2017.

## Disclosure statement

No potential conflict of interest was reported by the authors.

## References

Adorno, T., and M. Horkheimer. 1972. *Dialectic of Enlightenment*. New York: Verso.

Amsden, A. 1989. *Asia's Next Giant: South Korea and Late Industrialization*. New York: Oxford University Press.

Bockman, J. 2013. "Neoliberalism." *Contexts* 12 (3): 14–15.

Castells, M. 2009. *The Power of Identity*. 2nd ed. Malden, MA: Wiley-Blackwell.

Cherry, J. 2005. "'Big Deal' or Big Disappointment? The Continuing Evolution of the South Korean Developmental State." *The Pacific Review* 18 (3): 327–354.

Choi, Y. H. 2013. "The Korean Wave Policy as a Corporate-state Project of Lee Government: The Analysis of Structures and Strategies Based on the Strategic-relational Approach." *Economy and Society* 97 (3): 252–285.

C-Korea. 2010. "Cultural Industry Enriching Koran Competitiveness." http://www.industrykorea.net/gov_press_view00.htm.

Contents Industry Promotion Committee. 2011. *The First Contents Industry Promotion Basic Plan, 2011–2013*. Seoul: MCST.

Enric, Castello. 2007. "The Production of Television Fiction and Nation Building." *European Journal of Communication* 22 (1): 49–68.

Fifield, A. 2017. "South Korean President Removed from Office over Corruption Scandal." *Washington Post*, March 10. https://www.washingtonpost.com/world/asia_pacific/south-korean-president-impeached-from-office-over-corruption-scandal/2017/03/09/23666a46-0488-11e7-a391-651727e77fc0_story.html?utm_term=.e1113fcdb5d7.

Friedman, M. 1982. *Capitalism and Freedom*. Chicago, IL: The University of Chicago Press.

Fulcher, J. 2000. "Globalisation, the Nation-state and Global Society." *The Sociological Review* 48 (4): 522–543.

Harvey, D. 2005. *A Brief History of Neoliberalism*. Oxford: Oxford University Press.

Harvey, S. 2006. "Indigenous Culture and the Politics of Place: Regulation for Regionalism in British Broadcasting." In *Trading Culture: Global Traffic and Local Cultures in Film and Television*, edited by Harvey Sylvia, 47–57. Eastleigh: John Libbey Publishing.

Heo, I. H. 2015. "Neoliberal Developmentalism in South Korea: Evidence from the Green Growth Policymaking Process." *Asia Pacific Viewpoint* 56 (3): 351–364.

Herman, E., and R. McChesney. 1997. *The Global Media: The New Missionaries of Corporate Capitalism*. London: Cassell.

Hesmondhalgh, D., and A. Pratt. 2005. "Media and Cultural Policy as Public Policy." *International Journal of Cultural Policy* 11 (1): 95–109.

Hjarvard, S. 2003. *Media in a Globalized Society*. Copenhagen: Museum Tusculanum Press.

Hun, C. 2017. "South Korea's Blacklist of Artists Adds to Outrage over Presidential Scandal." *New York Times*, January 17. https://www.nytimes.com/2017/01/12/world/asia/south-korea-president-park-blacklist-artists.html?_r=0.

Hundt, D. 2005. "A Legitimate Paradox: Neo-liberal Reform and the Return of the State in Korea." *Journal of Development Studies* 41 (2): 242–260.

Hundt, D. 2015. "Neoliberalism, the Developmental State and Civil Society in Korea." *Asian Studies Review* 39 (3): 466–482.

Jin, D. Y. 2011a. *Hands on Hands Off: The Korean State and the Market Liberalization of the Communication Industry*. New York: Hampton Press.

Jin, D. Y. 2011b. "Cultural Politics in Japanization and the Korean Wave: The Changing Role of Nation-states in the midst of Cultural Globalization." In *Hallyu: Influence of Korean Popular Culture in Asia and beyond*, edited by D. K. Kim and M. S. Kim, 91–129. Seoul: Seoul National University.

Jin, D. Y. 2016. *New Korean Wave: Transnational Popular Culture in the Age of Social Media*. Urbana: The University of Illinois Press.

Jung, S. 2013. "Performing Trans-nationality, Trans-sexuality, and Trans-textuality." In *Asian Popular Culture in Transition*, edited by L. Fitzsimmons and J. Lent, 108–130. London: Routledge.

Kang, N. H. 2012. The Vacillation of Culture in Neoliberal South Korea. SOAS-AKS Working Papers in Korean Studies 21, April.

Kim, S. 2000. *Korea's Globalization*. Cambridge: Cambridge University Press.

Kim, M. G. 2007. *Korea's Cultural Policy at Global Cultural Forum 2007 Seoul*. Seoul: Ministry of Culture and Tourism.

Kim, J. S. 2011. "A Case Study on the Reduction of Korea's Screen Quota." *Culture & Society* 10 (5): 289–326.

Kim, S. H., C. H. Han, and J. H. Jang. 2008. "State-society Relations in South Korea after Democratization: Is the Strong State Defunct?" *Pacific Focus* 23 (2): 252–270.

Kim, T. Y., and D. Y. Jin. 2016. "Cultural Policy in the Korean Wave: An Analysis of Cultural Diplomacy Embedded in Presidential Speeches." *International Journal of Communication* 10: 5514–5534.

Korea Press Foundation. 2003. *Korea Media Yearbook 2002/2003*. Seoul: Korean Press Foundation.

Korean Creative Content Agency. 2016. *2016 Contents Industry Perspective*. Naju: KOCCA.

Korean Film Council. 2016. *2015 Korean Cinema Summary*. Busan: KOFIC.

Kwon, S. H., and J. Kim. 2014. "The Cultural Industry Policies of the Korean Government and the Korean Wave." *International Journal of Cultural Policy* 20 (4): 422–439.

Lee, B. M. 2007. "An Evaluation of Cultural Industry Policies in Korean Participatory Government and Future Policy." *Humanities Contents* 9: 205–235.

Lee, M. B. 2008. Presidential Inauguration Speech, February 28.

Lee, H. W. 2012. "S. Korea's President-elect Promises to Expand Support for Arts and Entertainment." *The Hollywood Reporter*, December 20. http://www.hollywoodreporter.com/news/s-koreas-president-elect-promises-405840.

Lee, H. K. 2013. "Cultural Policy and the Korean Wave: From National Culture to Transnational Consumerism." In *The Korean Wave: Korean Media Go Global*, edited by Y. N. Kim, 185–198. London: Routledge.

Lee, Y. I., and W. S. Kim. 2010. "South Korea's Meandering Path to Globalisation in the Late Twentieth Century." *Asian Studies Review* 34 (3): 309–327.

Lim, H. C., and J. H. Jang. 2006. "Between Neoliberalism and Democracy: The Transformation of the Developmental State in South Korea." *Development and Society* 35 (1): 1–28.

Limb, J. U. 2014. "Gov't Spend KRW 452.2 Billion on Creative Industries." *Korea.net*. http://www.korea.net/NewsFocus/Policies/view?articleId=124424#pagePrint.

Liow, E. D. 2011. "The Neoliberal-developmental State: Singapore as Case-study." *Critical Sociology* 38 (2): 241–264.

MCST (Ministry of Culture, Sports and Tourism). 2009. *White Paper on Cultural Policies*. Seoul: MCST.

MCST (Ministry of Culture, Sports and Tourism). 2012. *2011 Content Industry Statistics*. Seoul: MCST.

MCST (Ministry of Culture, Sports and Tourism). 2013. 2013 Major Policy Plans: An Annual Report to the President, March 28.

MCST (Ministry of Culture, Sports and Tourism). 2015. *2015 Budget of the Ministry*. Seoul: MCST.

MCST (Ministry of Culture, Sports and Tourism). 2016. *The Export of 2014 Cultural Products*. Seoul: MCST (press release).

Ministry of Culture and Tourism. 2001. *2001 Culture Policy White Paper*. Seoul: Ministry of Culture and Tourism.

Ministry of Culture and Tourism. 2004. *2004 Cultural Industries Whitepaper*. Seoul: MCT.

Mosco, Vincent. 1996. *The Political Economy of Communication*. London: Sage.

Nye, J. 2004. "Soft Power and American Foreign Policy." *Political Science Quarterly* 119 (2): 255–270.

Pang, E. S. 2000. "The Financial Crisis of 1997–98 and the End of the Asian Developmental State." *Contemporary Southeast Asia* 22 (3): 570–593.

Paquet, D. 2005. "The Korean Film Industry: 1992 to the Present, New Korean Cinema." In *New Korean Cinema*, edited by Chi-Yun Shin and Julian Stringer, 32–50. Edinburgh University Press.

Park, Y. W. 2012. "An Analysis of the Transition of the Cultural Content Industry Policy in Korea – Focused on the Government Finance." *Journal of Arts Management and Policy* 22: 299–332.

Park, G. H. 2013. Presidential Inauguration Speech, February 25.

Pieterse, J. N. 2004. "Neoliberal Empire." *Theory, Culture and Society* 21 (3): 119–140.

The Proposed South Korea-U.S. Free Trade Agreement (KORUS FTA). 2007. *Congressional Research Service*. Washington, DC: Institute for International Economics.

Roh, M. H. 2003. Presidential Inauguration Speech, February 28.

Roh, M. H. 2006. Congratulatory Address on the Export Day, October 30.

Ryoo, W. J. 2008. "The Political Economy of the Global Mediascape: The Case of the South Korean Film Industry." *Media, Culture & Society* 30 (6): 873–889.

Ryoo, W. J. 2009. "Globalization, or the Logic of Cultural Hybridization: The Case of the Korean Wave." *Asian Journal of Communication* 19 (2): 137–151.
Sánchez Ruiz, E. 2001. "Globalization, Cultural Industries, and Free Trade: The Mexican Audiovisual Sector in the NAFTA Age." In *Continental Order: Integrating North America for Cybercapitalism*, edited by V. Mosco and D. Schiller, 86–119. New York: Rowman & Littlefield.
Shin, J. Y. 2005. "Globalization and New Korean Cinema." In. *New Korean Cinema*, edited by Chi-Yun Shin and Julian Stringer, 51–62. Edinburgh: University of Edinburgh Press.
Sinclair, J. 2007. "Cultural Globalization and American Empire." In *Media in the Age of Marketization*, edited by G. Murdock and J. Wasko, 131–150. Cresskill, NJ: Hampton Press.
Singh, J. P. 2010. "Global Cultural Policies and Power." In *International Cultural Policies and Power*, edited by J. P. Singh, 1–15. New York: Palgrave Macmillan.
Strange, S. 1996. *The Retreat of the State*. Cambridge: Cambridge University Press.
Stuart, R. 2001. "Death of the Nation-state? Global Mass Culture in the Twenty-first Century: A Roundtable Discussion." *American Review of Canadian Studies* 31 (3): 427–440.
Suh, C. S., and S. H. Kwon. 2014. "Whither the Developmental State in South Korea? Balancing Welfare and Neoliberalism." *Asian Studies Review* 38 (4): 676–692.
The United States-Korea Free Trade Agreement. 2007. Report of the Industry Trade Advisory Committee on Services and Finance Industries (ITAC 10).
Wong, J. 2004. "The Adaptive Developmental State in East Asia." *Journal of East Asian Studies* 4: 345–362.
Wu, H., and J. M. Chan. 2007. "Globalizing Chinese Martial Arts Cinema: The Global-local Alliance and the Production of Crouching Tiger, Hidden Dragon." *Media, Culture and Society* 29 (2): 195–217.
Yim, H. S. 2003. *Creative Culture Society and Cultural Policy*. Seoul: Jinhan Publishing.
Yoon, S. W. 2009. "Internalizing Neoliberal Globalization in Korea – A Case for Developmental Neoliberalization." *Economy and Society* 83: 40–68.

# Trade and culture: the United States

Gilbert Gagné

**ABSTRACT**

The US government has long held that cultural goods and services represent an economic sector like any other and should be liberalized. The American cultural and digital industries enjoy a strong competitive advantage and constitute a leading export sector. This US stance has antagonized many countries pursuing cultural policies. This has led the US government to soften its trade strategy and accept financial measures, as well as a broader array of 'traditional' cultural regulatory instruments. At the same time, the United States insists on the absence of restrictions in digital networks, through which cultural contents are to be increasingly distributed and accessed. Under the negative-list negotiating approach, whereby everything is liberalized save for specific exceptions, states parties to US trade agreements have secured a varying array of measures. However, only a handful, essentially industrial countries, have secured digital exceptions, the latter coupled with conditions raising questions concerning their applicability.

## Introduction

Trade and culture normally belong to different spheres. While trade is generally understood as 'the activity of buying and selling goods and services, especially between countries,' culture mainly refers to 'the arts of describing, showing, or performing that represent the traditions or the way of life of a particular people or group' (Cambridge Dictionaries Online). Yet, these two concepts intersect when cultural goods and services are involved. Alongside visual, performing, and literary arts, the latter also include newspapers, magazines, books, movies, video and music recordings, radio and television, and now multimedia. To the extent that these reflect the way of life of specific communities, issues have arisen as to whether or the extent to which cultural products (encompassing goods and services) should be exempted from trade disciplines. Some states, such as the United States and Japan, important exporters of cultural products, have held that culture represents an economic sector like any other and should be liberalized, with cultural products subject to standard trade disciplines. On the other hand, states, such as France and Canada, concerned about the impact of foreign cultural products on their cultural identity and/or insistent on the pursuit of cultural policies and measures to foster their national cultures, have sought to wholly or partially exempt cultural products from economic liberalization. Between these extreme positions, in a globalizing world, most countries have proved favourable to a more or less pronounced form of cultural exception in trade agreements.

Such conflicting views as to the treatment of cultural products in international economic law have led to the so-called trade and culture debate. The debate has also proved ever more salient in the context of the digital revolution. Essentially, such debate stems from the difficulties in conciliating, on the one hand, the need to ensure sufficient policy space and flexibility for states' authorities for the pursuit of effective cultural policies, and, on the other hand, predictability and non-discrimination[1] in international trade exchanges. The terms of this long-standing debate have evolved with the advent of the twenty-first century. Now acknowledging the concerns for cultural identity in international trade negotiations, the position of the United States in particular has somehow softened, from outright liberalization to an acceptance of circumscribed and clearly defined exceptions. This article argues that this evolving US trade strategy on cultural products, rather than states' leverage or negotiation dynamics, mostly explains the scope of the provisions and/or exceptions found in US preferential free trade agreements (FTAs) enabling states parties to continue pursuing cultural policies. The evolving US views and preferences on the treatment of cultural products in trade agreements have mainly been translated in a series of FTAs negotiated in the early years of the twenty-first century.

The article is structured around three sections. Section one discusses the US views and interests toward the treatment of cultural products in international trade agreements. It does so by considering how the notion of culture and states' cultural policies are perceived in the United States, followed by the economic and trade importance of cultural industries for the United States, notably with the digital revolution. Section two focuses on the evolving US cultural trade agenda, first concentrating on the US positions and main negotiation outcomes at the multilateral level, then pointing to the adoption by the US Congress of the Trade Promotion Authority (TPA) in 2002, and describing the new or revised US trade strategy on cultural products. Section three turns to the implementation of the revised US approach through the negotiation and conclusion of FTAs. The key features of US FTAs are emphasized, as well as the essentials of the commitments and/or exceptions secured by states parties, as they pertain to the cultural sector, while the section ends with the more recent and/or ongoing US trade negotiations. Some concluding remarks follow, summarizing the evolution of the US strategy seeking to conciliate cultural policies with trade liberalization.

## US views and interests on cultural products

In this section, the key factors behind the US stance on the trade and culture debate are briefly stressed, starting with the perception of culture and cultural policies in the United States and, then, the place of cultural industries and digital platforms in the American economy.

### *Culture and cultural policies*

In the United States, culture tends to be understood in terms of fine arts, literature, opera, ballet, and classical music, i.e. 'high' culture. What corresponds to mass or popular 'culture,' through broadcasting, films, book and magazine publishing, sound recordings, and new media, is seen as the 'entertainment industry.' However, in most other countries, more aspects of cultural production at all levels are associated with cultural identity and, thus, are accorded greater political significance than in the United States, especially in terms of the need to protect them (Gagné 2003/2004, 30).

There is long-standing suspicion in the United States of government involvement in the arts and in the production of content viewed by its citizens. There is no Department of Culture and the US government does not normally subsidize and/or regulate (in the latter case, with the exception of obscenity as well as radio and television licenses) cultural industries.[2] Arts policy is rather financed largely through indirect subsidies, such as tax deductions, mainly at the state and/or local level, as well as through contributions and bequests from private donors, the latter activity in turn eligible for tax relief (see Cowen 2006). In general, any action that interferes with the free flow of ideas is seen as intrinsically wrong. Such a stance owes to US political culture and constitutional regime, its adherence to free trade principles (i.e. trade unfettered by government-imposed barriers), as well as to free speech, holding as valuable diversity of viewpoints and programming. Governments should refrain from intervening in the cultural lives of their citizens, who have the right to decide for themselves what they see, read, listen to, and do (Balassa 2012, 88–90).

Hence, there is the local culture model, or culture-as-identity, which understands culture as a way of life, a public good deserving of state support, and the global market model, or culture-as-commerce, which sees culture as a commodity to be treated like other commodities (Armstrong 2000, 370; see also Shi 2013, 20–31). No other country embraces the 'pure' market model more fiercely than the United States.

### *US cultural industries and exports*

The United States is the world's largest producer and exporter of cultural products, which also constitute one of its most profitable export sectors (Acheson and Maule 1999, 47–50; Bruner 2008, 355–56). This helps explain why Americans are so insistent on the free flow of information. In fact, the stance of people and governments in favour either of free trade or of an exception for cultural products usually rests on varying combinations of both principles and interests, most often difficult to disentangle. As Mulcahy (2000, 181–82) stresses, with a dominant popular culture able to indemnify its costs over a populous and prosperous society largely immune to cultural expressions not projecting an American sensibility, the United States can afford a 'cultural open-door policy' as it has little to fear from foreign competition. Moreover, the communication industries have long proved a key element in ensuring US world hegemony and, then, a pillar of American foreign policy (see: Schiller 2000; McCarthy 2015; see also: Nye and Owens 1996; Nye 2004).

The United States, and particularly Hollywood, has proved for the past century to be the nucleus of global entertainment. More recently, Silicon Valley has proved to be the nucleus of the digital revolution. With an economy increasingly based on services and knowledge, the United States has sought to prevent any restrictions in digital trade. The digital revolution indeed represents growing economic opportunities and is to profoundly alter the ways in which cultural contents are created, distributed, and accessed. As a consequence of digitization, notably with multimedia, which creates a whole new range of products, an explosion in demand for audiovisual content is expected. Internet 'majors,' i.e. Google, Apple, Facebook, and Amazon, and other US firms, such as Netflix, are the global driving force of the digital economy and the main beneficiaries of the explosion of content available on the Internet, as they provide the access to services and much of the content (Thiec 2014, 99).

The US exports of audiovisual services (movies and television programming, books and sound recordings, broadcasting and recording of live events) reached $20.4 billion in 2016, while the sales by foreign affiliates of US audiovisual firms (motion picture, video, and sound recording) totalled $12.3 billion in 2015 (USITC 2018, 23, 61, 64).[3] Thus, in the production and exchanges of cultural contents, the United States enjoys a strong competitive advantage from which it wants to benefit fully, or at least to the fullest extent possible, and strongly objects to what it perceives as restrictions under the guise of cultural concerns.

## The evolving US cultural trade agenda

This second section discusses the evolving US strategy on the treatment of cultural products in trade agreements. It first reviews the shift in the US position from its submissions to the World Trade Organization (WTO), followed by the granting of the TPA to the US executive in 2002, and, finally, the key characteristics of the new or revised US strategy.

### *The US cultural trade strategy at the multilateral level*

Up until 1998, the official US position was that cultural products were no different from other goods and services and, as a result, must be treated exactly like any other products in trade agreements (WTO, Council for Trade in Services 1998). A first indication that this position was subject to a significant change in both tone and substance came at the end of 2000 in the US communication to the WTO on audiovisual and related services (WTO, Council for Trade in Services 2000). This revision translates serious concern from both government and industry that the US position against content quotas and subsidies during the Uruguay Round of multilateral trade negotiations from 1986 to 1993 had hardened opposition to future liberalization commitments in the audiovisual sector. At the conclusion of the Round, within which services for the first time figured on the agenda, only 18 states made commitments relating to audiovisual services in the General Agreement on Trade in Services (GATS).[4] Although the United States committed itself almost completely, i.e. in all categories of audiovisual services, few of the other 17 states' commitments covered every sub-sector and mode of supply. Several of these states also inscribed limitations on market access and national treatment in sub-sectors with bound commitments.[5]

The United States was also mindful of ongoing discussions spearheaded by Canada and France that were to lead in 2005 to the adoption of the Convention on the Preservation and Promotion of the Diversity of Cultural Expressions within the United Nations Educational, Scientific and Cultural Organization. Adopted almost unanimously, the United States being one of only two countries to have opposed it, the Convention notably recognizes the special character of cultural goods and services, as well as the right of states to implement cultural policies (UNESCO 2005). The perspective of having the audiovisual sector entirely removed from multilateral trade disciplines was not taken lightly, and the United States set about to improve its image on the trade and culture debate (Balassa 2012, 79–80).

In order to cast the Doha Round in a new light, the US government emphasized that the audiovisual sector in 2000 was 'significantly different from the audiovisual sector of the Uruguay Round period when negotiations focused primarily on film production, film distribution, and terrestrial broadcasting of audiovisual goods and services' and went on to stress that '[e]specially in light of the quantum increase in exhibition possibilities available in today's digital environment, it is quite possible to enhance one's cultural identity and to make trade in audiovisual services more transparent, predictable, and open' (WTO, Council for Trade in Services 2000, paras 2 and 9). Directly referring to the trade and culture debate that marked much of the Uruguay Round discussion, the US communication refutes the notion that the controversy over the audiovisual sector in the WTO is an '"all-or-nothing" game' in which 'the only available options were to exclude culture from the WTO or to liberalize completely all aspects of audiovisual and related services' (WTO, Council for Trade in Services 2000, para 5).

In an attempt to lay the groundwork for a constructive negotiation, the communication, acknowledging the 'public concern for the preservation and promotion of cultural values and identity,' outlines a proposal where the promotion and preservation of a nation's cultural identity and liberalization of trade in audiovisual services may in fact 'reinforce each other' (WTO, Council for Trade in Services 2000, paras 1 and 9). It is recognized, in particular, that public funding of audiovisual services is 'a sensitive issue for many [WTO] Members where local theatrical film production ... is dependent on government support' (WTO, Council for Trade in Services 2000, para 8). The earlier 1998 communication mentioned that '[t]he U.S. delegation is of the view that development of trade disciplines for the audiovisual sector need not necessarily restrict government subsidies for domestic film production and distribution, as long as these are not derived from discriminatory practices' (WTO, Council for Trade in Services 1998, 3).

In three concluding sub-paragraphs, the 2000 US communication itemizes specific negotiation proposals. The first calls for a 'clear, accurate and comprehensive' classification of audiovisual services, respecting the principle of technological neutrality. The second proposal reiterates that 'GATS disciplines are relevant to the audiovisual sector, as they are to virtually any services sector' and the US objective of 'negotiated commitments ... that establish clear, dependable, and predictable trade rules with due account taken of the sector's specific sensitivities.' The third suggests 'developing an understanding on subsidies that will respect each nation's need to foster its cultural identity by creating an environment to nurture local culture ... while ensuring that the potential for trade distortive effects is effectively contained or significantly neutralized,' although this was made contingent on 'negotiated commitments for audiovisual services' (WTO, Council for Trade in Services 2000, para 10; see also Grant and Wood 2004, 372–73; Balassa 2012, 82–83).

In preparation for the Doha Round, unlike the previous multilateral negotiations, the United States did not make rollback[6] requests and has expressed its willingness to accept most existing subsidies in the audiovisual sector. The United States rather requested that governments commit themselves to their current levels of market access, i.e. a standstill[7] on existing audiovisual regulations. Yet, some countries were quick to point out that the US standstill request was less benign than it appeared. It would notably involve a legally binding commitment on the part of states not to impose any further restrictions in the new and more lucrative technologies, such as video-on-demand and pay-per-view television (Wunsch-Vincent 2003, 15–16; Balassa 2012, 81–82).

A similar US stance on cultural products, combining increased flexibility and concern for unfettered digital trade, was reflected in a presentation by the Motion Picture Association of America (MPAA), the main arm of the American audiovisual industry, before the US Congress in May 2001 (Motion Picture Association of America (MPAA) 2001). Since government authorities are bound to consult with and consider the views of various economic sectors in setting US trade objectives and priorities, both the government and industry have been involved in this shift in US cultural trade strategy.

Then, in July 2002, in the US proposals for liberalizing trade in audiovisual services, while countries were requested to schedule commitments reflecting current levels of market access in sub-sectors such as motion picture and home video entertainment production and distribution, radio and television production, and sound recording, the US government strongly insisted on the need to keep free of trade barriers in electronically delivered audiovisual products ((United States) Mission – Geneva 2002).

By 2008, only nine countries had made offers regarding audiovisual services so as to expand the scope of the GATS, six of which with existing commitments in the sector (Roy 2008, 361). If, unlike the Uruguay Round, audiovisual and cultural services have not been a hot topic in the Doha talks, it is partly because the trade and culture debate has unfolded in other settings, i.e. accession negotiations to the WTO and the proliferation of FTAs principally concluded by the United States. Hence, between 1996 and 2013, 16 among 25 new members of the WTO made liberalization commitments in audiovisual services, mainly as a result of US pressure (Rioux et al. 2015, 31; Vlassis and Hanania 2014, 27, 37). Although, as of June 2016, the total number of countries with audiovisual commitments was 36, given that the WTO counted 162 members, this service sector remains one in which the fewest WTO members have obligations.

### *The trade promotion authority of 2002 and US cultural objectives*

The US Congress adopted in June 2002 the TPA, in effect until 30 June 2007, in order to facilitate a parallel series of multilateral and preferential trade negotiations. The 2002 TPA was designed to further the US objectives, notably by strengthening intellectual property rights, as well as anticipating and preventing new trade barriers in the digital environment (United States 2002). The stalemate of the Doha Round has brought the United States to pursue its new approach on cultural products essentially through FTAs. Before 2002, the United States had FTAs with Canada, Israel, Jordan, and Mexico. Under the 2002 TPA, the US government, between late 2000 and 2007, successfully negotiated 11 preferential trade agreements, all in the form of FTAs. These are all in force and involve 16 countries throughout the world. Besides the one with Costa Rica, the Dominican Republic, El Salvador, Guatemala, Honduras, Nicaragua, and the United States (CAFTA-DR), the other US FTAs are bilateral and have been concluded with Singapore, Chile, Australia, Morocco, Bahrain, Oman, Peru, Colombia, Panama, and South Korea. The bilateral character of most FTA negotiations, coupled with the asymmetry of the negotiating parties and the resort to the negative-list approach, make them interesting, and indeed better, venues for securing US views and interests on trade in cultural products.

## *The new US trade strategy on cultural products*

There are four main characteristics to the new or revised US negotiating stance or strategy pertaining to the treatment of cultural products in trade agreements (see Wunsch-Vincent 2003, 11; Bernier 2004, 3–19). The first is the adoption of the most liberal approach possible for making trade commitments. The United States seeks wide-ranging liberalization coupled with a predictable trade framework based on clearly defined provisions. To serve this objective, the US FTA negotiations are conducted following the top-down or negative-list approach, under which, in the fields of services and investment, all sectors and measures are liberalized, save for those subject to specific reservations or exceptions in a list or schedule. Two types of lists are provided. Exceptions in Annexes I allow the maintenance and renewal of measures in a given domain. Yet, following the standstill clause, any renewed or revised measure could not be more trade restrictive than the existing one; while, under the ratchet mechanism, any subsequent liberalization of measures is to be automatically bound. On the other hand, under exceptions in Annexes II, also known as reservations for future measures, states keep full discretion to not only maintain existing, but adopt new or more restrictive, measures in a sector or sub-sector.

This was the approach proposed by the United States for the multilateral negotiations on services, notably for the Doha Round, but WTO members held to the positive-list approach. Then, the United States resolved to use its favoured approach in its FTA program, which had already been resorted to for the negotiations of the North American Free Trade Agreement (NAFTA). A crucial aspect of this method is that, unless a party succeeds in excluding a future service, all new services are to be automatically covered and, consequently, freely traded, with key implications for digital trade in cultural products.

The second characteristic of the new US strategy refers to the broad acceptance that financial support schemes for culture and content production need not be dismantled. Except for very trade-distorting financial support schemes, the United States has come to a more detached view of subsidies. Yet, the United States already excluded subsidies from the services chapters of its FTAs prior to the 2002 TPA. One reason for the US opening on subsidies is that, in contrast with regulatory measures, they are generally less trade-distorting, have a lesser impact on market access and, hence, on the interests of US industries. When considered in context, the US concession on subsidies is more apparent than real. Production of audiovisual and cinematographic content in most countries is practically impossible without financial support. The United States is aware that any attempt to seriously curtail the resort to subsidies for audiovisual products is to be fiercely resisted. Besides, the United States itself has offered considerable subsidies to its audiovisual sector, although often at the state level (Bernier 2004, 6–7; see also Balassa 2012, 82).

Unlike the first two characteristics of the revised US strategy, which are common to all its FTAs in the twenty-first century, the scope of the last two depends on the specific exceptions or reservations secured by states parties. The third characteristic, perhaps the most surprising, as Bernier (2004, 3) points out, consists in the abandonment of traditional demands that local content requirements and other barriers to trade in the audiovisual sector be entirely suppressed, so far as traditional technologies are concerned. Thus, most domestic cultural quotas subject to reservations are the existing ones; they may only be maintained, and it is often on condition that they are reduced. Far less common are reservations leaving latitude to states to adopt future content requirements and, even more so, in the digital field.

The fourth and last characteristic, at the core of the new US strategy, is that states commit themselves to keep digital networks free of cultural protectionism. As a leader in high- technology and intellectual-property-intensive industries, the United States has most to lose from restrictions in digital trade.

Let us now look at the various FTAs through which the United States has been able to translate its new cultural trade strategy into legal rights and obligations at the international level.

## US free trade agreements and cultural agenda

This third section begins by highlighting some essential components of US FTAs relating to cultural products, followed by the key exceptions obtained by states parties to these FTAs, to finish with the more recent and/or ongoing American trade initiatives.

### *Key features of US FTAs and cultural products*

The texts of the US FTAs negotiated under the 2002 TPA conform to a standard model or template and, thus, are quite similar. Although the numbering of the chapters as well as their scope and content may vary slightly, they address basically the same issues more or less in the same order. What really differ from one FTA to another are the lists of exceptions and, at times, some precedents. The chapters in US FTAs most relevant as regards the treatment of cultural products and, hence, states' ability to pursue cultural policies, are those on cross-border trade in services, investment, and electronic commerce, as well as, to a lesser degree, those on telecommunications and intellectual property rights. These chapters deal primarily with cultural 'services,' thereby reflecting the key concerns over cultural products in trade agreements, since they are associated with measures such as domestic content regulations in the media. Cultural goods are rarely singled out for special treatment in FTAs and usually treated like any other merchandise.

The chapters on electronic commerce pertain to trade in digital products.[8] While cultural goods and services come under different WTO agreements, i.e. the GATT and the GATS, the term 'digital products' in US FTAs encompasses both cultural goods and services, so as to make them subject to similar, more liberalizing, provisions. Regarding telecommunications, whereas the audiovisual, computer, and telecommunications sectors used to differ in terms of contents, networks, and regulations, they now tend to converge. Digital technologies merge the market segments of telecommunications, centered on transmission and networks, and of audiovisuals, centered on programming and contents, so as to relate the availability of contents to network accessibility. As a result, the key US actors in the telecommunications sector are to play an increasing role in the dissemination of digital cultural contents, notably through the Internet access services they provide. As for the chapters aimed at strengthening the protection and enforcement of intellectual property rights,[9] the United States is the world's first producer and exporter of products to which such rights apply, and loses more revenue from infringements of intellectual property rights than any other country. Each party to US FTAs should have ratified or acceded to the main existing, mostly multilateral, treaties dealing with copyrights. While the WTO Agreement on Trade-Related Aspects of Intellectual Property Rights provides for a minimal protection of 50 years following the publication or the death of an author (TRIPS, art. 12), the United States has obtained from its FTA partners an extension of copyrights to 70 years.[10]

### *US FTAs and cultural commitments/reservations*

As it seeks extensive liberalization, the United States has relatively few reservations in its FTAs. The US reservations, including those pertaining to cultural products, are also largely identical in all its FTAs. Under Annex I, in the field of radiocommunications, consisting of all communications by radio, including broadcasting, the United States reserves the right to restrict foreign ownership of radio licenses. Under Annex II, the US government reserves the right to adopt or maintain any measure according differential treatment to persons of other countries due to application of reciprocity measures or through international agreements involving sharing of the radio spectrum, guaranteeing market access, or national treatment with regard to the one-way satellite transmission of direct-to-home and direct broadcasting satellite television and digital audio services. Another reservation provides that equivalent treatment may be accorded to persons of any country that limits ownership by US persons in an enterprise engaged in the operation of a cable television system in that country. The latter exception is included in the NAFTA and the CAFTA-DR, as well as in the US FTAs with Singapore, Australia, Oman, and Panama.

Let us now turn to the exceptions in favour of cultural policies secured by states parties to US FTAs. The one with Israel, first to be concluded by the United States in the post-war period, only covers trade in goods, with no provisions relating specifically to the cultural sector. In the FTA with Canada, despite US objections, there is a general exemption of cultural industries, later incorporated into the NAFTA, coupled with a right to retaliate with 'measures of equivalent commercial effect' against any action inconsistent with the FTA were it not for the exemption (see Goff in this issue). In contrast, with some clearly specified exceptions, Mexico significantly liberalized its cultural sector under the NAFTA. As for the FTA with Jordan, it provides for even more wide-ranging liberalization of cultural services, although commitments have been entered into following the positive-list approach.

With respect to the US FTAs negotiated under the 2002 TPA, there are as well various cultural exceptions. Since subsidization measures are not subject to the national treatment and MFN obligations of the services and investment chapters, states preserve a wide margin of manoeuvre to adopt financial measures as part of national cultural policies. Table 1 summarizes the measures of cultural regulation maintained by states parties to US FTAs. The table only includes the FTAs in force. The US-Israel FTA, with no coverage of services, and the US-Jordan FTA, with positive-list services commitments, are excluded for lack of comparability. Since such regulatory exceptions vary considerably in number, scope, substance, and/or details, the table only indicates, under general categories, the most important ones for states' ability to pursue cultural policies. These have been secured by governments either in direct form or through broader exceptions. Nearly all states parties to US FTAs, to different degrees, have secured reservations as regards the ownership, control, and/or management of cultural enterprises, as well as licenses for television and radio broadcasting. In addition, half of the parties, namely Australia, Chile, Colombia, Costa Rica, the Dominican Republic, Peru, Singapore, and South Korea, not to forget Canada and Mexico under the NAFTA, have obtained exceptions so as to ensure domestic content in public radio and television. An almost equal number of countries have taken MFN exemptions in favour of audiovisual co-production arrangements.

**Table 1.** Main types of cultural regulatory exceptions across states parties to existing US FTAs.

| | States Parties | | | | | | | | | | | | | | | | | | |
|---|---|---|---|---|---|---|---|---|---|---|---|---|---|---|---|---|---|---|---|
| Cultural Regulatory Exceptions | US | AU | BH | CA | CL | CO | CR | DR | ES | GU | HO | KR | MO | MX | NI | OM | PA | PE | SG |
| Restrictions re. property/ control/management and licensing of cultural enterprises | • | • | • | • | • | • | • | • | • | | • | • | | • | • | • | • | • | • |
| Domestic content requirements | | | | | | | | | | | | | | | | | | | |
| - Public radio and/or television | | • | | • | • | • | • | • | | | | • | | • | | | | • | • |
| - Subscription television | | | | • | | • | | | | | | • | | • | | | | | |
| - Advertising | | • | | • | | • | • | • | | | | | | | | | | | |
| - Cinema (screen quotas) | | | | | | • | | | | | | • | | • | | | | • | |
| Audiovisual cooperation agreements | | • | | • | • | • | • | | | | | • | • | | | | | • | |
| Digital or new technologies | | | | | | | | | | | | | | | | | | | |
| - Interactive audio and/or video | | • | | X | | • | | | | | | • | | X | | | | | |

X: Inapplicable, as the NAFTA predates digital developments.

US – United States, AU – Australia, BH – Bahrain, CA – Canada, CL – Chile, CO – Colombia, CR – Costa Rica, DR – Dominican Republic, ES – El Salvador, GU – Guatemala, HO – Honduras, KR – Korea, MO – Morocco, MX – Mexico, NI – Nicaragua, OM – Oman, PA – Panama, PE – Peru, SG – Singapore.

With regard to broadcasting (television and radio), the maintenance of a number of restrictions – including foreign equity limitations and content quotas – is the norm rather than the exception, although most often listed under Annexes I and set to ensure the United States a predictable level of market access. Such restrictions are more numerous for traditional free-to-air television, and where capacity – or shelf-space – is necessarily limited. There are fewer restrictions where the United States has more interests, e.g. satellite television, foreign programming for cable television, and interactive audio/video services (Roy 2008, 367–68). On the other hand, alongside Jordan, eight parties to existing US FTAs – Bahrain, El Salvador, Guatemala, Honduras, Morocco, Nicaragua, Oman, and Panama – have not secured any significant reservations concerning the audiovisual sector.

There is significant variation in the number and scope of exceptions for the regulation of the cultural sector across states parties to US FTAs. This begs the question of the reason(s) for such variation. Since most US FTA partners are developing countries, none seemed to have much more bargaining power or leverage than another in its dealings with the United States. With scant information on the various negotiations, one may wonder if states' exceptions for cultural policies were the object of tough bargains and/or entailed further concessions to the US side. In view of the negative-list approach, governments subscribe to trade obligations simply by not (thinking about) including policies and measures in their lists of exceptions. A state, therefore, ought to be prepared to formulate requests for exceptions to the benefit of its cultural sector and to hold on to such requests. Thus, an essential reason why some countries were better able than others at maintaining flexibility to pursue cultural policies has to do with the importance they attach to such policies for their cultural identity, often related to the level of mobilization of domestic cultural industries.

Further, such variations and outcomes are attributable to the revised US trade strategy, which allows for the maintenance of regulatory measures for cultural industries, and makes the United States willing to accommodate specific cultural concerns. It does not appear, either, to be the result of difficult trade-offs. The United States does not seem to have required anything important in return for such concessions concerning the 'traditional' instruments of cultural policy, which the American government and industry do not see as involving major costs. This is indeed the conclusion reached by the US Advisory Committee on Services in its reports on the US FTAs in which states parties secured such exceptions (see, e.g. CAFTA, ISAC-13 Report, 10; US-Peru FTA, ITAC-10 Report, 8–9). It also explains why US authorities may not have felt strongly about this type of exceptions. In fact, a relatively greater number of countries' exceptions for the cultural sector in US FTAs is often accompanied by a greater number of exceptions in various sectors. Chase (2015, 236–38) noticed that neither countries' economic size nor trade flows appears to fully explain the varying US ability to secure concessions on audiovisual services from FTA partners.

States' leverage seems determinant, however, in the case of exceptions relating to new or digital media. Only Australia, Colombia, and South Korea have obtained exceptions concerning digital cultural content. Under Annexes II, these may nonetheless only be used if domestic digital audiovisual content is found to be 'not readily available' to domestic consumers and to ensure that access to such content is 'not unreasonably denied.' Following 'consultations,' any measure to be implemented should be 'no more trade restrictive than necessary' and, in Colombia's case, with US agreement. Thus, such exceptions are coupled with conditions so onerous as to question their applicability (Gagné 2016, 108–110). The developed country status of both Australia and South Korea, their economic weight, as well as their concerns and interests for effective cultural policies, appear to be the key factors behind their respective exceptions pertaining to new media and, compared with Colombia, the less onerous conditions attached to them.

### *The trade promotion authority of 2015 and US trade negotiations*

If the 2002 TPA expired in 2007, US trade negotiations had not stopped and the Obama administration secured in June 2015 the renewal of the TPA, which has since been extended to

1 July 2021. The revised US trade strategy on cultural products has remained, arguably with a further emphasis on a free, open, and global digital marketplace (United States 2015). The United States has notably taken part in three major sets of preferential trade negotiations: the Trans-Pacific Partnership (TPP), conducted from 2010 and 2015, which came to include 12 countries of the Pacific Rim[11]; the Trade in Services Agreement (TiSA), which has grouped 23 WTO members (the EU counted as one); and the Transatlantic Trade and Investment Partnership (TTIP) between the United States and the European Union. Yet, these have either been disavowed or put on hold by the Trump administration. The United States has rather renegotiated some of its existing FTAs, notably the NAFTA and the one with South Korea, and expressed an interest for bilateral FTAs, as with the United Kingdom and Japan.

The exceptions in the TPP relating to the cultural sector are specified and delimited. Among cultural policy instruments, while the financial ones are still essentially exempted, a whole series of country-specific 'traditional' regulations, of varying scope, have been kept in place. For countries that were not already parties to a US FTA, significant commitments in the cultural sector had to be made to satisfy the ambitious American agenda, especially relating to digital trade. With respect to partners to existing US FTAs, Canada's cultural exemption was reformulated so as to limit, if not to prevent, its applicability to the digital marketplace (see Gagné 2016, 119–120 and Goff in this issue). The US government was seemingly satisfied with the results of its FTAs negotiated under the 2002 TPA, as it secured no further commitments pertaining to cultural products. Many parties to these US FTAs even secured more extensive exceptions for the pursuit of cultural policies under the TPP. The United States ensured, however, that, unless otherwise specified, the more liberalizing rules would have prevailed, thereby safeguarding the bargains from its FTA negotiations under the 2002 TPA.

As for the TiSA and TTIP negotiations, many issues remain to be solved if they are to conclude successfully, notably with respect to cultural products and digital trade. In both cases, US cultural and digital liberalization objectives may need to be accommodated with the principles of cultural exception/diversity, as advocated by the European Union and Canada (see Richieri Hanania and Goff in this issue).

While the cultural sector was not among the points of contention in the US-Korea FTA renegotiation, a key question in the NAFTA renegotiation was whether Canada's exemption of cultural industries would apply to trade in digital products or be coupled with conditions along those figuring in the TPP. In an unprecedented rebuff of the US digital trade agenda, Canada's overall cultural exemption has been maintained in what is now known as the United States-Mexico-Canada Agreement (USMCA), which was signed on 30 November 2018. To the extent that the Canadian government, as the vanguard of cultural exception/diversity, made the preservation of its complete ability to pursue cultural policies a sine qua non condition for its participation in the USMCA, the United States has seemingly relented. Yet, this may have been made easier since the retaliatory clause has also been maintained. The latter could be triggered by any measure to be adopted by Canada adversely impacting US trading interests in digital products (see Goff in this issue).

## Concluding remarks

The main consequence of US FTAs is to constrain, often significantly, the ability of states parties to carry out public policies benefiting the cultural sector. This is the case as a result of US insistence on limiting measures of regulation of cultural activities and preventing any such measures for digital trade. Under its revised trade strategy on cultural products, as Bernier (2004, 19–20) emphasizes, the United States accepts to make concessions. Financial cultural policy instruments are exempted, while a varying array of regulatory measures, notably national content quotas, could be maintained. Yet, such 'concessions,' through the maintenance of 'traditional' instruments of cultural policy, are usually conditioned upon the absence of any restrictions with regard to the electronic commerce of digital products. When state measures of cultural regulation are subject to specific reservations, it is because US authorities consider that, owing to the digital revolution, they are to become increasingly obsolete. Hence, such FTAs provide the United States with unlimited gains in the future in exchange for well-circumscribed concessions in the present. Aside from Canada under the NAFTA and USMCA, Australia, Colombia, and South Korea are the only three existing US FTA partners to have secured digital cultural exceptions. These, however, are coupled with such conditions that they do not significantly confront the US policy of absence of cultural protectionism in digital platforms.

## Notes

1. The principle of non-discrimination, central in the international trading regime, has both external and internal dimensions. The external one consists of the most-favoured-nation (MFN) treatment, whereby any trade advantage a country gives to another must be extended, immediately and unconditionally, to all other countries. As for the internal dimension of non-discrimination, it revolves around national treatment, which requires countries to treat imported products no less favourably than domestic products with respect to internal taxes and regulations.
2. Yet, under the regulatory oversight of the Federal Communications Commission, US broadcasters have nonetheless had 'public-interest obligations' and been subject to local and children's programming requirements, closely resembling quotas in their design and impact (Grant and Wood 2004, 212–15).
3. Despite problems in measuring the extent of international trade in services, figures on US exports of cultural services are indicated in order to give an idea of their economic magnitude.
4. While heavily influenced by the General Agreement on Tariffs and Trade (GATT), regulating since 1947 trade in goods, the GATS entails a different normative framework and more modest obligations. Unlike the GATT, market access (i.e. the conditions set by countries for the delivery of specific services into their territory) and national treatment (according to which imported and domestic services should be treated equally) are not general obligations. Following the bottom-up or positive-list negotiating approach, such obligations only apply if and to the extent that specific commitments are listed in a country's schedule.
5. Under the United Nations Provisional Central Product Classification (UN CPC) code, used as an optional guiding tool by states for the GATS negotiations, 'audiovisual services' are classified as a sub-sector of 'communication services' and divided into six sub-categories: motion picture and video tape production and distribution (CPC 9611); motion picture projection (CPC 9612); radio and television (CPC 9613); radio and television transmission (CPC 7524); sound recording; and 'other' unclassified audiovisual services, such as multimedia. The first four sub-categories, with their corresponding codes, are also further divided. Most cultural services other than audiovisual are included within 'recreational, cultural and sporting services.' These comprise: entertainment (including theatre, live bands, and circus) (CPC 9619); news agency (CPC 962); libraries, archives, museums, and other cultural services (CPC 963); sporting and other recreational services (CPC 964); and an 'other' sub-category. Among the remaining cultural services, advertising (CPC 871) as well as printing and publishing (CPC 88442) belong to 'other business services.'Given the specifics of services, compared with goods, the WTO has defined trade in services to span four modes of supply: Mode 1 – cross-border, where a service is supplied from the territory of a country into the territory of another; Mode 2 – consumption abroad, where a service is supplied in the territory of a country to the consumers of another; Mode 3 – commercial presence, where a service is supplied through the establishment of a legal entity of a country in the territory of another (i.e. foreign direct investment); Mode 4 – movement of natural persons, where a service is supplied by a national of a country in the territory of another.Under the GATS, a sector or sub-sector included in a country's list of specific commitments does not automatically entail full compliance with the market access (Article XVI) and national treatment (Article XVII) obligations. States rather decide, for each mode of supply, whether to undertake full commitments (i.e. without any limitations), partial commitments (i.e. inscribing in their schedules measures or types of measures inconsistent with Articles XVI or XVII to be maintained or adopted in the future), or no commitment at all (i.e. keeping flexibility to maintain or adopt any measure inconsistent with Articles XVI and/or XVII with regard to a given mode of supply).
6. To reduce the scope of various measures or regulations, and notably their trade effects, or to eliminate them altogether.
7. To ensure that measures or regulations remain the same or do not expand in scope, so as to prevent any further trade effects.
8. Digital products include computer programs, texts, videos, images, sound recordings, and other products that are digitally encoded and produced for commercial sale or distribution, regardless of whether they are fixed on

a carrier medium (CD, DVD or other) or transmitted electronically. This definition was gradually refined or fine-tuned as successive US FTAs were being negotiated.

9. Intellectual property rights are understood as exclusive rights granted to creators and inventors to control the use made of their productions. For literary and artistic works, the most relevant for cultural products, these correspond to copyright and related or neighbouring rights.
10. It would be cumbersome to refer to the articles or page numbers of specific provisions and/or exceptions in various US FTAs. All US FTAs are included in the list of references, with their web links, from which their texts, provisions, and exceptions can be accessed.
11. Australia*, Brunei, Canada*, Chile*, Japan, Malaysia, Mexico*, New Zealand, Peru*, Singapore*, the United States, and Vietnam. Countries with an asterisk already had an FTA with the United States.

## Disclosure statement

No potential conflict of interest was reported by the author.

## Funding

This work was supported by the Social Sciences and Humanities Research Council of Canada [435-2016-0778].

## References

Acheson, K., and C. Maule. 1999. *Much Ado about Culture: North American Trade Disputes*. Ann Arbor: University of Michigan Press.

Armstrong, S. 2000. "Magazines, Cultural Policy and Globalization: The Forced Retreat of the State." *Canadian Public Policy* 26(2): 369–385. doi:10.2307/3552107.

Balassa, C. 2012. "The Impact of the U.S. Position in the Trade and Culture Debate: Negotiation of the Convention on the Diversity of Cultural Expressions." In *The UNESCO Convention on the Diversity of Cultural Expressions: A Tale of Fragmentation of International Law*, edited by T. Kono and S. Van Uystel, 71–93. Cambridge: Intersentia.

Bernier, I. 2004. "The Recent Free Trade Agreements of the United States as Illustration of Their New Strategy regarding the Audiovisual Sector." April-June. http://www.diversite-culturelle.qc.ca/fileadmin/documents/pdf/conf_seoul_ang_2004.pdf

Bruner, C. M. 2008. "Culture, Sovereignty, and Hollywood: UNESCO and the Future of Trade in Cultural Products." *New York University Journal of International Law and Politics* 40: 351–436.

*Cambridge Dictionaries Online*. http://dictionary.cambridge.org/us/.

Chase, K. A. 2015. "Audiovisual Goods and Services in Preferential Trade Agreements." In *Trade Cooperation: The Purpose, Design and Effects of Preferential Trade Agreements*, edited by A. Dür and M. Elsig, 218–245. Cambridge: Cambridge University Press.

Cowen, T. 2006. *Good and Plenty: The Creative Successes of American Arts Funding*. Princeton: Princeton University Press.

Gagné, G. 2003/2004. "Cultural Sovereignty, Identity, and North American Integration: On the Relevance of the U.S.-Canada-Quebec Border." *Québec Studies* 36: 29–49. doi:10.3828/qs.36.1.29.

Gagné, G. 2016. *The Trade and Culture Debate: Evidence from US Trade Agreements*. Lanham, MD: Lexington Books.

Grant, P. S., and C. Wood. 2004. *Blockbusters and Trade Wars: Popular Culture in a Globalized World*. Vancouver: Douglas & McIntyre.

McCarthy, D. R. 2015. *Power, Information Technology, and International Relations Theory: The Power and Politics of US Foreign Policy and the Internet*. Basingstoke: Palgrave Macmillan.

Motion Picture Association of America (MPAA). 2001. "Impediments to Digital Trade." Testimony by Bonnie J.K. Richardson, Vice President, Trade & Federal Affairs, Motion Picture Association of America, Washington, DC, before the House Commerce Committee Subcommittee on Commerce. Trade & Consumer Protection. May 22.

Mulcahy, K. V. 2000. "Cultural Imperialism and Cultural Sovereignty: U.S.-Canadian Cultural Relations." *American Review of Canadian Studies* 30(2): 181–206. doi:10.1080/02722010009481050.

Nye, J. S. 2004. *Soft Power: The Means to Success in World Politics*. New York: Public Affairs.

Nye, J. S., and W. A. Owens. 1996. "America's Information Edge." *Foreign Affairs* 75(2): 20–36. doi:10.2307/20047486.

Rioux, M., C. Deblock, G. Gagné, D. Tchéhouali, K. Fontaine-Skronski, and A. Vlassis. 2015. *Pour Une Culture En Réseaux Diversifiée: Appliquer La Convention Sur La Protection Et La Promotion De La Diversité Des Expressions Culturelles (CDEC) À L'ère Du Numérique [For a Diversified Networked Culture: Bringing the Convention on the Protection and Promotion of the Diversity of Cultural Expressions (CPPDCE) in the Digital Age]*. Centre d'études sur l'intégration et la mondialisation, Université du Québec à Montréal, February. http://www.ieim.uqam.ca/IMG/pdf/rapportcdecvfinale.pdf

Roy, M. 2008. "Beyond the Main Screen: Audiovisual Services in PTAs." In *Opening Markets for Trade in Services: Countries and Sectors in Bilateral and WTO Negotiations*, edited by J. A. Marchetti and M. Roy, 340–377. Cambridge: Cambridge University Press.

Schiller, H. I. 2000. *Living in the Number One Country: Reflections from a Critique of American Empire*. New York and London: Seven Stories Press.

Shi, J. 2013. *Free Trade and Cultural Diversity in International Law*. Oxford and Portland, OR: Hart.

Thiec, Y. 2014. "From a Moratorium in the Conflict between Trade and Culture to the Creation of a Digital Deal for Cultural Diversity." In *Cultural Diversity in International Law: The Effectiveness of the UNESCO Convention on the Protection and Promotion of the Diversity of Cultural Expressions*, edited by L. R. Hanania, 95–106. London and New York: Routledge.

Vlassis, A., and L. R. Hanania. 2014. "Effects of the CDCE on Trade Negotiations." In *Cultural Diversity in International Law: The Effectiveness of the UNESCO Convention on the Protection and Promotion of the Diversity of Cultural Expressions*, edited by L. R. Hanania, 25–39. London and New York: Routledge.

Wunsch-Vincent, S. 2003. "The Digital Trade Agenda of the U.S.: Parallel Tracks of Bilateral, Regional and Multilateral Liberalization." *Aussenwirtschaft* 58: 7–46.

## Official Documents

UNESCO. 2005. "Convention on the Protection and Promotion of the Diversity of Cultural Expressions." adopted 20 October 2005, effective 18 March 2007. https://en.unesco.org/creativity/convention/what-is/convention-text doi:10.1094/PDIS-91-4-0467B.

## GATT/WTO

Agreement on Trade-Related Aspects of Intellectual Property Rights (TRIPS). adopted 15 April 1994, effective 1 January 1995. https://www.wto.org/english/docs_e/legal_e/31bis_trips_01_e.htm

General Agreement on Tariffs and Trade (GATT). adopted 20 October 1947, effective 1 January 1948. https://www.wto.org/english/docs_e/legal_e/gatt47_e.pdf

General Agreement on Trade in Services (GATS). adopted 15 April 1994, effective 1 January 1995. https://www.wto.org/english/docs_e/legal_e/26-gats.pdf

WTO, Council for Trade in Services. 1998. "Communication from the United States, Audiovisual Services." Doc. S/C/W/78, December 8.

WTO, Council for Trade in Services. 2000. "Communication from the United States, Audiovisual and Related Services." Doc. S/CSS/W/21. December 18.

## United States: Free Trade Agreements

United States – Israel Free Trade Agreement. signed 22 April 1985, effective 1 September 1985. https://ustr.gov/sites/default/files/files/agreements/FTA/israel/Israel%20FTA.pdf

United States – Canada Free Trade Agreement. signed 2 January 1988, effective 1 January 1989. http://www.international.gc.ca/trade-agreements-accords-commerciaux/assets/pdfs/cusfta-e.pdf

North American Free Trade Agreement (NAFTA). signed 17 December 1992, effective 1 January 1994. https://www.nafta-sec-alena.org/Home/Legal-Texts/North-American-Free-Trade-Agreement doi:10.3168/jds.S0022-0302(94)77044-2.

United States – Jordan Free Trade Agreement. signed 24 October 2000, effective 17 December 2001. https://ustr.gov/trade-agreements/free-trade-agreements/jordan-fta/final-text

United States – Singapore Free Trade Agreement. signed 6 May 2003, effective 1 January 2004. https://ustr.gov/trade-agreements/free-trade-agreements/singapore-fta/final-text

United States – Chile Free Trade Agreement. signed 6 June 2003, effective 1 January 2004. https://ustr.gov/trade-agreements/free-trade-agreements/chile-fta/final-text

United States – Australia Free Trade Agreement. signed 18 May 2004, effective 1 January 2005. https://ustr.gov/trade-agreements/free-trade-agreements/australian-fta/final-text

Dominican Republic – Central America – United States Free Trade Agreement (CAFTA-DR). signed 5 August 2004, effective 1 March 2006. https://ustr.gov/trade-agreements/free-trade-agreements/cafta-dr-dominican-republic-central-america-fta/final-text

United States – Morocco Free Trade Agreement. signed 15 June 2004, effective 1 January 2006. https://ustr.gov/trade-agreements/free-trade-agreements/morocco-fta/final-text

United States – Bahrain Free Trade Agreement. signed 14 September 2004, effective 1 August 2006. https://ustr.gov/trade-agreements/free-trade-agreements/bahrain-fta/final-text

United States – Oman Free Trade Agreement. signed 19 January 2006, effective 1 January 2009. https://ustr.gov/trade-agreements/free-trade-agreements/oman-fta/final-text

United States – Peru Trade Promotion Agreement. signed 12 April 2006, effective 1 February 2009. https://ustr.gov/trade-agreements/free-trade-agreements/peru-tpa/final-text

United States – Colombia Trade Promotion Agreement. signed 22 November 2006, effective 15 May 2012. https://ustr.gov/trade-agreements/free-trade-agreements/colombia-fta/final-text doi:10.1094/PDIS-11-11-0999-PDN.

United States – Panama Trade Promotion Agreement. signed 28 June 2007, effective 31 October 2012. https://ustr.gov/trade-agreements/free-trade-agreements/panama-tpa/final-text doi:10.1094/PDIS-11-11-0999-PDN.

United States – Korea Free Trade Agreement. signed 30 June 2007, effective 15 March 2012. https://ustr.gov/trade-agreements/free-trade-agreements/korus-fta/final-text doi:10.1094/PDIS-11-11-0999-PDN.

Trans-Pacific Partnership (TPP). signed 4 February 2016. https://ustr.gov/trade-agreements/free-trade-agreements/trans-pacific-partnership/tpp-full-text

## United States: Official Documents

(United States) Mission – Geneva. 2002. *Press Release*, July.

United States. 2002. "Bipartisan Trade Promotion Authority Act of 2002 (2002 TPA)." Public Law 107-210, 6 August 2002.

United States. 2015. "Bipartisan Congressional Trade Priorities and Accountability Act of 2015 (2015 TPA)." Public Law, 29 June 2015.

Industry Sector Advisory Committee on Services for Trade Policy Matters (ISAC-13). *Report to the President, the Congress and the United States Trade Representative on the U.S.-Central America Free Trade Agreement* (CAFTA). 17 March 2004.

Industry Trade Advisory Committee on Services and Finance Industries (ITAC-10). *Report to the President, the Congress and the United States Trade Representative on the U.S.-Peru Free Trade Agreement* (US-Peru FTA). 1 February 2006. https://ustr.gov/archive/assets/Trade_Agreements/Bilateral/Peru_TPA/Reports/asset_upload_file209_8983.pdf

United States International Trade Commission (USITC). 2018. *Recent Trends in U.S. Services Trade: 2018 Annual Report*, Publication Number: 4789, Investigation Number: 332-345. Washington, DC: USITC, June. https://www.usitc.gov/publications/332/pub4789.pdf

# China and the "culture and trade" debate: a holistic approach

Rostam J. Neuwirth

**ABSTRACT**
Over the past century, the 'culture and trade' debate has constantly evolved, particularly in the wake of rapid and still accelerating technological and scientific advances. These changes, manifest in an increasing convergence of many new technologies and industries, meant that the strict separation of culture from trade by means, for instance, of general or special exceptions in international trade agreements, such as the 1947 General Agreement on Tariffs and Trade (GATT) or the 1988 Canada–United States Free Trade Agreement (CUSFTA), can no longer be sustained. It means that in light of the emergence of oxymoronic concepts like 'the cultural and creative industries', the debate can no longer be framed along binary modes of thinking that oppose the liberalization of international trade and the protection and promotion of the diversity of cultures. Instead a more holistic approach seems to be needed, which appears to coincide with the approach taken by the People's Republic of China (PRC), which joined the WTO in 2001. The present paper examines the holistic approach by the PRC, which seeks to combine rather than separate culture and trade in its domestic, regional and global law and policymaking.

## Introduction

> *New technological advances, by not only changing our lives but also our perception thereof, confirmed that the areas of "culture and trade" cannot be separated, not technologically, not conceptually, not factually and certainly not legally* (Neuwirth 2013a, 418).

At any given moment in time, an attempt to make a brief assessment of the state of play of the 'culture and trade debate' poses a difficult task. This task has certainly not become easier over time, in the context of the debate evolving at a faster pace and over shorter intervals, and the relevant legal and other documents constantly increasing in number and in scope (Neuwirth 2010). Consequently, at the beginning of the twenty-first century, a sound combination of knowledge of historical developments, awareness of present affairs and divinatory skills in foreseeing the future is needed. In this regard, a focus on the People's Republic of China (PRC) does not facilitate the task, because the PRC itself has both been the cause of the evolutionary changes and felt the effects of the accelerated pace of change in the world (Brandt and Rawski 2008; Guthrie 2009). Put differently, the PRC's own internal transformation since the initiation of the opening-up policy in the late 1970s has been mirrored externally and has also been shaped by the PRC in the global transformation of the world (see also Zucca 2018 on how the PRC may shape the global (constitutional) order in the future).

Generally, we are now living in a globalized world where an accelerating pace of change seems to become noticeable (Gleick 2000). For law and policymaking a faster pace of change poses serious challenges, in particular, in how law can 'preserve its integrity over time, while managing to address the newly emerging circumstances that continually arise throughout our history' (Johnson 2007, 845). In other words, when the dust has settled, all things in their context appear to be completely changed, and previous efforts, whether successful or not, no longer seem adequate or relevant. As a second and related characteristic, law and policymaking are also threatened by the implications of greater complexity and the blurring of former lines of distinctions, largely driven by trends of technological and industrial convergence (Lee and Olson 2010). Both these trends were aptly summarized by Yuval Noah Hariri as follows:

> While some experts are familiar with developments in one field, such as artificial intelligence, nanotechnology, big data or genetics, no one is an expert on everything. No one is therefore capable of connecting all the dots and seeing the full picture. Different fields influence one another in such intricate ways that even the best minds cannot fathom how breakthroughs in artificial intelligence might impact nanotechnology, or vice versa. Nobody can absorb all the latest scientific discoveries, nobody can predict how the global economy will look in ten years, and nobody has a clue where we are heading in such a rush (Hariri 2017, 44).

In their combination, the regulatory challenges caused by an acceleration of change and an increasing complexity literally surface in so-called 'essentially oxymoronic concepts', i.e. mainly oxymora and paradoxes, which are rhetorical figures of speech combining apparently contradictory terms or ideas (Neuwirth 2018, 253–256). In practical terms, they often cause serious legal conflicts between obligations laid down in different international treaties (Jenks 1953, 425–426).

Put in a nutshell, these trends also largely characterize the evolution of the culture and trade debate, which for centuries was characterized by their mutual separation resulting from dualistic thinking and binary logic. Throughout the 20$^{th}$ century, it can be said that their separation was reinforced by the opposing positions between the United States (US) on the one hand and the European Union (EU), France and Canada on the other (Murray 1997; Garrett 1994). Accordingly, the conflict consisted in the US largely focusing on the trade aspects of related goods and services while denying their cultural aspects as it is reflected in the preferred use of 'entertainment industries' over 'cultural industries' (Bhagwati 2000). By contrast, the EU, France and Canada appeared to have emphasized the importance of the related industries' cultural aspects.

Eventually, the 2005 UNESCO Convention on the Protection and Promotion of the Diversity of Cultural Expressions recognized at least the cultural industries' dual character, i.e. to have both 'an economic and a cultural nature' (Recital 18 of the Preamble). Yet, as they did at the establishment of the WTO in 1994 that both partners seem to have concluded an 'agreement to disagree' (Elliott and Luce 1993, 1) rather than fully understanding their dual character as it is rooted in the oxymoronic quality of the notion of 'culture industry'.

In simple terms, this means that – especially in the legal realm – the cognitive shift necessary to deal with apparent contradictions juxtaposed in language by oxymora and paradoxes has not yet materialized, neither in the US nor in the EU. Moreover, the culture and trade debate is generally too fragmented and often follows a dichotomous approach by emphasizing either more the cultural or more the trade aspects. This dualism is further aggravated by the dominant scientific taxonomies and their further subdivision in specialized journals or books, which either focus on trade law issues (Bhattasali, Li, and Martin 2004; Hufbauer, Wong, and Sheth 2006; Zhang 2006; Barfield 2007; Zeng 2007), on intellectual property law issues (Zhou 2011; Pang 2012), on social issues (Su 2015), on cultural policy issues (Keane 2004; Zhang 2010; Vlassis 2016), or special fields, such as communications (Su 2011), diplomacy (Pan 2013) or tourism (Sofield and Li 1998). However, a gradual realization of their close connection came with the decision in the *China – Publications and Audiovisual Products* case, which explicitly dealt with the consistency of Chinese measures with WTO obligations that were aimed at the cultural industries (Pauwelyn 2010; Neuwirth 2010; Yu 2011; Ya Qin 2011).

By contrast, this article suggests that China's legal approach to the culture and trade debate is more holistic, at least in cognitive terms. Expressed in other words, such an alternative cognitive approach corresponds at least to the necessities in contemporary global law and policymaking in general, where greater coherence is much needed. It can therefore be said that it is not a Chinese prerogative per se but perhaps a contribution that China can, due to its language, philosophical tradition and politico-legal setting, make to the solution of the problems related to these challenges. One reason is that China does not separate or at least consider incompatible the two areas of culture and trade in law and policymaking. However, it does not mean that China may not treat them differently in related agreements or policies but it still makes a difference eventually when it comes to the interpretation and implementation of the relevant rules. As the cognitive level is hard to make out in concrete terms, it is difficult to grasp and fix in language the level of ideas.

Yet, despite these difficulties, it is with the assistance of a reasonable degree of abstraction derived from a critical analysis of past developments, the present trends may still be translated into recommendations, and may even allow this article to make some reliable predictions about the future that are of fundamental importance to human history. To possibly identify trends deriving from differences at the cognitive level, Section 1 of the contribution first provides a brief chronology of the milestones that have already been reached in the global culture and trade debate, in order to extract some information about the fundamental concepts and drivers of change in this debate. Section 2 then looks at the local changes in the PRC's governmental cultural and trade policies, notably in connection with its accession to the World Trade Organization (WTO) in 2001, so as to pave the way for finding connections between the local, regional, and global levels, with a view to extracting the main trends and resulting challenges for law and policymaking in the future. Finally, the conclusion makes some general recommendations as to the optimal features of law and policy that will secure the lasting reconciliation between cultural and economic issues that is necessary for the success of a sustainable development strategy, locally and globally.

## 1. The changing landscape of 'culture and trade': a 'binary' view

> *However, while the concept, 'culture industry', was deliberately coined to create a contradictory contrast that juxtaposes culture and industry, the terms creative industry or creative economy display some beginning tendencies to resolve that paradox by gradually dissolving the apparent inherent contradiction* (Neuwirth 2015, 32).

In fast motion, the history of the 'culture and trade' relationship over the millennia may best be characterized as one of contestation, chiefly featuring the division between culture and trade that resulted from dualistic thinking and binary logic. At an early stage, their dichotomy was exemplified by the Roman law, where cultural products were legally qualified as '*res extra commercium*' or 'things which cannot be the object of exchange or of any legal commercial transaction' (Berger 1953, 677). Later, this thinking gave rise to the separation of international intellectual property rights into one category of laws protecting commercial or 'industrial' rights (1883 Paris Convention for the Protection of Industrial Property) and a second category for cultural or 'literary and artistic' rights (1886 Berne Convention for the Protection of Literary and Artistic Works).

In international trade law, a similar bifurcation was introduced into the 1947 General Agreement on Tariffs and Trade (GATT) by means of the general exceptions enshrined in Article XX GATT and the special exception in Article IV GATT related to cinematograph films (Jackson 1969, 293; Neuwirth 2006, 109–132). As a result of the failure of the International Trade Organization, the separation of culture from trade in the GATT is also reflected in the wider institutional split between the international trading regime and the United Nations Organization, which continues until today.[1] Equally, the separation of culture from international trade continued in the working group established to determine the precise classification of television as a good or a service (GATT 1961). Remaining unsolved, the issue re-emerged in the context of the negotiation of the 1988 US–Canada Free Trade Agreement, which – together with similar audiovisual policies inside the European Communities – also affected the successful completion of the

Uruguay Round negotiations for the establishment of the WTO. Even after the creation of the WTO in 1995, the position did not change very much, as the dichotomy was legally maintained; this is reflected in the panel decision in the *Canada – Periodicals* case, which stated that 'cultural identity was not at issue' (WTO Panel Report 1997, para. 5.45). Equally, conditions did not change after the adoption of a separate Convention on the Protection and Promotion of the Diversity of Cultural Expressions through UNESCO in 2005, as can be seen from the legal irrelevance of this Convention in the *China – Publications and Audiovisual Products* case, which – by and large – maintained the bifurcation in the regulation of cultural and trade matters (WTO Appellate Body Report 2009).

These are but a few examples of the way in which the international community has advanced along dichotomous lines, and there are numerous examples in other areas. For instance, European integration was divided between the Council of Europe and the European Economic Community (Neuwirth 2008, 37–38). Similarly, the regimes governing military security were divided between the 1949 North Atlantic Treaty Organization (NATO) and the 1955 Warsaw Pact (Wagner 1978). On a wider scale, the security divide was mirrored by a geographical divide between the east and the west that was then replaced by one between the north and the south (Neuwirth 2018, 128 and 131–134). Despite the indivisibility of human rights, this field too saw a split in 1966, with two separate covenants, one on civil and political rights and the other on cultural, social, and economic rights (United Nations General Assembly 1952).

Going back to the divide between culture and trade, there were few who saw the intrinsic connections between the two areas. For example, Max Horkheimer and Theodor W. Adorno still saw them as contrasting, but did at least merge them conceptually into the oxymoron of 'the culture industry' (Adorno 1991, 98). Later, economists followed suit in expanding their economic interest to the realm of culture, paving the way for the equally oxymoronic notions of 'the cultural economy' (Frey 2000, 1–5) and later 'the creative economy' (Venturelli 2001). Even the trade negotiators of the US and the EU found an oxymoron to bring a temporary settlement to their differences as to the treatment of culture within international trade, by means of an 'agreement to disagree' (Elliott and Luce 1993, 1). These are only a few examples of a growing trend by which the former dividing line between culture and trade became blurred, and culture and trade increasingly progressed towards convergence, which was also expressed in a shift from the 'cultural' to the 'creative industries' (Garnham 2005). Convergence, however, is not limited to the cultural or creative industry sectors. The concept has also concentrically expanded to affect the understanding of the economy as a whole (Throsby 2008), whence the term 'convergenomics' (Lee and Olson 2010).

Strangely, at present, each emerging trend appears to be instantly accompanied by an opposite force. For instance, the trend towards industrial convergence is accompanied by a trend towards regulatory divergence (Neuwirth 2015), globalization by localization (Khondker 2005), integration by fragmentation (Rosenau 1997, 99–117), and cooperation by competition (Esty and Geradin 2000). More recently, however, these dichotomies are gradually being replaced by a growing number of paradoxes or oxymora, like those of 'fragmegration', 'glocalisation', or 'coopetition'. This overarching trend had already been noted by James N. Rosenau in 1995, when he described the challenges of global governance by the need to 'discern powerful tensions, profound contradictions, and perplexing paradoxes' (Rosenau 1995, 13). In the same year, Charles Handy described the present era as the 'Age of Paradox' (Handy 1995). Given the noticeable intensification of these apparently contradictory trends, I introduced the notion of 'essentially oxymoronic concepts' in 2013 to better analyze and address the rise in the number of notable oxymora and paradoxes (Neuwirth 2013b), which has now prompted me to define the present era as the 'Time of Oxymora' (Neuwirth 2018). Given that an oxymoron denotes 'a figure of speech or expressed idea in which apparently contradictory terms appear in conjunction' (Soanes and Stevenson 2008, 1040), these oxymoronic concepts are seen to clash with the strict rules of dualistic thinking or exclusive logic. As such, they appear to undermine or challenge the current paradigms in various sciences and the law (Neuwirth 2018; Kapur et al. 2011, 1). They have been found to challenge the law, in particular, because the law is largely built on dichotomous thinking as it was expressed in the following terms:

> For the lawyer's purpose every situation which confronts him is dealt with as falling into one or the other of two categories which are apparently supposed to be mutually exclusive and separated by a sharp boundary. Either this is a battery or not a battery, a trespass or not a trespass, etc. (Cook 1933, 333).

The prima facie aversion of lawyers to face the contradictions found in paradoxes or oxymora has also surfaced in the field of cultural and trade policymaking, where it was noted:

> Paradox is a rich source for artistic creation; it is, however, a poor basis for the development of cultural trade policy (Dymond and Hart 2002, 32).

Generally, it is often forgotten that what divides two concepts, like the border between two countries, is also the point that connects them. Hence, the previous quote may have become obsolete in view of the shared approach of, and the convergence between, culture and trade or business, which is seen in terms like 'the cultural and creative industries'. Moreover, in the 'Age of Paradox' or 'Time of Oxymora', educators are insisting that paradoxical or oxymoronic learning may be the only way to tackle future challenges (Eliason 1996, 341; Lewis and Dehler 2000; Bryant 2006; Thomas and Seely Brown 2011). This may not be a surprise, as many concepts applied to describe the imminent future, such as 'artificial intelligence', 'virtual reality', or 'cyborgs', can be considered oxymora. Similarly, machines and computers are already using fuzzy logic or similar concepts in their computation (Zadeh 1996, 110). It has been asked whether we have 'entered a world order in which Western dualistic thinking has somewhat lost its validity' (Steiner 2002, 216). If this were true, it would perhaps also explain the rise of the PRC and the Asian continent in the present century, as cultural geographers note the greater emphasis of Asian philosophy and education on holistic thinking, which can be translated into a better ability to embrace contradictions (Peng and Nisbett 1999; Nisbett 2003). It is therefore useful to look at culture- and trade-related developments within the PRC.

## 2. The PRC's glocal strategy on 'culture and trade': a holistic view

> *When persistence is successful, there is no blame [...] (I CHING – The Book of Change* 2006, 49).

It is difficult to assess the PRC's overall contribution to the 'global culture and trade debate'. Most recently, this contribution is perhaps best characterized by two key dates and developments: first, the beginning of the so-called 'reform and opening-up' policy of 1978, and, second, the PRC's accession to the WTO on 11 December 2001 (Bhala 2000). The two events are actually closely related, as the later of them merely marked the international legal recognition of the accomplishment of the earlier one's domestic objectives. However, China's influence on culture and trade goes much further back in history. The fact is that – contrary to frequently found stereotypes (Dimitrov 2009; Mertha 2005) – China has been a prolific innovator and inventor in both culture and trade (and in many more fields) (Temple 2007). It was even stated that for 'a large part of the last two millennia, China was the world's largest and most advanced economy' (Dahlman and Aubert 2001, xv). Historically, China could even be seen as a pioneer of the cultural industries long before the term was coined in 1947, given its central role in the invention of paper and the early development of book printing and publishing technologies around the seventh century (Gunaratne 2001; Carter 1955). In this respect, it is encouraging to note that the stereotypical image of the PRC in the media as a recidivist 'copycat' (Ngai 1995, 4; Zaracostas and Carvajal 2007, 10; Yu 2017, 2B) is gradually being changed and corrected (Rein 2014). The assumption that the PRC is a haven for intellectual property infringements is based on inadequate information and overly simplistic assumptions about the organization of the industries involved. For instance, it completely disregards the complexities related to counterfeiting and piracy, by neglecting the potential of the positive externalities caused by piracy and counterfeiting (Neuwirth 2017). Second, it also disregards the fact that it is well known that the logical path of creativity is from imitation via innovation to originality, and that most countries at some point in history have followed this path (Gibbons 2011). This path is also detected in the rise of so-called '*shanzhai* products', which are products that have evolved from being mere counterfeit or pirated products to products that are more innovative than the originals (Zhu and Shi 2010).

For the future evolution of the global culture and trade debate, it is important to assess the central contribution that the PRC has already made, both internally and externally, or locally and globally. It is possible that the key point is that China and its people never actually and conceptually separated culture and trade or saw them as mutually exclusive and contradictory. This may also be reflected in the particular characteristics of the present political and legal system, which appears to have better integrated (or at least not divided) not only politics and economics but, as a result of the greater coherence of policy making, even culture and trade. With regard to the legal system of the PRC, it was stated that it 'is the product of policy decisions by the Party/state to build an institutional framework to support economic growth' (Potter 2001, 1) and that the main 'motivating forces China's turn toward rule of law has been the belief that legal reforms are necessary for economic development' (Peerenboom 2002, 450). At the same time, the particular nature of the PRC's politico-legal system may explain the difficulties of an outsider trying to understand its complexity (Ruskola 2003, 656). In this regard, a brief explanation of different policies formulated and implemented by the PRC at different levels helps to cast light on the politico-legal system.

### *2.1. Local Cooperation: One Country, Two Systems*

There is no doubt that the governance of internal affairs and the governance of external affairs – like the governance of cultural and that of trade matters – are best considered as complementary, as they are intrinsically linked. In this regard, it is noteworthy that the PRC's global rise probably started a long time ago, with the most recent landmark change being the adoption of the 1949 Common Program of the Chinese People's Political Consultative Conference ('Common Program'), which triggered the subsequent constitutional history of the present PRC. Since 1949, the PRC's rapid development may confirm the paradoxical theory of change of Arnold Beisser, which contends that change cannot 'take place through a coercive attempt' (Beisser 1970, 77). Accordingly, the history of the Chinese people displays a long line of persistent internal efforts and struggles as outlined by the Preamble of the Constitution of the PRC. These persistent internal efforts were only (re-)aligned with the external world following the opening-up policy in the late 1970s. During that time, the fifth five-year plan (1976–1980) was adopted, which, in addition to the objective of economic development, also foresaw the modernization of China. In the subsequent plan (the sixth five-year plan, 1981–1985), the general objectives to pursue the principle of 'adjust, reform, rectify and improve' so as 'to further overcome the various challenges to economic development' were complemented by specific objectives, one of which included education, science and culture, as follows:

> 5) To assemble the country's scientific and technological [sic] for scientific and technological research and to promote the application of new technologies, and to strenuously develop *education, science and culture* to accelerate the construction of an ideological and material civilization.[2]

During the same period, the Constitution of the PRC was adopted by the 5th National People's Congress on 4 December 1982. In its most recently amended version, the Preamble also displays signs of a combined consideration of various economic and culture-related aspects, as follows:

> [...] the Chinese people of all ethnic groups will continue to [...] develop the *socialist market economy*, develop socialist democracy, improve the socialist legal system, work hard and self-reliantly to modernize the country's industry, agriculture, national defense and science and technology step by step, and *promote a coordinated development* of material, political and spiritual civilizations to turn China into a socialist country that is *prosperous, powerful, democratic and culturally advanced.*[3]

The Constitution thus also reflects a conceptual approach that combines economic objectives with the objective of cultural development, or actually perceives all these objectives as part of one greater common goal. Generally, law and policymaking in the PRC seems to be characterized by a strong spirit of persistence, planning, and patience in the pursuit of reforms and objectives that are very often set out for the very long term. Such long-term thinking also surfaces in the words of Deng Xiaoping when he discussed the 50-year term for the Basic Law of the HK Special Administrative Region as follows:

> Even after 50 years our policy will not change either. That is, for the first 50 years it cannot be changed, and for the second there will be no need to change it (Xiaoping 1993, 267).

In the present times of ever faster change, such long-term thinking in policymaking, or the ability to formulate and carry out a vision, is rare in most countries and has certainly been absent for a long time in Europe. In such uncertain times, a long-term vision for the policy goals that are to be achieved is more likely to lead to success when pursued with a coherent approach and not an approach for which effort turns into regret and leads to more changes only a few months later. Similar considerations about continuity were also voiced in support of the most recent amendment to the Constitution of the PRC, which saw the former presidential term limit of two consecutive terms abolished by an amendment of Article 79 of the Constitution of the PRC (Shirk 2018).

Another example of the persistent pursuit of a long-term strategy comes from a field of major significance for culture and trade, namely the protection and enforcement of intellectual property rights. In 2008, the State Council of the PRC issued the Outline of the National Intellectual Property Strategy, the introduction to which states:

> Since the reform and opening up policy was introduced, China has maintained a sustainable and rapid economic and social development, and has made advances in science and technology and cultural creations, while the capacity for innovation has been constantly improved, and knowledge is playing an increasingly prominent role in China's economic and social development. China is now experiencing a new historical beginning, and it is of great strategic importance for the country to develop and utilize knowledge-based resources in order to transform the pattern of economic development, ease the constraints posed by demand for resources and environmental concerns, improve the nation's core competitiveness and meet the increasing material and cultural demands of the people (State Council of the People's Republic of China 2008).

One of the major strategic goals outlined is to become by 2020 'a country with a comparatively high level in terms of the creation, utilization, protection and administration of IPRs'. Only two years before the deadline, the PRC has already made considerable progress in the field of IPRs, as can be seen in the highest number of patent, trademark and industrial design filings recorded in 2017 (WIPO 2017, 7), marking a continuing shift from 'Made in China' to 'Created in China' (Moon 2018). The speed of progress is quite remarkable, given that China was still the defendant in the *China – Intellectual Property Rights* case of 2009, in which it was accused of serious violations of intellectual property rights (WTO Panel Report 2009a). At the same time, China was also challenged before the WTO by the US for breaches of other laws and regulations in the audiovisual sector (WTO Panel Report 2009b).

Since then, the PRC has made similar efforts in the promotion of the creative economy and cultural industries, and these are set to continue given that the acceleration of the development of the 'modern cultural industries' features prominently among other cultural and related sectors in the latest five-year plan, namely the 13th Five-Year Plan for Economic and Social Development of the People's Republic of China (2016–2020) (Central Committee of the Communist Party of China 2016, 192–193 [Section 3]).

In parallel, there are ambitious efforts to also shift China from a producing to a creating country, as it is reflected in the 'Made in China 2025' plan that was issued by the State Council in 2015 (State Council of the People's Republic of China 2015d). The plan itself does not mention the cultural or creative industries but rather focuses on innovation, which is, however, closely related to creativity. It *inter alia* aims to adapt its institutions for innovation and to 'promote trans-industrial and interdisciplinary collaborative innovation, digitalization, network technologies, and smart technologies in manufacturing' (State Council of the People's Republic of China 2015c).

The overall success of the broad strategies and goals pursued by the PRC, such as the 'Made in China 2025' plan, necessarily depends on the wider context of global trade, which is why there is also a need for the coherent coordination of the internal and the external (that is to say, wider regional and global policies). In this respect, it is worth mentioning that the PRC has also gained valuable experience with its constitutional approach of 'One Country, Two Systems', which allows its two Special Administrative Regions (SARs), Hong Kong and Macau, both to be an inalienable part of the PRC but, at the same time, to be members of the WTO (Yang 2006; Chen 2003; Neuwirth 2011).

However, the future of the domestic regulation is likely to be influenced by the current global trade climate, particularly the US-China series of trade conflicts, which are bringing further uncertainty not only to the future of the 'culture and trade debate' but the entire multilateral trading system in general (Malawer 2017). Moreover, such international trade disputes also often require the responding party to change its domestic laws in order to bring them into conformity with international trade obligations. In this regard it is noteworthy that since President Trump took office in January 2017, the US has initiated a number of additional cases against China. China in turn, has also initiated several against the US. In terms of particular relevance to culture and trade issues, the following pending cases deserve to be mentioned:

The first case sees the United States complain in March 2018 (again) about Chinese measures concerning the protection of intellectual property rights.[4] In this case consultations were initially requested by the US as it claimed various violations of the TRIPS Agreement, namely that 'China denies foreign patent holders the ability to enforce their patent rights against a Chinese joint-venture party after a technology transfer contract ends' and 'also imposes mandatory adverse contract terms that discriminate against and are less favorable for imported foreign technology'.[5] In this case, a request for the establishment of a panel was submitted on 19 October 2018.[6]

In a second case, the European Union requested on 1 June 2018 consultations with China on Certain Measures on the Transfer of Technology.[7] The EU argues that China's domestic legislation is discriminatory by imposing 'a different set of rules on the import of technology, including industrial property rights, other intellectual property rights and undisclosed information'.[8]

These two cases are most relevant for the culture and trade debate but meanwhile a few other cases have been initiated both by China against the US[9] and by the US against China.[10] Overall, the lingering trade disputes are centered around China's legal system in general and various measures that notably encourage innovation in the domestic manufacturing sectors while curbing the involvement of foreign companies. They focus perhaps less explicitly on cultural aspects but reflect a more general trend from the core cultural industries to the creative industries and their most novel technologies expressed in concepts like cloud computing, big data, the internet of things and e-commerce or nanomaterials and biotechnologies. In spite of the explicit absence of culture, it can be expected that progress in these areas and innovation in general will also benefit the core cultural industries and creation of cultural content. This can already be seen by the rise of giant Chinese information technology firms like Tencent, Xiaomi, Alibaba or Baidu (Tse 2015).

In this respect, however, China will have to seek a proper balance between giving or restricting its population a wider access to global information, especially if it wants them to produce innovative and appealing products that appeal to a global consumer outside of China as well. In this regard it is worth mentioning that upon accession to the WTO China has originally limited the importation of motion pictures for theatrical release to 20 films per year (WTO 2002, 21). In the wake of the decision in the *China Publications and Audiovisual Products* case, China and the US had agreed to allow the importation of at least fourteen (14) enhanced format revenue-sharing films per calendar year beginning in 2012 (WTO 2012). In this regard, a 2018 report noted that China has facilitated the importation and distribution of U.S. films significantly, but still not sufficiently and to the full extent of the agreement reached (United States Trade Representative 2018, 483–485).

Overall, it seems too early to predict how the current trade rows will impact the future regulatory framework of culture and trade issues. It will certainly be important to monitor closely how changes brought by these trade disputes will affect the culture and trade debate globally and locally. Most likely, it will see a shift from the explicit regulation of cultural industries to broader policy goals under the broader concepts of the digital or creative economy. In this regard, it will be decisive to create a consistent regulatory framework suitable for a sustainable and inclusive growth, to maximize policy coherence with a view of balancing and complementing apparent opposites, like tradition and innovation, risks and dangers, or sustainability and development. In short, it means to be able to tackle the contradictions inherent in oxymora and paradoxes.

### *2.2. Global Cooperation: Bilateral treaties plus the 'BRICS' and the 'Belt and Road Initiative' (BRI)*

With regard to international trade and as an example of the PRC's growing significance as a global economic power, the PRC has, to date, concluded and notified 15 regional trade agreements (RTAs) to the WTO and has made an early announcement of three more.[11] At least two more new bilateral RTAs, namely with Georgia and the Maldives, have been signed, and several others are being negotiated (e.g. with Sri Lanka, Israel, Mauritius, and Moldova) (MOFCOM 2018). Moreover, existing RTAs are in the process of being upgraded and several new ones are under consideration. Additionally, several plurilateral ones, like the Regional Comprehensive Economic Partnership (RCEP), the agreement between China and the Gulf Cooperation Council, and the China–Japan–Korea RTA are being negotiated (MOFCOM 2018). In general, the Chinese government explains the rationale for the conclusion of RTAs as follows:

> The Chinese Government deems Free Trade Agreements (FTAs) as a new platform to further opening up to the outside and speeding up domestic reforms, an effective approach to integrate into global economy and strengthen economic cooperation with other economies, as well as particularly an important supplement to the multilateral trading system (MOFCOM 2018).

Complementing these efforts are various other policy initiatives that do not necessarily fit within a concrete legal definition, like the BRICS association, which is characterized as a 'cooperation and dialogue platform', or the 'Belt and Road Initiative' (BRI), which will be discussed later. It is also noteworthy that the PRC has concluded about 145 Bilateral Investment Treaties (BITs) (UNCTAD 2018).

First, focusing on the substantive issues related to the existing RTAs, it is important to note that all these RTAs share a primary focus on trade or economic issues. Nonetheless, they differ so that they can better meet the specific economic or political features of the respective trading partner. For example, the PRC has also notified two FTAs with its own two SARs, Hong Kong and Macau, each of which is – as laid down in the 'One Country, Two System' principle – an 'inalienable part' of the PRC but which are separate WTO members (Chiu 2006; Neuwirth 2011). The PRC has RTAs with countries located all over the world, including partners as different as Switzerland, Chile, New Zealand, the Maldives, and South Korea. More generally, following a rapid global trend of 'regionalizing multilateralism', the newer agreements have evolved and have usually expanded in scope and depth; for example, the Georgia FTA entered into force on 1 January 2018 and mentions 'electronic commerce' (Ch. 12.2 Georgia FTA).

The existing agreements concluded by the PRC, however, seem to share the objective of closer trade cooperation while also aiming to 'reinforce and expand cooperation, collaboration and mutual interchanges in the cultural areas' (see e.g. Chile FTA (Art. 104(1) (d); see also Art. 118(2)(c) Costa Rica FTA). Several agreements thus contain an explicit clause on cultural cooperation (e.g. Art. 110 Chile FTA, Article 17.23 South Korea FTA; and Art. 156 Peru FTA), or list culture under 'sports and recreation activities' (Art. 122 Costa Rica FTA).

Other RTAs also mention cultural aspects in the context of intellectual property rights; for example, the RTA with South Korea states that the objective of a chapter on IPR is 'to facilitate international trade and economic, social and cultural development through the dissemination of ideas, technology and creative works' (Art. 15.1(a)) South Korea FTA). Still others refer to cultural aspects in the context of 'genetic resources, traditional knowledge and folklore' (Art. 145 Peru FTA; see also Art. 11.9 Switzerland FTA).

The agreements with a stronger trade focus and no explicit reference to cultural cooperation are those signed with Pakistan, Australia, Iceland, New Zealand, and Singapore. However, even the more trade-focused agreements often contain clauses on culture-related topics, such as intellectual property rights (e.g. Art. 111 Chile FTA; Art. 112 Costa Rica FTA; Ch. 11 Georgia FTA; Iceland FTA; Switzerland FTA; Ch. 15 South Korea FTA; Ch. 11 Australia FTA) or traditional Chinese medicine (Australia FTA).

In sum, it is difficult to establish a clear pattern of the treatment of cultural aspects in the different RTAs concluded by the PRC, especially given that the scope of RTAs and the global context evolve so quickly. However, a report published in 2017 compares and summarizes ten of China's RTAs and concludes that the Chinese bilateral FTAs usually do not contain a reference to the 2005 UNESCO Convention and that China has made no or little commitments in certain sectors of cultural services (Guèvremont and Otašević 2017, 65–68). Otherwise, there exist notable differences between these agreements as to the treatment of cultural goods and services, the preferential treatment relating to culture, and the status of electronic commerce.

This finding comes as no surprise given the rather diverse backgrounds in terms of size, economy, geography, language or culture, of the different trading partners. Yet, a more holistic conception of the PRC of 'trade relations', a conception that is less likely to separate trade from other 'non-trade' (or, better, 'trade-related') issues, occasionally surfaces in these agreements. This can be seen in the Peru FTA, where the objectives for the cooperation are outlined as follows:

> 1. The Parties reaffirm the importance of all forms of cooperation, with particular attention to economic, trade, financial, technical, educational and cultural cooperation, as means to contribute to implementing the objectives and principles derived from this Agreement (Art. 149 China-Peru FTA).

At the same time, the very same agreement also exempts the cultural industries from the MFN commitment (Art. 131(3) b) China-Peru FTA). In this respect, it is also important to consider that the 'black letter text' of an RTA is not likely to reflect its actual impact on the treatment, protection, or promotion of the diversity of cultural expressions or culture as a whole. Here, too, the finding by a Canadian court seems to confirm that 'pure law is an oxymoron', since the law always needs a context within which it is to be considered (Ontario Superior Court of Justice 2011, 22).

In this regard, it must be noted that China was formerly not involved in the drafting and negotiation of the rules establishing the WTO, which also governs the establishment of RTAs (Art. XXIV GATT and Art. V GATS). Therefore, the present negotiation of RTAs do not well reflect the Chinese approach to culture and trade, as they are constrained by rules written in the past and by a system for the classification of goods and services, which has been outlived by the rapid pace of technological and scientific innovation and progress.

It is therefore perhaps more enlightening to look at China's other policy initiatives, which may not face the same constraint. For instance, the point about integrating culture into other areas (or at least not confining it to a separate field of cooperation), perhaps as part of an overall aim of achieving greater policy coherence, may also be exemplified in the cooperation known as 'BRICS' between Brazil, Russia, India, China and South Africa, which was formalized in 2011. Despite, or because of, their differences, the BRICS partners are making good progress and show vast potential for mutual cooperation (Neuwirth, Svetlicinii, and de Castro Halls 2017). Some find it strange that the cooperation between the BRICS countries has, strictly speaking, thus far not resulted in a free trade agreement but instead produced only three major international legal instruments, two of which, the New Development Bank (or 'BRICS Bank') and the Treaty for the Establishment of a BRICS Contingent Reserve Arrangement (Itabaiana Martins, Pires Ferreira, and Basílio Weber 2017), are more economic in nature, while the third is the Agreement on Cooperation in the Field of Culture (Hanania Richieri and Vlassis 2017). In the Agreement on Culture, the BRICS countries pledge the following:

> In accordance with this Agreement, and laws and policies of their states, the Parties shall develop and promote cooperation and exchanges in the field of culture, including the art of music and dancing, choreography, theatre, circus, archives, publishing and libraries, museums, cultural heritage, fine, decorative and applied arts, audio-visual works, and in other creative activities provided for by this Agreement.[12]

A similar finding of a more coherent or integrated approach to culture and trade can be made by considering the recent Belt and Road Initiative (BRI) that was launched in 2013 by the PRC (State Council of the People's Republic of China 2015a). With the aim of reviving the Silk Road, the BRI constitutes a vast project to connect Asia, Europe and Africa by land (the belt) and by sea (the road) (Mayer 2018; Deepak 2018). However, it is important to mention that officials have stated that 'the Silk Road Economic Belt and the 21st Century Maritime Silk Road initiatives will be "open" to all nations and are not limited by geography' (State Council of the People's Republic of China 2015c). As for the close entwinement of economic and cultural aspects in the BRI, its Action Plan opens with the following words:

> More than two millennia ago the diligent and courageous people of Eurasia explored and opened up several routes of *trade and cultural exchanges* that linked the major civilizations of Asia, Europe and Africa, collectively called the Silk Road by later generations. For thousands of years, the Silk Road Spirit – "peace and cooperation, openness and inclusiveness, mutual learning and mutual benefit" – has been passed from generation to generation, promoted the progress of human civilization, and contributed greatly to the prosperity and development of the countries along the Silk Road. Symbolizing communication and cooperation between the East and the West, the Silk Road Spirit is a *historic and cultural heritage* shared by all countries around the world (State Council of the People's Republic of China 2015b).

More specifically still, the same text also states that the BRI embraces 'the trend toward a multipolar world, economic globalization, cultural diversity and greater IT application' and is 'designed to uphold the global free trade regime and the open world economy in the spirit of open regional cooperation'. As a last example of the relationship and non-separation of culture and trade, the Action Plan also puts together 'economic integration and cultural inclusiveness' as well as 'trade and cultural exchange activities' (State Council of the People's Republic of China 2015b).

The bilateral and regional initiatives of the PRC confirm its growing global role. Moreover, the many initiatives now seem to complement each other to form a broader picture of the plan the PRC is pursuing globally, notably through multilateral means and channels. For instance, in the forefront of the BRICS Agreement on Culture, the leaders explored the possibility of establishing, at UNESCO, 'a "BRICS-UNESCO Group", aiming at developing common strategies within the mandate of the Organization' (BRICS Sanya Declaration 2011). In this regard, it is important to reiterate that even though the BRI and the BRICS cooperation have a regional character, their objectives are designed to support the multilateral order. This is exemplified by the statement that the BRI should be open to all interested parties, as well as the most recent 2017 BRICS Xiamen Declaration, which reiterates the aim to uphold development and multilateralism by 'working together for a more just, equitable, fair, democratic and representative international political and economic order' (BRICS Xiamen Declaration 2017). The BRICS cooperation also values a combined approach to economic and cultural matters. In this context, too, it was found that 'the success of the BRICS issue narrative on culture depends on the coherency and persuasiveness of parallel narratives in the areas of global governance, international security and economic partnerships' (Van Noort 2018).

In sum, the principal question is what kind of framework for culture and trade will be developed in parallel with the work towards a future global legal order of governance. The PRC's role in shaping such a future global legal order will depend on its ability to influence the many debates that are held under the overall description of 'global governance debate', and particularly to deal with the apparent contradictions underlying the paradoxes and oxymora. With China's economic power on the rise, its influence on political matters is also expected to grow but this is not usually enough. This is why many commentators are also increasingly looking at the 'soft power' of the PRC.

The assessment of the PRC's soft power evaluates its diplomacy, in general, and its media and cultural industries, in particular, and is being made individually and also collectively within the BRICS countries (Kurlantzick 2007; Straubhaar 2015; Vlassis 2016; Stuenkel 2016). Perhaps another good example to demonstrate that no strict separation exists between cultural and economic goals is found by looking at the PRC's soft diplomacy, like the work of the 700 Confucius Institutes or Confucius classrooms that China has set up around the world since 2004 (Hartig 2012). These institutes are primarily set up to promote Chinese culture and language, but they are also used in more practical ways 'to do business and open markets' or provide 'an effective mechanism for the scientific contribution to economic globalization' (Hartig 2012, 68). They are also said to meet a growing demand abroad 'due to China's economic growth and increasing political influence' (Yang 2010, 239). The case of the Confucius Institutes once more confirms the intrinsic links between culture and trade, and also shows that China does not seem to see the necessity to separate them organizationally (or at least finds better ways of integrating them with a single goal).

In sum, the many domestic as well as foreign policy activities of the PRC seem to seamlessly complement and not necessarily to contradict each other. From the perspective of an outsider, the government seems to perform an invisible coordination of all the levels, local, regional, and global, as well as all the fields, political, legal, economic, and cultural.

## Conclusion

*According to China, the Panel failed to perform such a "holistic approach" to treaty interpretation [...]* (WTO Panel Report 2009b, 18).

In 2015, the editors of a book investigated, in broad terms, the question of the role of China in the international economic order and whether this role will move things in new directions or even change existing paradigms (Toohey, Picker, and Greenacre 2015). At the time, and while finding strong evidence in the affirmative, namely that China 'will increasingly contribute to and influence IEL [international economic law], perhaps even going so far eventually as to be a standard-setter', the editors left the final answer to the reader (Picker and Toohey 2015, 7–8). Perhaps an answer can be found when looking at the role of China in the global culture and trade debate. This debate has evolved for centuries in the past but was, in law and for regulatory purposes, often divided into two separate areas, for instance by the use of special or general exceptions. It took a long time for the two to merge, at least conceptually, which is most visibly in the old oxymoron of the 'culture industry', coined by Adorno and Horkheimer, which eventually also made its entry into the world of international trade law by virtue of Article 2012 of the 1988 Canada-United States Free Trade Agreement and Article 4(5) of the 2005 UNESCO Convention on the Protection and Promotion of the Diversity of Cultural Expressions.

While the areas of culture and of trade may have converged conceptually, their separation still widely persists in law today, as it is reflected in the WTO covered agreements' use of exceptions or the institutional clash between the WTO and UNESCO. During the Uruguay Round negotiations, the legal separation was reinforced by the opposite views on the nature and treatment of cultural industries held by the United States on the one hand and the EU, France and Canada on the other. While the US generally denied these industries any cultural nature, the EU and Canada usually overemphasized the cultural importance. Both sides only concur in their underlying cognitive mindset, which is based largely on dualistic thinking and binary logic. This is where China appears to have a different mindset, one which does not necessarily see apparent opposites, as expressed in oxymora or paradoxes, as mutually incompatible. This mindset was circumscribed here by China taking a more holistic approach towards the issue of culture and trade as it expressed it in the *China – Publications and Audiovisual Products* case decided before the WTO.

As China was not actively involved in the negotiation and drafting of the present multilateral trading rules governed by the WTO, which also apply to RTAs within its scope, the third and more holistic approach is not yet easily detected. Generally, China not seeing culture and trade as belonging to different areas can be seen in the fact that China ratified the UNESCO Convention in January 2007 and also embraces multilateralism under the WTO. From a closer perspective though, China's holistic approach is less visible in trade relations under the WTO, including the numerous RTAs it concluded, which have to comply with WTO rules and existing services classifications (which are not apt to deal with the dynamic nature and growing complexity of cultural and creative industries). In other words, China's contribution to the debate will still need some more time to materialize but some trends may become discernible from other policy initiatives outside the WTO framework, such as the Belt and Road Initiative (BRI) or the BRICS cooperation. At present, what seems certain already is that the culture and trade debate will continue albeit in a different regulatory environment (Neuwirth 2010).

The reason is that at the beginning of the twenty-first century things are evolving faster and further, and the 'paradox' can no longer be regarded as 'a rich source for artistic creation' but only as a 'poor basis for the development of cultural trade policy' (Dymond and Hart 2002, 32). On the contrary, understanding paradoxes, often expressed in oxymoronic concepts, and taking a holistic approach to apparent opposites are key nowadays to successful law and policymaking in general and to the appropriate combination of cultural and trade laws and policies in particular (Neuwirth 2013b). Such oxymoronic or paradoxical thinking, it is argued, is particularly essential in an age of constant change, which is both driven by and results in a growing convergence of industries and technologies, blurring the old lines not only of established legal fields but of all areas of policymaking (Neuwirth 2018). At the same time, participants in the debate about culture and trade must make sure that they develop a cognitive mindset that allows them to talk to each other and not past each other. This is of particular relevance in the context of the ongoing series of trade conflicts involving the US and China as well as the EU and other countries. These conflicts are already renewing efforts to reform the multilateral trading system governed by the WTO (European Union 2018; Government of Canada 2018).

Against this backdrop, China's more coherent and perhaps holistic approach (or else its ability to see the complementarity rather than the contradiction between apparent opposites) to different policy fields and phenomena, like those of culture and trade, appears as an advantage. In practical terms, the conceptual advantage lies in the support from its politico-legal system and a tendency for long-term planning. A further advantage is found in a script made of characters (rather than a linear alphabet) and a more unitary mindset (focusing on complementarity rather than solely mutual exclusivity) that has developed over thousands of years and is well acquainted philosophically with rapid and constant change. Hence, there is little doubt that China will play a central role in the future of the culture and trade debate, both jointly and separately, in the field of culture as exemplified by support for the 2005 UNESCO Convention on the Protection and Promotion of the Diversity of Cultural Expressions and in international trade as highlighted by its rise as a global economic player and strong support for the multilateral trading regime under the aegis of the WTO.

Certainly, there are also multiple dangers or obstacles related to the latest trends and advances in science and technology, and these will have great repercussions for both culture and trade. The dangers are real at the local, regional, and global level. For the PRC, some of the advantages may also have a serious downside, namely that changes may happen too fast or else that a chosen strategy, because it was pursued coherently, may turn out to be counterproductive or wrong. In other words, progress usually involves learning through serious mistakes, and these feature in the history of the PRC as of any place in the world. However, a relentless will to learn, combined with persistence, planning, and patience, may compensate for negative effects or help to overcome them in the long run.

With a share of almost a fifth of the total world population, China's recent return to the global scene marks a great opportunity for the global governance debate in terms of global democratic representation. This is particularly true as every place on earth and every culture has an important role to play in shaping the destiny of humanity, as recognized by international cultural law in general and the UNESCO Convention on the Protection and Promotion of the Diversity of Cultural Expressions, which states in the Preamble that 'cultural diversity is a "defining characteristic of humanity" creating "a rich and varied world"' (Recital 1 and 3). Most of all, the PRC has already contributed to the advent of a new stage in the understanding of the relationship between culture and trade, by realizing that they are intrinsically linked and are like two sides of the same coin. China is also implementing these lessons practically under the aegis of the multilateral trading system, by way of numerous bilateral initiatives and other plurilateral efforts, like the BRICS cooperation and the Belt and Road Initiative. Because of this enhanced global cooperation in both fields, through local, regional, and global channels, one can continue to hope that the world remembers that human creativity and ingenuity really know no limitations in terms of territory, culture, race, time, or space and that culture everywhere has always flourished best without such boundaries. The best possible conditions to favor the concentration of human creativity and ingenuity have been found in different places at different times, like in Baghdad in the ninth century, Florence during the Renaissance, and Vienna at the turn of the nineteenth century, to mention but a few (Janik and Toulmin 1973; Hamilton Morgan 2008; Belting 2011). This begs the next open question: Where will the next center be? Will it be Beijing or Shanghai, or will the entire globe itself finally become a flourishing center where art, science, culture, and trade, through law, contribute to the sustainable and inclusive development of all people?

## Notes

1. WTO. 1996. *Decision of the General Council on Conditions of Service applicable to the Staff of the WTO Secretariat of 7, 8 and 13 November 1996*. WTO Doc. WT/L/197 (18 November 1996) ('NOTING that the WTO is a sui generis organization established outside the United Nations system').
2. See the 6th Five-Year Plan (1981–1985) [*Italics* added]. http://www.china.org.cn/english/MATERIAL/157619.htm.
3. Recital 7 of the Preamble of the Constitution of the People's Republic of China (4 December 1982/last amended on 11 March 2018) [*Italics* added]. http://en.pkulaw.cn/display.aspx?cgid=311950&lib=law.
4. WTO. 2018. *China – Certain Measures Concerning the Protection of Intellectual Property Rights (Request for Consultations by the United States)*. WT/DS542/1 (26 March 2018). For an earlier China copyright case, see WTO Panel Report. 2009. *China – Measures Affecting the Protection and Enforcement of Intellectual Property Rights*. WT/DS 362/R (26 January 2009).
5. WTO. 2018. *China – Certain Measures Concerning the Protection of Intellectual Property Rights (Request for Consultations by the United States)*. WT/DS542/1 (26 March 2018).
6. WTO. 2018. *China – Certain Measures Concerning the Protection of Intellectual Property Rights (Request for Consultations by the United States)*. WT/DS542/8 (19 October 2018).
7. WTO. 2018. *China – Certain Measures on the Transfer of Technology (Request for Consultations by the EU)*. WT/DS549/1 (6 June 2018).
8. WTO. 2018. *China – Certain Measures on the Transfer of Technology (Request for Consultations by the EU)*. WT/DS549/1 (6 June 2018).
9. See WTO. 2018. *United States – Tariff Measures on Certain Goods from China (Request for consultations by China)*. WT/DS543/1 (5 April 2018); WTO. 2018. *United States – Certain Measures on Steel and Aluminium Products (Request for consultations by China)*. WT/DS544/1 (9 April 2018); WTO. 2018. *United States – Safeguard Measure on Imports of Crystalline Silicon Photovoltaic Products (Request for consultations by China)*. WT/DS562/1 (16 August 2018); WTO. 2018. *United States – Certain Measures Related to Renewable Energy (Request for consultations by China)*. WT/DS563/1 (16 August 2018); and WTO. 2018. *United States – Tariff Measures on Certain Goods from China II (Request for consultations by China)*. WT/DS565/1 (27 August 2018).
10. See WTO. 2017. *China – Subsidies to Producers of Primary Aluminium (Request of Consultations by the United States)*. WT/DS519/1 (17 January 2017); and WTO. 2018. *China – Additional Duties on Certain Products from the United States (Request for consultations by the United States)*. WT/DS558/1 (19 July 2018).
11. The notified agreements include the following countries or regional economic integration organizations (REIOs): ASEAN; Asia Pacific Trade Agreement (APTA); Asia Pacific Trade Agreement (APTA) (Accession of China); Australia; Chile; Costa Rica; Hong Kong, China; Republic of Korea; Macao, China; New Zealand;

Singapore; Iceland; Pakistan; Peru; and Switzerland. The three early announcements relate to The Cross-Straits Economic Cooperation Framework Agreement (ECFA), Norway and Moldova; see WTO. *RTA Database*. http://rtais.wto.org/UI/PublicSearchByMemberResult.aspx?MemberCode=156&lang=1&redirect=1.

12. Article 1 of the Agreement between the Governments of the BRICS States on Cooperation in the Field of Culture Ufa, Russia (9 July 2015). http://en.brics2015.ru/load/381755.

## Acknowledgments

The author would like to thank the editor of this special issue for the initial incentive to write this article and Lilian Hanania Richieri as well as the two anonymous reviewers for their critical but constructive comments.

## Disclosure statement

No potential conflict of interest was reported by the author.

## Funding

This work was supported by a Multi-Year-Research-Grant (MYRG) provided by the University of Macau [grant number MYRG2015-00222-FLL]

## ORCID

Rostam J. Neuwirth http://orcid.org/0000-0002-0641-5261

## References

Adorno, T. W. 1991. *The Culture Industry*. London: Routledge.

Barfield, C. 2007. "The Dragon Stirs: China's Trade Policy for Asia and the World." *Arizona Journal of International and Comparative Law* 24 (1): 93–119.

Beisser, A. 1970. "A Paradoxical Theory of Change." In *Gestalt Therapy Now: Theory, Techniques, Applications*, edited by J. Fagan and I. L. Shepherd, 70–80. Palo Alto: Science and Behavior Books.

Belting, H. 2011. *Florence and Baghdad: Renaissance Art and Arab Science*. Boston: Belknap Press.

Berger, A. 1953. *Encyclopedic Dictionary of Roman Law*. Philadelphia: The American Philosophical Society.

Bhagwati, J. 2000. "'Culture and Trade: America's Blind Spot'." In *The Wind of the Hundred Days: How Washington Mismanaged Globalization*, edited by J. Bhagwati, 209–213. Cambridge: MIT Press.

Bhala, R. 2000. "Enter the Dragon: An Essay on China's WTO Accession Saga Symposium: Interfaces: From International Trade to Economic Law." *American University International Law Review* 15 (6): 1469–1538.

Bhattasali, D., S. Li, and W. Martin, eds. 2004. *China and the WTO: Accession, Policy Reform, and Poverty Reduction Strategies*. Washington: World Bank.

Brandt, L., and T. G. Rawski. 2008. *China's Great Economic Transformation*. Cambridge: Cambridge University Press.

BRICS. 2011. Sanya Declaration (adopted by the BRICS Leaders at their 3rd meeting in Sanya, Hainan, China, on 14 April 2011). https://brics2017.org/English/Documents/Summit/201701/t20170125_1405.html

BRICS. 2017. Xiamen Declaration (4 September 2017). http://pibphoto.nic.in/documents/rlink/2017/sep/p20179401.pdf

Bryant, M. 2006. *Oxymoron? A Practical Guide to Fun and Effective Teaching*. New York: iUniverse.

Carter, T. F. 1955. *The Invention of Printing in China: And Its Spread Westward*. New York: Ronald Press Co.

Central Committee of the Communist Party of China. 2016. *The 13th Five-Year Plan for Economic and Social Development of the People's Republic of China (2016–2020)*. Beijing: Central Compilation & Translation Press. http://en.ndrc.gov.cn/newsrelease/201612/P020161207645765233498.pdf

Chen, A. H. 2003. "The Concept of 'One Country, Two Systems' and Its Application to Hong Kong." In *Understanding China's Legal System*, edited by C. Stephen Hsu, 353-373. New York: NYU Press.

Chiu, Y. W. P. 2006. "CEPA: A Milestone in the Economic Integration between Hong Kong and Mainland China." *Journal of Contemporary China* 15 (47): 275–295. doi:10.1080/10670560500534921.
Cook, W. W. 1933. ""Substance" and "Procedure" in the Conflict of Laws." *The Yale Law Journal* 42 (3): 333–358. doi:10.2307/791291.
Dahlman, C. J., and J.-E. Aubert. 2001. *China and the Knowledge Economy: Seizing the 21st Century*. Washington: The World Bank.
Deepak, B. R., ed. 2018. *China's Global Rebalancing and the New Silk Road*. Singapore: Springer.
Dimitrov, M. K. 2009. *Piracy and the State: The Politics of Intellectual Property Rights in China*. Cambridge: Cambridge University Press.
Dymond, W. A., and M. M. Hart. 2002. "Abundant Paradox: The Trade and Culture Debate." *Canadian Foreign Policy Journal* 9 (2): 15–33. doi:10.1080/11926422.2002.9673281.
Eliason, J. L. 1996. "Using Paradoxes to Teach Critical Thinking in Science." *Journal of College Science Teaching* 25 (5): 341–345.
Elliott, L., and E. Luce. 1993. "US and Europe Clear Obstacles to GATT Deal." *The Guardian (London)*, December 15.
Esty, D. C., and D. Geradin. 2000. "Regulatory Co-Opetition." *Journal of International Economic Law* 3 (2): 235–255. doi:10.1093/jiel/3.2.235.
European Union. 2018. "Concept Paper: WTO Modernisation." http://trade.ec.europa.eu/doclib/docs/2018/september/tradoc_157331.pdf
Frey, B. S. 2000. *Arts & Economics: Analysis & Cultural Policy*. Berlin: Springer.
Garnham, N. 2005. "From Cultural to Creative Industries." *International Journal of Cultural Policy* 11 (1): 15–29. doi:10.1080/10286630500067606.
Garrett, L. L. 1994. "Commerce versus Culture: The Battle between the United States and the European Union over Audiovisual Trade Policies." *North Carolina Journal of International Law and Commercial Regulation* 19 (3): 553–577.
GATT (General Agreement on Tariffs and Trade). 1961. *Application of GATT to International Trade in Television Programmes*. L/1615 (16 November 1961).
Gibbons, L. J. 2011. "Do as I Say (Not as I Did): Putative Intellectual Property Lessons for Emerging Economies from the Not so Long past of the Developed Nations." *SMU Law Review* 64 (3): 923–973.
Gleick, J. 2000. *Faster: The Acceleration of Just about Everything*. New York: Vintage Books.
Government of Canada. 2018. "Strengthening and Modernizing the WTO: Discussion Paper." September 21, 2018. http://international.gc.ca/gac-amc/campaign-campagne/wto-omc/discussion_paper-document_travail.aspx?lang=eng
Guèvremont, V., and I. Otašević. 2017. *Culture in Treaties and Agreements: Implementing the 2005 Convention in Bilateral and Regional Trade Agreements*. Paris: UNESCO. http://unesdoc.unesco.org/images/0024/002498/249829e.pdf
Gunaratne, S. A. 2001. "Paper, Printing and the Printing Press: A Horizontally Integrative Macrohistory Analysis." *International Communication Gazette* 63 (6): 459–479. doi:10.1177/0016549201063006001.
Guthrie, D. 2009. *China and Globalization: The Social, Economic and Political Transformation of Chinese Society*. 2nd ed. London: Routledge.
Hamilton Morgan, M. 2008. *Lost History: The Enduring Legacy of Muslim Scientists, Thinkers, and Artists*. Washington: National Geographic Society.
Hanania Richieri, L., and A. Vlassis. 2017. "For a BRICS Agenda on Culture and the Creative Economy." In *The BRICS-Lawyers' Guide to Global Cooperation*, edited by R. J. Neuwirth, A. Svetlicinii, and D. D. C. Halis, 333–351. Cambridge: Cambridge University Press.
Handy, C. 1995. *The Age of Paradox*. Boston: Harvard Business School Press.
Hariri, Y. N. 2017. *Homo Deus: A Brief History of Tomorrow*. New York: Harper Collins.
Hartig, F. 2012. "Confucius Institutes and the Rise of China." *Journal of Chinese Political Science* 17: 53–76. doi:10.1007/s11366-011-9178-7.
Hufbauer, G. C., Y. Wong, and K. Sheth. 2006. *US-China Trade Disputes: Rising Tide, Rising Stakes*. Washington: Institute for International Economics.
Itabaiana Martins, C., L. Pires Ferreira, and R. Basílio Weber. 2017. "The BRICS Bank: On the Edge of International Economic Law and the New Challenges of Twenty-First-Century Capitalism." In *The BRICS-Lawyers' Guide to Global Cooperation*, edited by R. J. Neuwirth, A. Svetlicinii, and D. D. C. Halis, 200–220. Cambridge: Cambridge University Press.
Jackson, J. H. 1969. *World Trade and the Law of GATT*. Indianapolis: The Bobbs Merril Company.
Janik, A., and S. Toulmin. 1973. *Wittgenstein's VIENNA*. New York: Simon and Schuster.
Jenks, C. W. 1953. "The Conflict of Law-Making Treaties." In *British Yearbook of International Law* 30, 401–453.
Johnson, M. L. 2007. "Mind, Metaphor, Law." *Mercer Law Review* 58 (3): 845–868.
Kapur, N., A. Pascual-Leone, T. Manly, and J. Cole. 2011. "The Paradoxical Nature of Nature." In *The Paradoxical Brain*, edited by N. Kapur, 1–13. Cambridge: Cambridge University Press.
Keane, M. 2004. "Brave New World." *International Journal of Cultural Policy* 10 (3): 265–279. doi:10.1080/1028663042000312516.
Khondker, H. H. 2005. "Globalisation to Glocalisation: A Conceptual Exploration." *Intellectual Discourse* 13 (2): 181–199.

Kurlantzick, J. 2007. *Charm Offensive: How China's Soft Power Is Transforming the World*. New Haven: Yale University Press.

Lee, S. M., and D. L. Olson. 2010. *Convergenomics: Strategic Innovation in the Convergence Era*. Farnham: Gower.

Lewis, M. W., and G. E. Dehler. 2000. "Learning through Paradox: A Pedagogical Strategy for Exploring Contradictions and Complexity." *Journal of Management Education* 24 (6): 708–725. doi:10.1177/105256290002400604.

Malawer, S. S. 2017. "Trump's China Trade Policies: Threats and Constraints." *China and WTO Review* 1: 109–120. doi:10.14330/cwr.2017.3.1.05.

Mayer, M., ed. 2018. *Rethinking the Silk Road: China's Belt and Road Initiative and Emerging Eurasian Relations*. Singapore: Palgrave Macmillan.

Mertha, A. C. 2005. *The Politics of Piracy: Intellectual Property in Contemporary China*. Ithaca: Cornell University Press.

MOFCOM (Ministry of Commerce). 2018. "*China FTA Network*." http://fta.mofcom.gov.cn/english/index.shtml

Moon, L. 2018. "How the Mainland Went from 'Made in China' to 'Created in China'." *South China Morning Post (Hong Kong)*, January 11, 2018.

Murray, T. M. 1997. "The U.S.-French Dispute over GATT Treatment of Audiovisual Products and the Limits of Public Choice Theory: How an Efficient Market Solution Was "Rent-Seeking." *Maryland Journal of International Law and Trade* 21 (2): 203–224.

Neuwirth, R. J. 2006. *The Cultural Industries in International Trade Law: Insights from the NAFTA, the WTO, and the EU*. Hamburg: Dr. Kovač.

Neuwirth, R. J. 2008. "The European Union and the Ambivalence Towards the Process of European Integration." *NUJS Law Review* 1 (1): 33–53.

Neuwirth, R. J. 2010. "The "Culture and Trade Debate" Continues: The UNESCO Convention in Light of the WTO Reports in China – Publications and Audiovisual Products: Between Amnesia or Déjà Vu?" *Journal of World Trade* 44 (6): 1333–1356.

Neuwirth, R. J. 2011. "Governing 'Glocalisation': A View from the Macau Special Administrative Region of China." *City University of Hong Kong Law Review* 3 (1): 89–109.

Neuwirth, R. J. 2013a. "The Future of the Culture and Trade Debate: A Legal Outlook." *Journal of World Trade* 47 (2): 391–419.

Neuwirth, R. J. 2013b. "Essentially Oxymoronic Concepts." *Global Journal of Comparative Law* 2 (2): 147–166. doi:10.1163/2211906X-00202002.

Neuwirth, R. J. 2015. "Global Market Integration and the Creative Economy: The Paradox of Industry Convergence and Regulatory Divergence." *Journal of International Economic Law* 18 (1): 21–50. doi:10.1093/jiel/jgv012.

Neuwirth, R. J. 2017. "Counterfeiting and Piracy in International Trade: The Good, the Bad and the … Oxymoron of 'Real Fakes'." *Queen Mary Journal of Intellectual Property Law* 7 (4): 444–467. doi:10.4337/qmjip.2017.04.03.

Neuwirth, R. J. 2018. *Law in the Time of Oxymora: A Synaesthesia of Language, Logic and Law*. New York: Routledge.

Neuwirth, R. J., A. Svetlicinii, and D. de Castro Halis, eds. 2017. *The BRICS-Lawyers' Guide to Global Cooperation*. Cambridge: Cambridge University Press.

Ngai, A. 1995. "China's Fertile Copycat Industry." *South China Morning Post (Hong Kong)*, January 29.

Nisbett, R. E. 2003. *The Geography of Thought: How Asians and Westerners Think Differently … and Why*. New York: Free Press.

Ontario Superior Court of Justice. 2011. *Silveira v. Ontario (Minister of Transportation)*. (2011) O.J. No. 3157.

Pan, S. 2013. "Confucius Institute Project: China's Cultural Diplomacy and Soft Power Projection." *Asian Education and Development Studies* 2 (1): 22–33. doi:10.1108/20463161311297608.

Pang, L. 2012. *Creativity and Its Discontents: China's Creative Industries and Intellectual Property Rights Offenses*. Durham: Duke University Press.

Pauwelyn, J. 2010. "Squaring Free Trade in Culture with Chinese Censorship: The WTO Appellate Body Report on China – Audiovisuals." *Melbourne Journal of International Law* 11 (1): 119–140.

Peerenboom, R. 2002. *China's Long March toward Rule of Law*. Cambridge: Cambridge University Press.

Peng, K., and R. E. Nisbett. 1999. "Culture, Dialectics, and Reasoning about Contradiction." *American Psychologist* 54 (9): 741–754. doi:10.1037/0003-066X.54.9.741.

Picker, C. B., and L. Toohey. 2015. "China in the International Economic Order: New Directions and Changing Paradigms." In *China in the International Economic Order: New Directions and Changing Paradigms*, edited by L. Toohey, C. B. Picker, and J. Greenacre, 1–8. Cambridge: Cambridge University Press.

Potter, P. B. 2001. *The Chinese Legal System: Globalization and Local Legal Culture*. London: Routledge.

Rein, S. 2014. *The End of Copycat China: The Rise of Creativity, Innovation, and Individualism in Asia*. New Jersey: John Wiley & Sons.

Rosenau, J. N. 1995. "Governance in the 21st Century." *Global Governance* 1 (1): 13–43. doi:10.1163/19426720-001-01-90000004.

Rosenau, J. N. 1997. *Along the Domestic-Foreign Frontier: Exploring Governance in a Turbulent World*. Cambridge: Cambridge University Press.

Ruskola, T. 2003. "Law without Law, or Is "Chinese Law" and Oxymoron?" *William & Mary Bill of Rights Journal* 11 (2): 655–669.

Shirk, S. L. 2018. "The Return to Personalistic Rule." *Journal of Democracy* 29 (2): 22–36. doi:10.1353/jod.2018.0022.
Soanes, C., and A. Stevenson, eds. 2008. *Concise Oxford English Dictionary*. 11th ed. Oxford: Oxford University Press.
Sofield, T. H. B., and F. M. S. Li. 1998. "Tourism Development and Cultural Policies in China." *Annals of Tourism Research* 25 (2): 362–392. doi:10.1016/S0160-7383(97)00092-3.
State Council of the People's Republic of China. 2008. *Outline of the National Intellectual Property Strategy* (issued by the State Council of the People's Republic of China on 25 June 2008).. http://www.wipo.int/wipolex/en/text.jsp?file_id=125982
State Council of the People's Republic of China. 2015a. *"The Belt and Road Initiative."* http://english.gov.cn/archive/publications/2015/03/30/content_281475080249035.htm
State Council of the People's Republic of China. 2015b. *"Action Plan on the Belt and Road Initiative."* http://english.gov.cn/archive/publications/2015/03/30/content_281475080249035.htm
State Council of the People's Republic of China. 2015c. *"China's Belt and Road Plan 'Open' to All Nations."* http://english.gov.cn/news/top_news/2015/04/18/content_281475091262006.htm
State Council of the People's Republic of China. 2015d. *"Made in China 2025."* http://www.cittadellascienza.it/cina/wp-content/uploads/2017/02/IoT-ONE-Made-in-China-2025.pdf
Steiner, D. 2002. "Globalization and Its Challenge to Higher Education: Some Reflections of a European Americanist Educator and Life-Long Learner." In *Which "Global Village"? Societies, Cultures, and Political-Economic Systems in A Euro-Atlantic Perspective*, edited by V. G. Lerda, 213–228. Westport: Praeger.
Straubhaar, J. 2015. "BRICs as Emerging Cultural and Media Powers." In *Mapping BRICS Media*, edited by K. Nordenstreng and D. K. Thussu, 87–104. London: Routledge.
Stuenkel, O. 2016. "Do the BRICS Possess Soft Power?" *Journal of Political Power* 9 (3): 353–367. doi:10.1080/2158379X.2016.1232285.
Su, W. 2011. "Resisting Cultural Imperialism, or Welcoming Cultural Globalization? China's Extensive Debate on Hollywood Cinema from 1994 to 2007." *Asian Journal of Communication* 21 (2): 186–201. doi:10.1080/01292986.2010.539301.
Su, W. 2015. "From Culture for the People to Culture for Profit: The PRC's Journey toward a Cultural Industries Approach." *International Journal of Cultural Policy* 21 (5): 513–528. doi:10.1080/10286632.2014.931382.
*I CHING: The Book of Change*. 2006. Translated by T. Cleary. Boston: Shambhala.
Temple, R. 2007. *The Genius of China: 3,000 Years of Science, Discovery, and Invention*. 3rd ed. London: Carlton Publishing.
Thomas, D., and J. Seely Brown. 2011. *A New Culture of Learning: Cultivating the Imagination for A World of Constant Change*. Lexington: CreateSpace Independent Publishing Platform.
Throsby, D. 2008. "The Concentric Circles Model of the Cultural Industries." *Cultural Trends* 17 (3): 147–167. doi:10.1080/09548960802361951.
Toohey, L., C. B. Picker, and J. Greenacre, eds. 2015. *China in the International Economic Order: New Directions and Changing Paradigms*. Cambridge: Cambridge University Press.
Tse, E. 2015. *China's Disruptors: How Alibaba, Xiaomi, Tencent, and Other Companies are Changing the Rules of Business*. New York: Penguin.
UNCTAD. 2018. "International Investment Agreements Navigator." http://investmentpolicyhub.unctad.org/IIA/CountryBits/42
United Nations General Assembly. 1952. "Preparation of Two Draft International Covenants on Human Rights". Resolution 543 (5 February 1952). http://www.un.org/documents/ga/res/6/ares6.htm
United States Trade Representative. 2018. *2017 Report to Congress on China's WTO Compliance*. https://ustr.gov/sites/default/files/files/Press/Reports/China%202017%20WTO%20Report.pdf
Van Noort, C. 2018. "Brics Issue-Narrative on Culture: Strategic or Trivial?"." *International Journal of Cultural Policy* 24 (6): 786–797. doi:10.1080/10286632.2018.1459589.
Venturelli, S. 2001. *From the Information Economy to the Creative Economy: Moving Culture to the Center of International Public Policy*. Washington: Center for Arts and Culture.
Vlassis, A. 2016. "Soft Power, Global Governance of Cultural Industries and Rising Powers: The Case of China." *International Journal of Cultural Policy* 22 (4): 481–496. doi:10.1080/10286632.2014.1002487.
Wagner, N. 1978. "NATO and the Warsaw Pact." *Scientia Militaria* 8 (4): 40–46.
WIPO. 2017. *World Intellectual Property Indicators 2017*. Geneva: World Intellectual Property Organization (WIPO).
WTO. 1996. *Decision of the General Council on Conditions of Service Applicable to the Staff of the WTO Secretariat of 7, 8 and 13 November 1996*. WTO Doc. WT/L/197 (18 November 1996).
WTO. 2002. *The People's Republic of China: Schedule of Specific Commitments*. GATS/SC/135 (14 February 2002).
WTO. 2012. *China – Measures Affecting Trading Rights and Distribution Services for Certain Publications and Audiovisual Entertainment Products (Joint Communication from China and the United States)*. WT/DS363/19 (11 May 2012). doi:10.1094/PDIS-11-11-0999-PDN.
WTO Appellate Body Report. 2009. *China – Measures Affecting Trading Rights and Distribution Services for Certain Publications and Audiovisual Entertainment Products*. WT/DS363/AB/R (21 December 2009).
WTO Panel Report. 1997. *Canada – Certain Measures Concerning Periodicals*. WTO Doc. WT/DS31/R (30 June 1997).

WTO Panel Report. 2009a. *China – Measures Affecting the Protection and Enforcement of Intellectual Property Rights*. WT/DS 362/R (26 January 2009).

WTO Panel Report. 2009b. *China – Measures Affecting Trading Rights and Distribution Services for Certain Publications and Audiovisual Entertainment Products*. WT/DS 363/R (12 August 2009).

Xiaoping, D. 1993. *Deng Xiaoping Wenxuan*. Beijing: People's Press. [English translation available at: http://www.chinadaily.com.cn/china/19thcpcnationalcongress/2010-10/26/content_29714426.htm]

Ya Qin, J. 2011. "Pushing the Limits of Global Governance: Trading Rights, Censorship and WTO Jurisprudence – A Commentary on the China-Publications Case." *Chinese Journal of International Law* 10 (2): 271–322. doi:10.1093/chinesejil/jmr017.

Yang, C. 2006. "The Pearl River Delta and Hong Kong: An Evolving Cross-Boundary Region under 'One Country, Two Systems'." *Habitat International* 30: 61–86. doi:10.1016/j.habitatint.2004.06.004.

Yang, R. 2010. "Soft Power and Higher Education: An Examination of China's Confucius Institutes." *Globalisation, Societies and Education* 8 (2): 235–245. doi:10.1080/14767721003779746.

Yu, L. 2011. "WTO and National Cultural Policy: Rethinking China Measures Affecting Trading Rights and Distribution Services for Certain Publications and Audiovisual Entertainment Products." *Revue Juridique Themis* 45 (3): 457–493.

Yu, R. 2017. "Trump Takes on China's Trade Deals; President Directs Officials to Probe Possible Piracy Practices in Effort to Save U.S. Jobs." *USA TODAY*, August 3.

Zadeh, L. A. 1996. "Fuzzy Logic = Computing with Words." *IEEE Transactions on Fuzzy Systems* 4 (2): 103–111. doi:10.1109/91.493904.

Zaracostas, J., and D. Carvajal 2007. "China and Russia Cited as Major Piracy Locales." *The International Herald Tribune*, January 30. doi:10.1094/PDIS-91-4-0467B.

Zeng, K., ed. 2007. *China's Foreign Trade Policy: The New Constituencies*. London: Routledge.

Zhang, W. 2010. "China's Cultural Future: From Soft Power to Comprehensive National Power." *International Journal of Cultural Policy* 16 (4): 383–402. doi:10.1080/10286630903134300.

Zhang, X. 2006. *International Trade Regulation in China: Law and Policy*. Oxford: Hart.

Zhou, W. 2011. "Pirates behind an Ajar Door, and an Ocean Away: U.S.-China WTO Disputes, Intellectual Property Protection, and Market Access." *Temple International & Comparative Law Journal* 25 (1): 139–177.

Zhu, S., and Y. Shi. 2010. "Shanzhai Manufacturing – An Alternative Innovation Phenomenon in China." *Journal of Science and Technology Policy in China* 1 (1): 29–49. doi:10.1108/17585521011032531.

Zucca, L. 2018. "Two Conceptions of Global Constitutional Order." https://papers.ssrn.com/sol3/papers.cfm?abstract_id=3188161

# The end of cultural policy?[1]

Per Mangset

**ABSTRACT**
The article discusses whether we are approaching the end of public cultural policy in Western democracies, because contemporary cultural policy is not adapted to major transformation processes in contemporary societies. I discuss seven different challenges/scenarios that public cultural policy has to confront today: (1) It appears to be very difficult to democratise culture. (2) Public authorities consistently continue to support cultural institutions that may be obsolete. (3) Professional artists are still poor, despite public support schemes. (4) Public cultural policy is still predominantly national, despite the globalisation of cultural production and distribution. (5) Public authorities increasingly justify subsidies to culture with reference to the beneficial effects that art and culture could have outside the cultural field. Therefore, one might argue that other public bodies could take better care of cultural affairs. (6) A specific public cultural sector may appear to 'imprison' culture in a bureaucratic 'iron cage'. (7) Finally, one might argue that a public cultural policy has no sense in a period of stagnating public finances. In addition, I discuss several counterarguments to these challenges, without coming to a definite conclusion. I have based the analysis on available comparative research about the public cultural policies of Western democracies, predominantly Norwegian cultural policy.

## Introduction

Cultural policy—defined as the structured actions of specific public authorities responsible for the cultural sector—is a relatively recent historical phenomenon. Many countries in the Western world established their primary public bodies in this policy field after WWII: the UK created 'the Arts Council of Great Britain' in 1946; France established the first European ministry of culture in 1959; and the Nordic countries organised specific public bodies responsible for local and regional culture in the 1970s, introducing welfare-oriented scholarships for individual artists at the same time.

Of course, I know that many countries introduced various kinds of public support and control of cultural life long before WWII, for example royal patronage of the arts in medieval and Renaissance Europe, and film censorship in many countries from the early twentieth century. It is also a fact that both communist and fascist states conducted active cultural policies—often linked to propaganda—during several decades of the twentieth century. However, these policy regimes are since long brought to an end, e.g. communist Soviet Union (1922–91) and East Germany (1949–90), and Nazi Germany (1933–45). Thus, I think it is still legitimate to say that the modern, sectorial public cultural policy in Western democracies is primarily a post-WWII phenomenon.

The new, post-WWII cultural policies formulated great and bold goals for the democratisation of culture and support for artistic creation. Did they succeed? Now we can summarise many decades' experience of the results of different cultural policy regimes. The ideal cultural policy regime, however, is still elusive. Modern public cultural policy was more or less a by-product of the post-war welfare state: Public authorities should take care of new areas of citizens' lives, even their cultural well-being. During the following decades, however, major social transformations have taken place in Western societies, i.e. increasing globalisation; privatisation, liberalisation, market-isation and digitalisation; financial crises in many countries; the rise of religious fundamentalism; migration crises; terrorism, etc. We now have 50–70 years' substantial experience of public cultural policy in most Western countries: Have these public cultural policies achieved their great and bold goals? Have the policy instruments that public cultural authorities apply proved to be adequate? Some countries, after decades of active public cultural policy, are now experiencing a certain legitimation crisis. Democratisation of culture has proved to be difficult to achieve; artists still experience more or less permanent poverty and insecurity. It seems, therefore, that contemporary public cultural policy is not adapted to major transformation processes in contemporary Western societies. Are we now facing the end of modern cultural policy?

Two German scholars, Annette Zimmer and Stefan Toepler, asked this question in a seminal article published more than 20 years ago (Zimmer and Toepler 1996). Based on a comparative analysis of three different cultural policy regimes (i.e. Germany, Sweden and USA), they asked whether one 'now' (in 1996) was about to experience 'the end of cultural policy as we know it', or even 'the end of cultural policy proper', that is whether a 'post-cultural policy age has [had] begun' (op. cit. 190). As far as they could see, at that stage, a levelling of differences between these three cultural policy regimes had taken place. They saw a general development towards more liberal and privatised cultural policies—and a parallel retraction of public authorities from the cultural field—in all three countries.

In this article, I will continue this discussion, based on the development of the cultural policies of Western countries both before 1996 and in the subsequent decades: Are we now confronted with the 'end of cultural policy', that is has 'the post-cultural policy age' begun? I then have to emphasise that I talk about 'cultural policy' in a quite narrow sense, that is as a primarily sectorial and structured public cultural policy. I focus in particular on the cultural policy of Norway, but I will also compare with the cultural policies of other Western democracies.

Empirically, I base my analysis on previous comparative studies of the cultural policies of various countries that I conducted myself (i.e. Mangset 2003, 2006, 2009, 2012b, 2013; Mangset and Hylland 2017) and on other available international cultural policy research (see references). Therefore, I will often refer to research about Norwegian cultural policy, but also try to compare it with the cultural policies of other Western countries. It is certainly partly for pragmatic reasons that I take Norwegian cultural policy as a starting point and as primary empirical example. One main purpose of this article is to question the efficiency and adequacy of actual public cultural policies in contemporary societies. The Nordic countries (Sweden, Denmark, Finland and Norway in particular) have all developed quite strong, focused and welfare-oriented cultural policies since WWII. The Norwegian government, for instance, significantly increased its cultural budget between 2005 and 2013. At the time of the change of government in 2013, almost 1% of the general government budget was being spent on culture (NOU 2013: 4). When we discuss the efficiency of public cultural policy, it may, therefore, be reasonable to take an apparently successful Nordic country as a starting point.

## Stability and change

Are we, then, approaching the end of cultural policy? It is of course hard to predict the future, including the future of public cultural policy. I do not really intend to make predictions in this article, rather to discuss potential future scenarios that might be helpful to reflect on for cultural policy researchers. Many scholars—especially before the new millennium—predicted fundamental paradigmatic transformations of Western and/or global culture and/or societies: Ulrich Beck (1992) described a forthcoming 'risk society', Zygmunt Bauman (2000) expected an increasingly 'liquid modernity', while Samuel Huntington (1993) predicted an even more threatening 'clash of civilisa-tions'. Spokespeople for cultural field interests often sketch rather pessimistic scenarios: Public authorities do not appreciate cultural interests enough! Support to culture is (always) declining! I will not contradict any of these predictions or scenarios here, just confront them with an alternative description of social change, especially in the cultural policy field. Based on an evaluation of a quite recent and comprehensive Norwegian cultural policy reform (2005–13), the Norwegian researcher Erik Henningsen writes that 'cultural policy in Norway evolves in a sedimentary fashion, through the gradual addition of new layers to the established arrangements, rather than through changes in the makeup of the sector' (Henningsen 2015, 28). According to Henningsen, the changes in this sector in Norway have been gradual and sedimentary rather than abrupt and dramatic during this specific period (2005–13). The French cultural policy researcher, Vincent Dubois, has promoted similar perspectives in an analysis of 'Cultural Policy Regimes in Western Europe' (2013, 1):

> The evolutions of cultural policies result from the interaction between these two levels, the political and the cultural one. They mostly consist in adding new layers of institutions, orientations and discourses rather than in radical changes, in a way that contemporary cultural policies can be viewed as the sedimentation of previous ones.

These diagnoses may also be valid for the development of public cultural policy in other countries.

The establishment of modern post-war public cultural policy was closely linked to the creation of a specific administrative apparatus, that is to the creation of ministries of culture and/or arts councils at the national level and of cultural administrations at the regional and local levels. It is well known, however, that such political and administrative structures may be unstable and variable in several policy fields.[2] If a policy field that previously had its own separate ministry (e.g. development aid or cultural diplomacy) is integrated into a broader departmental structure (e.g. into a ministry of foreign affairs), it does not necessarily imply that it gets lower priority. There may be several pragmatic and political reasons for restructuring the Governmental policy landscape. In some countries, such restructurings are more frequent than in other countries. Thus, the absence or the disappearance of a ministry of culture does not necessarily imply the 'end of cultural policy'. Nevertheless, it would probably signal lower priority.

In the following, I will discuss seven different challenges that modern public cultural policy may have to confront today. The legitimacy of modern public cultural policy may be at stake. Do these challenges undermine the foundations of cultural policy? I present these challenges primarily as scenarios, i.e. as potential future developments under certain circumstances, not necessarily as probable predictions. In the end, I will also present seven potential counterarguments to the challenges/scenarios, in order to stimulate further reflection and discussion.

## Democratisation of culture

Democratising culture has been the most important objective of, and rationale for, a modern cultural policy in many countries since WWII. The French Minister of Culture from 1959 to 1969—André Malraux—tried (with limited success) to convey high culture to the general French public by establishing a network of spectacular cultural houses ('maisons de la culture') throughout France during the 1960s (Looseley 1995; Urfalino 1996). In the 1940s, 50s and 60s, Nordic cultural authorities created itinerary public cultural institutions (in the fields of theatre, visual art and music) that aimed to distribute high culture to the whole country, that is both to the centre and the periphery (Mangset 1992, Vestheim 1995). The principal idea was that culture is a social good that should be available to everyone in a democratic society, including to working-class people and to people living far from urban centres. Traditionally, cultural policy tried to democratise culture within a very hierarchical cultural field: One would make the best works of art and the most valuable culture (i.e. high culture) accessible to everybody. Since then, however, substantial research in various countries has shown that the democratisation goals are difficult, if not impossible, to reach. In the late 1990s, a prominent French researcher in the field of cultural participation —Olivier Donnat—concluded that there had been no substantial reduction in the gap between social groups between 1973 and 1997, as far as traditional cultural activities (e.g. visits to theatres, art museums or symphony orchestras) were concerned (Donnat 1999, 111). Another French veteran in the social sciences, Jean-Claude Passeron, also concluded that no substantial democratisation of culture had taken place during this period (Passeron 2003, 380).

Many international studies of cultural participation and 'class cultures' in recent decades have been inspired by the French sociologist Pierre Bourdieu's seminal study 'The Distinction' (1984 [1979]). He analysed the profound sociocultural distinctions in France, based on data from the 1960s and 70s. Bourdieu focused, in particular, on the access of different social classes to economic, cultural and/or social capital. A follow-up-study of cultural participation in the UK, conducted around 2006, largely confirmed Bourdieu's major findings about different class cultures (in the UK after 2000) (Bennett et al. 2009). But they also found that *class* distinguished somewhat less, *gender, ethnicity* and *age* somewhat more, than Bourdieu had found in France back in the 1960s and 70s. Several recent Nordic studies have also shown that sociocultural distinctions (based on class, educational level, age and domicile/centrality) of cultural participation persist rather steadily (Rosenlund 2000; Danielsen 2006; Jarness 2013). It may seem, however, that high culture has a lower standing in Norway than in some other European countries, and that those who prefer high culture to mass culture often tend to hide, euphemise and even deny their elite cultural preferences (Jonvik 2015; Skarpenes 2007). According to another international research tradition, many middle- and upper-class people today tend to be 'omnivorous' in their cultural consumption preferences (Peterson 1992; Danielsen 2006; Jarness 2013). Their cultural consumption patterns are quite broad, i.e. they tend to consume both high and mass culture, while lower-class people are more 'univorous', i.e. they unilaterally prefer to consume only specific aspects of low culture (for instance only country music or only brass bands). Nevertheless, most empirical research in this field seems to confirm that there are still persistent distinctions in cultural participation due to differences in educational level, social class, etc., both in Norway and in many other countries.

In the 1970s and 80s, several countries (e.g. the Nordic countries and Germany) tried to overcome the democratisation problem by relativising the cultural hierarchies. They introduced a 'new cultural policy' that aimed to wipe out the quality distinctions between high and low culture. They tried to give amateur culture, folk culture and/or socioculture higher standing, broadly similar to traditional high culture (Girard 1973; Mangset 1992; Vestheim 1995; Höpel 2011). This 'new cultural policy' did not really contribute to removing sociocultural distinctions, however; it merely broadened the scope of cultural expressions recognised and supported by cultural policy. The 'new cultural policy' is now more or less an obsolete remnant of the 1970s and 80s. Few, if any, countries promote this kind of sociocultural policy in national policy documents any more, at least not rhetorically.

Altogether, it must be fair to say that the success of the cultural democratisation policy has been limited. The relative failure of cultural democratisation has contributed to a legitimation crisis for public culture policy in some countries, especially in France (Dubois 2003, 2010; Martin 2011). Why should public authorities continue to conduct an active public cultural policy if democratisation of culture is futile?

## Obsolete vestiges of a handicraft economy?

In their influential book about the cultural economy—published in 1966—the American economists Baumol and Bowen asked the somewhat provocative rhetoric question: 'Might it not argue the contrary – that live performance [i.e. theatre performances, symphony orchestras, opera and ballet performances] is an obsolete vestige of a handicraft economy which deserves no public assistance precisely because effective demand for it is inadequate?' (Baumol and Bowen 1966, 377). It may seem here as if Baumol and Bowen were primarily trying to provoke and tease the reader. Since its publication in 1966, their study has served as a strong argument *for* public subsidies to the performing arts rather than the contrary. It is worth wondering, however, if several technological innovations during the last 100–150 years have not made traditional live performances superfluous.

The Norwegian researcher Yngvar Kjus, for instance, asks: 'Why would people spend time and money on concerts when they could get better-quality music at home, cheaply and readily?' Based on his own studies, he responds that live concerts still give 'unique access to psychological and social experiences with music' that record listening does not give (Kjus 2018, 151). Nevertheless, it is worth wondering why a substantial part of public subsidies to culture—and a substantial part of public cultural policy concerns in general—favours cultural institutions that took shape during the nineteenth century or earlier, institutions that still often present their performances in a more or less traditional way. Opera, for instance, is a very expensive performing art form with a rather limited audience in social terms.[3] Despite several attempts of renewal of this art form, many opera performances are still rather traditional.

During the twentieth and early twenty-first centuries, fundamental changes have taken place in the cultural field in general: Several media revolutions and a recent digital revolution have taken place from the early twentieth century to the present day. Consequently, people's cultural consumption patterns have changed significantly. Many scholars also claim that profound 'festivalisation' and 'eventualisation' processes are affecting contemporary cultural activity patterns in many countries (e.g. Tjora et al. 2013; Quinn 2010; Ronström 2014; Bennett, Taylor, and Woodward 2014). Thus, Henningsen, Håkonsen, and Løyland (2015) recently declared that Norwegian cultural life was currently undergoing a structural change from 'institutions to events'.

The rather obsolete performing arts institutions are still substantially subsidised by public authorities in most countries. Are we now approaching the end of the age when traditional performing arts institutions are at the centre of public cultural policy?

## Support to artists

Public support to professional artists—or at least to artistic creation—has been a major public cultural policy concern, especially in the Nordic countries (Heikkinen 2000, 2003; Mangset et al. 2008). The Norwegian Ministry of Culture, for instance, explicitly aims to 'strengthen artists' potential for increased incomes', in its' latest annual budget.[4] During the 1960s and 70s, public authorities in the Nordic countries introduced largely welfare-oriented support schemes to create a decent work and income situation for professional artists. In other countries, such as France and the UK, the authorities supported artistic *creation* rather than supporting artistic *professions* directly (Mangset 2006). Indeed, such support to creation also benefits artistic professions and individual artists economically. After several decades of public support of this kind, however, most professional artists in most countries still have to endure a rather modest work and income situation (Menger 2006; Heian, Løyland, and Mangset 2008; Heian, Løyland, and Kleppe 2015; Mangset et al. 2018). Throsby and Zednik (2011, 9) sum up the general findings of the relevant research thus:

> Over the last 20 years a number of studies in various countries have elaborated the nature of artistic labour markets in both theoretical and empirical terms (Alper & Wassall, 2006; Benhamou 2000; Filer 1989; Karhunen 1998; Throsby 1992; Wassall and Alper 1992). A persistent finding of this research has been that financial rewards for professional artistic practice are typically lower than in other occupations requiring similar levels of human capital (as indicated by education, training and experience); the resulting need to supplement their creative income with income from other sources means that the labour market profiles of many artists are characterized by multiple job-holding.[5]

Artistic work is still quite insecure. Many artists have to supplement their primary artistic work with odd jobs to make a decent living. Most professional artists earn much less from artistic work than other professionals with a similar educational level do from *their* work. These professions are also characterised by skewed income distribution: A few professional artists earn very high incomes, while the great majority have to endure quite low incomes. Some artistic categories are fairly well off economically (e.g. permanently employed performing artists), while some other categories experience precarity (e.g. some visual artists[6] and freelance dancers).

Several public support schemes have contributed to improving the work and income situation of many artists since the 1970s. Nevertheless, the real income of professional artists has not followed the spectacular rise in real income of other professions in recent decades, at least not in Norway (Heian, Løyland, and Mangset 2008; Heian, Løyland, and Kleppe 2015; Mangset et al. 2018). Artists tend to lag behind general income growth. From 2006 to 2013, the real income of Norwegian artists even declined, despite a substantial rise in real income among other professions.

The above-mentioned modest work and income structures within the professional artist field have persisted rather enduringly, despite substantial cultural policy efforts during the post-war period (Menger 2006; Throsby and Zednik 2011; NOU 2013:4 ; Mangset et al. 2018). Why should public authorities continue to conduct ambitious public artist policies if they do not contribute to improving artists' living conditions?

## National cultural policies in the age of globalisation

Modern public cultural policies originally developed primarily within the contexts of nation states, e.g. the Arts Council of Great Britain (1946), the first French Ministry of Culture (1959) and the new support schemes to individual artists in Norway in the late 1970s. Cultural production and distribution, however, became increasingly globalised over the following decades. Today, powerful media produce cultural content (film, TV series) for international—if not global—markets. The contemporary popular music industry is also predominantly global. The digital revolution since the 1990s has significantly reinforced these globalising tendencies. Performing artists also often pursue international careers, for example international musicians and dancers hired by orchestras and dance companies in foreign countries. Many visual artists exhibit their art at international exhibitions and biennials, for example Documenta, Venice and São Paulo. A small number climb successfully in an international prestige hierarchy (Moulin 1992).

Therefore, there seems to be a need for not only national cultural policies but also some kind of international regulations. International regulations and policies of this nature have developed quite slowly, probably most significantly in the fields of copyright and heritage. There is certainly still a mismatch, however, between an increasingly *globalised* cultural life and primarily *national* cultural policies. It is true that some international institutions (such as the Council of Europe, the EU and UNESCO) have been making substantial efforts for several decades to develop international cultural policies of this kind. In addition, many countries have developed their own foreign cultural policies.

It is still worth asking whether the predominantly national cultural policies are not—in our contemporary increasingly globalised cultural world—obsolete.

## Instrumental legitimisations of cultural policy

During the initial years of modern cultural policy, public authorities often legitimised support to culture with reference to the inherent values of art and culture. One should primarily appreciate 'high culture', one should value art 'for its own sake', or one considered high culture to have a 'civilising mission' (Arnold 2006 [1869]). Over the last 30–40 years, however, cultural politicians and interest groups have, increasingly, tried to justify support to culture by citing its positive effects *outside* the cultural field (e.g. Myerscough 1988; Arnestad 1989; Bamford 2008; Cuypers et al. 2012): Could art and culture contribute to economic growth, better health, regional development, sustainability or better educational achievements? Such arguments were very popular during the 1980s and 90s, but also met with severe criticism from researchers, not least from economists (e.g. Peacock 1991; Bille Hansen 1995; Puffelen 1996). Richard Florida's influential book 'The Rise of the Creative Class' (2002) gave a new boost to such instrumental ideas: Clusters of creative workers/ artists in cities could contribute to substantial economic growth and development, he said. His optimistic ideas inspired cultural politicians in many countries for a couple of decades after the publication of his book. In a recent book (2017) however, Florida tends to revise his previous theories about the 'rise of the creative class'.

Today, cultural politicians and consultancy firms speak about 'the spillovers' from the cultural and creative sectors rather than about 'economic impacts' or the 'creative class' (Fleming 2015). The basic ideas are fairly similar, however. The 'Tom Fleming Creative Consultancy' was recently

> commissioned by an international consortium consisting of Arts Council England (ACE), Arts Council of Ireland, european centre for creative economy (ecce), European Cultural Foundation, European Creative Business Network and Creative England (...) to investigate in detail the evidence base of the spillover effects of public investment (public money awarded directly or indirectly by government) in arts, culture and in the creative industries (Fleming 2015, 12).

All these above-mentioned arguments for cultural investments (economic impacts, spillover, etc.) situate the potentially positive effects of cultural activities and efforts *outside* the cultural field, e.g. within the 'departments' of industry, health, education and/or regional development. Why, then, do we need a specific public cultural policy? Could not industrial, educational or other public authorities be responsible for cultural affairs instead?

Such instrumental ideas have probably contributed to a certain restructuring of regional and local cultural policy in several countries in recent decades. Since the 1990s, cultural affairs in Norwegian regional administrations have, increasingly, been connected to either a) welfare or b) regional development (Vestby 2012; Mangset and Hylland 2017). Sweden implemented a new 'model' for regional cultural organisation in 2011, giving regional authorities increased responsibility for cultural planning. According to a recent evaluation of the reform, all Swedish regional cultural plans now focus on the instrumental aspects of regional culture, e.g. on the contributions that regional culture might make to economic development, social sustainability, etc. (Blomgren and Johannisson 2015). Gray (2017) reports similar developments in the arts policies of local governments in the UK, referring to 'an increasing exogenous instrumentalisation of the sector' (op. cit.:316). He also writes:

> The attachment of local authority arts activities can be seen particularly clearly in the case of local economic development and regeneration strategies in recent years. These have often been based on the idea that cultural and arts activities are an effective means by which local economies can be improved and local areas can be enhanced (Gray 2017, 318).

Many researchers have questioned the scientific credibility and reliability of such 'instrumental legitimations' (e.g. Peacock 1991; Bille Hansen 1995; Hjorth-Andersen 2013). Some researchers also criticise the 'depoliticising' effects and nature of the 'creative industry discourse' (Lee 2014). Even the 'Tom Fleming Creative Consultancy' draws quite cautious and sober conclusions about the spillover effects of the cultural and creative industries: 'This preliminary methodological review demonstrates that, despite being increasingly used in policy lexicon, little of the research and evaluation across Europe reviewed has been able to demonstrate causality' (Fleming 2015, 50).

Nevertheless, such legitimations certainly dominate contemporary cultural policy rhetoric in most Western countries. From the point of view of cultural politicians, it might therefore seem tempting to displace cultural policy decisions from specific cultural policy departments to other departments (e.g. industry, health, education). The integration of cultural affairs into wider regional and local units (e.g. regional development, education, health) in Norway points in that direction (Mangset and Hylland 2017). Such a scenario might imply the end of public cultural policy as a specific sectorial policy.

## Public cultural sector: a bureaucratic iron cage

On the contrary, one might also argue that the establishment of a specific cultural sector has 'imprisoned' culture in an unfortunate bureaucratic 'iron cage',[7] that is that a non-sectorial cultural policy would have been more beneficial and fruitful (Solhjell 2005; Engberg 2005). Some of the traditional critics of the new post-war sectorial cultural policy promoted such points of view: They pointed out that cultural policy in a wide sense had previously had a larger scope and impact than the new, narrow cultural sector; cultural policy was—from this perspective—a broader concern of civilisation. Education policy, urban development and construction policy (i.e. architecture) were also important cultural policy topics in this broader sense. Solhjell (2005), for instance, maintains that when cultural policy was established as a specific sectorial policy after WWII, it also became constricted to a much narrower sectorial policy than before. From this perspective, this sectorial constriction has been unfortunate and harmful to cultural policy in general. Perhaps one ought to restore a non-sectorial cultural policy?[8]

## Public cultural policy in an age of stagnating public finances

There has been much talk in cultural policy debates lately about fairly significant cutbacks in public support to culture in European countries. It is well known, both from cultural economics and political science, that 'culture' is a somewhat marginal public sector: Public authorities grant just a minor part of their operating budgets to culture (usually less than 1% at national level). During periods of recession, it also seems easier to make cuts to cultural budgets than to many other 'more vital' public budgets. Culture often appears as a residual category in public finances, where 'expenses often are indirectly determined' depending on the needs of other public (municipal) sectors (Hansen and Kjellberg 1980, 130). Neo-liberal ideology is also influencing cultural policy more than before in some European countries. This implies an increasing focus on private financing of culture—and potential cutbacks in public support. Would cultural production be able to survive on market income without any public subsidies?

The UK seems to have experienced such cutbacks in public cultural budgets in recent years. In 2011, the European expert website *Compendium of cultural policy and trends in Europe* predicted a substantial decline in public cultural budgets in the UK:

> It is relevant to note that in 2004 when central government expenditure on the arts in particular was still being increased, there was already evidence that spending by local authorities as a whole was beginning to decline. The situation since then has worsened and, although good data is not readily available, the most recent indicators are that significant reductions are underway or planned in the face of a 27% cutback in the central government allocation of funds to local government. At the end of 2010 there were estimates that more than 250 public libraries in England were threatened with closure, while a number of others were facing reductions in opening hours (public library provision is a statutory responsibility, so it would be difficult for local councils to axe their library services completely). However, several local authorities have announced the complete axing of their arts provision (a non-statutory service).[9]

*Compendium* reports similar cuts in other countries, for instance in the Netherlands, Spain, the Czech Republic and Ireland.[10]

It seems difficult, however, to find reliable comparative data on budget cuts in all or most European countries. But we have no reason to doubt that many countries have experienced cuts to or stagnating public cultural budgets, especially just after the financial crisis in 2009–2011. Norway is certainly a prosperous exception; we know that the Norwegian government's cultural budgets increased substantially between 2005 and 2013 (NOU 2013, 4). Several other Western countries have experienced more precarious public finances. A study of 13 European Union member states conducted by Čopič and colleagues connected the cutbacks primarily to the financial crisis of 2007–2008. The crisis may have contributed to cutbacks in cultural budgets in the following years, but the researchers did not find any long-term downward trend:

> The movements in cultural budgets during the financial crisis have possibly occurred as cyclical movements and not as part of a longer-term structural trend. The analysis shows clear downward deviations from the trend value for general, central and local budgets for culture. The analysis also shows that downward movements in cultural budgets on general, central and local levels were present during the crisis whereas a similar change has not been observed in the previous years as part of longer-term trends. This means that countries lowered the budgets for culture in the years 2009–2011 most likely as a consequence of the financial crisis and not of longer-term trends (Čopič et al. 2013, 6).

It is worth noting, however, that the public finances of Western welfare states appear more insecure than before. The post-war years of more or less automatic growth in public welfare may be over. An aging population, increased immigration and ecological challenges may all threaten our financial sustainability. Cultural policy, then, may appear a rather secondary concern. Why should public authorities continue to bother about it?

## *Some counterarguments*

Until now in this article, I have primarily emphasised 'negative' arguments, that is arguments that may indicate that the end of modern public cultural policy is approaching. One might of course also present several counterarguments to these apocalyptic 'predictions'. Let me finally evoke some such counterarguments:

(1) Democratisation of culture.

Despite the relative failure of the cultural democratisation policy, systematic public efforts in this field have certainly benefited many people in absolute terms. It is probably true that the democratisation policy has not substantially reduced the gap in cultural activity patterns between different social categories. Nevertheless, cultural democratisation programmes have encouraged many people, previously unfamiliar with such cultural expressions, to visit cultural institutions. It is also worth noting that the democratisation of culture policy may have helped to equalise *formal* opportunities: More people in principle have the opportunity to visit cultural institutions, whether they do so or not.

Perhaps democratisation of culture is not so futile after all?

(2) Performing arts institutions—obsolete vestiges of a handicraft economy?

Performing arts institutions (theatres, opera and symphony orchestras) may seem old-fashioned and obsolete in our digital age. There are no clear indications, however, that visits to such institutions or performances are decreasing. Instead, recent statistics from Statistics Norway demonstrate stability, or even a minor increase, in the proportion of the Norwegian population visiting such institutions (theatre/musical/cabaret, opera/operetta, ballet/dance, concerts) during a year (Vaage 2017). There is no general downward tendency in other countries either—at least not among EU countries—in terms of visits to performing arts institutions: According to Eurostat (EU 2016, 125), the proportion of the population visiting 'live performances' seems to have decreased somewhat from 2007 to 2011 in some European countries (e.g. Belgium, Estonia, Cyprus and Lithuania). However, the proportion has increased in other countries (e.g. Czech Republic, Germany, Italy and Slovakia), and overall appears to have remained stable in most European countries. Olivier Donnat (2009, 179) draws a similar picture of the development of attendance at 'live performances' in France from 1997 to 2008: Attendance at some live performances, for example theatre, appeared to have increased somewhat, while attendance at other live performances, for example classical music concerts, had decreased slightly.

But what about the alleged transformation of people's cultural activities from 'institutions to events' (Henningsen, Håkonsen, and Løyland 2015)? Is there a tendency for people in general to abandon traditional performing arts institutions and instead turn to festivals and cultural events? It does not appear to be the case, at least not in Norway, where visits to such institutions still greatly exceed visits to festivals (Mangset, Håkonsen, and Stavrum 2017).

Perhaps there are still good reasons to continue subsidising performing arts institutions?

(3) Support to artists.

Artist policy has certainly not eliminated poverty among artists. Nevertheless, the work and income situation of professional artists—at least in the Nordic countries—has certainly improved since the 1970s and 80s due to public support schemes. While it is true that the real income of Norwegian artists *decreased* somewhat between 2006 and 2013, their real income has probably *increased* for most of the post-war period, although most likely less than in many other professions: We know, for instance, that the real artistic income of Norwegian artists increased by 18% from 1993 to 2006, while the real income of the workforce as a whole increased by 40% (Mangset et al. 2018, 2). Unfortunately, we do not have solid diachronic empirical data on the development of artists' income situations in other European countries. However, it is not unlikely that they have experienced more or less parallel developments, that is that their real income has increased for several decades, but more modestly than in other professions.

Perhaps the income development and work insecurity of the artist population would have been even worse without an active public artist policy?

(4) National cultural policies in the age of globalisation.

One may also argue that *national* cultural policies are particularly desirable and necessary 'in the age of globalisation', namely because cultural globalisation challenges cultural diversity. Globalisation often implies cultural levelling. Powerful international corporations in the field of popular culture may challenge and threaten high-quality art. That is why cultural policy authorities in some countries—France in particular—have fought for the 'cultural exception' ('l'exception culturelle'), that is the principle that cultural products should be treated differently from other commercial products in international trade. There is certainly a need for some kind of international and/or supranational cultural policy to support and regulate cultural production and distribution in the age of globalisation, e.g. under the auspices of UNESCO, the EU and/or the Council of Europe.

Perhaps there is also a need for relatively strong national cultural policies as bulwarks against excessive globalisation of culture?

(5) Instrumental legitimations of cultural policy.

Instrumental legitimations are nothing new in cultural policy. All cultural policy is instrumental, according to Vestheim (2008). Over the last two or three decades, however, the tendency to legitimise cultural policy by means of its beneficial external effects—for instance economic impacts, regional development and/or health benefits—has certainly increased in many countries. The available research does not necessarily support the idea that art and culture have all those beneficial effects. Neither does it necessarily imply that it is a good idea to displace cultural policy decisions to other departments (such as departments of trade, regional development and/or health). It is also quite uncertain whether cultural industries and cultural entrepreneurialism would benefit from responsibility for them being moved from a ministry of culture to a ministry of trade, industry and fisheries.

(6) Public cultural sector: A bureaucratic iron cage.

Developing a 'non-sectorial' cultural policy, that is making cultural policy an aspect of the policy of every department, may appear an innovative and inspired idea. It is likely, however, that public cultural policy would be seriously weakened by spreading jurisdiction across many departments.

(7) Public cultural policy in an age of stagnating public finances.

Stagnating or declining public finances are not, in themselves, a good argument for cuts in public subsidies to culture, for at least two reasons: (1) While culture is a very small public sector, at least at the national level, cuts in public subsidies would do little to improve the general public budget situation. (2) Stagnating or declining public cultural budgets seem to be temporary rather than permanent in Western countries.

## Conclusion

The purpose of this article is not, strictly speaking, to *predict* the end of cultural policy, rather to present Pro and Con arguments to the general question: Are we approaching the end of cultural policy? I want to emphasise that it is not obvious that public authorities will maintain a public cultural policy—as a specific policy sector—in the future. I have presented seven arguments or challenges that indicate that the maintenance of this policy sector is not altogether self-evident. I have also presented several counterarguments to demonstrate that my apocalyptic 'predictions' are debatable. My principal message in the article is, therefore, that 1) it is not obvious that a sectorial cultural policy will persist in the future, 2) public cultural policy is facing legitimation crises in some countries, and 3) there is a need for further discussions on the rationales for public cultural policy.

This article focuses on the achievement of cultural policy objectives and on the legitimacy of public cultural policy. There are good reasons to doubt that public cultural policy regimes, in general, are able to fulfil their main objectives. This does not necessarily imply the end of cultural policy, however. Public cultural policy structures (e.g. ministries of culture, arts councils and local cultural administrations) may, of course, subsist without fulfilling their main objectives. Governments may also continue to conduct an active cultural policy after having abolished the specific cultural policy structures and/or integrated cultural policy into broader political and administrative structures. It is, of course, also possible that *some* countries will abolish their specific public cultural policy structures, while *others* will not.

Altogether, I maintain that a cultural policy regime that consistently fails to achieve its main objectives may, sooner or later, be exposed to a legitimation crisis.

## Notes

1. I have partly based this article on a preliminary discussion in the final chapter of our book (in Norwegian) 'Kulturpolitikk. Organisering, legitimering og praksis' (Mangset and Hylland 2017). The author of the present article was also the first author of that specific chapter.
2. Many previous Norwegian ministries have been abolished, and several new ministries have been established during the last 150 years, see: https://www.regjeringen.no/no/om-regjeringa/tidligere/departementer_embeter/regjeringssekr_dep/nedlagte-departementer-og-sekretariater-/id426142/, May 2018.—Norway had a Ministry for Church and Education—responsible even for cultural policy—before 1982. In 1982, Norway established its first Ministry of Culture, responsible even for science. Since then this Ministry's responsibilities has changed slightly several times. The French 'Sports ministry' may be another example of instability/changing responsibilities. The responsibilities of this ministry has changed slightly several times since WWII.
3. Just 8% of the Norwegian population attended opera/operetta in 2016, primarily people with a long-cycle tertiary education (Vaage 2017, 26).
4. Norwegian Governments culture budget 2018: «Regjeringen ønsker å legge til rette for vekst og utvikling i kulturlivet, og å styrke kunstneres muligheter for økte inntekter» (p. 13). (The Government aims to facilitate growth and development in cultural life, and to strengthen artists' potential for increased income", https://www.regjeringen.no/contentassets/9f6729dc46e2463091dca2d00227fa39/no/pdfs/prp201720180001kuddddpdfs.pdf, May 2018.
5. I have omitted a footnote in the original article.
6. The annual artistic income of a Norwegian visual artist was around 9000 Euros on average in 2013. Many visual artists of course earned much less, because of the skewed income structure (Heian, Løyland, and Kleppe 2015).

7. The metaphor 'bureaucratic iron cage' refers of course to Max Weber's famous writings about the bureaucratic order that may trap individuals into a system world (i.e. Weber 1967 [1930], 1971; DiMaggio and Powell 1991).
8. I do not know whether Solhjell would agree with all this.
9. http://www.culturalpolicies.net/web/unitedkingdom.php?aid=61, Jan. 2018.
10. https://www.culturalpolicies.net/web/index.php, May 2018.

## Disclosure statement

No potential conflict of interest was reported by the author.

## References


Alper, N. O., and G. H. Wassall. 2000. "More than once in a Blue Moon: Multiple Jobholdings by American Artists." (Research Rep. No. 40). Washington, DC: National Endowment for the Arts.

Arnestad, G. 1989. "Kultur for regional utvikling. Kultursatsing i eit utkantfylke mot slutten av 1980-åra." Report no. 8/89. Sogndal: Vestlandsforsking.

Arnold, M. 2006 [1869]. *Culture and Anarchy*. Oxford: Oxford University Press.

Bamford, A. 2008. *Wow-faktoren. Globalt forskningskompendium, om kunstfagenes betydning i utdanning*. Oslo: Musikk i skolen.

Bauman, Z. 2000. *Liquid Modernity*. Cambridge: Polity Press.

Baumol, W. J., and W. G. Bowen. 1966. *Performing Arts – The Economic Dilemma. A Study of Problems Common to Theater, Opera, Music and Dance*. Cambridge, Massachusetts/ London, England: M.I.T. Press.

Beck, U. 1992. *Risk Society: Towards a New Modernity*. New Delhi: Sage.

Benhamou, F. 2000. "The Opposition between Two Models of Labour Market Adjustment: The Case of Audiovisual and Performing Arts Activities in France and Great Britain over a Ten Year Period." *Journal of Cultural Economics* 24 (4): 301–319. doi:10.1023/A:1007660228755.

Bennett, A., J. Taylor, and I. Woodward. 2014. *The Festivalization of Culture*. Griffith, Australia: Ashgate.

Bennett, T., M. Savage, E. Silva, A. Warde, M. Gayo-Cal, and D. Wright. 2009. *Culture, Class, Distinction*. London/New York: Routledge.

Bille Hansen, T. 1995. "Measuring the Value of Culture." *The European Journal of Cultural Policy* 1 (2): 309–322. In. doi:10.1080/10286639509357988.

Blomgren, R., and J. Johannisson. 2015. "Kulturpolitik, styrning och legitimitet i svenska regional kulturplaner." In *Gränsløs. Tidskrift för studier av Öresundsregionens historia, kultur och samhällsliv*, 9–18. Sweden: Lunds Universitet/ University of Lund.

Bourdieu, P. 1979 [1984]. *La Distinction. Critique sociale du jugement*. Paris: Les Éditions du Minuit (English translation published in 1984 by Routledge & Kegan Paul).

Čopič, V., P. Inkei, A. Kangas, and A. Srakar 2013. "Trends in Public Funding for Culture in the EU." EENC Report, August 2013, http://www.interarts.net/descargas/interarts2573.pdf

Cuypers, K., S. Krokstad, T. L. Holmen, M. S. Knudtsen, L. O. Bygren, and J. Holmen. 2012. "Patterns of Receptive and Creative Cultural Activities and Their Association with Perceived Health, Anxiety, Depression and Satisfaction with Life among Adults: The HUNT Study, Norway." *Journal Epidemiology Community Health*, 66 (8): 698–703.

Danielsen, A. 2006. *Behaget i kulturen. En studie av kunst- og kulturpublikum*. Oslo: Norsk kulturråd.

DiMaggio, P. J., and W. W. Powell. 1991. "The Iron Cage Revisited: Institutional Isomorphism and Collective Rationality in Organizational Fields." In *The New Institutionalism in Organizational Analysis*, edited by W. W. Powell and P. J. DiMaggio. Chicago: University of Chicago Press.

Donnat, O. 1999. "La stratification sociale des pratiques culturelles et son évolution 1973–1997." *Revue française de sociologie* X-L 1: 111–119. doi:10.2307/3322521.

Donnat, O. 2009. "Les pratiques culturelles des français à l'ère numérique." In *Énquete 2008*, edited by Département des Études et de la Prospective - Ministère de la Culture (de France). Paris: La Découverte/Ministère de la Culture et de la Communication.

Dubois, V. 2003. "La statistique culturelle au ministère de la Culture, de la croyance à la mauvaise conscience." In *Le(S) public(S) de la culture*, edited by O. Donnat and P. Tolila. Paris: Presses de Sciences Po. Volume II (CD-rom).

Dubois, V. 2010. "Le « modèle français » et sa « crise »: ambitions, ambiguïtés et défis d'une politique culturelle." In *Tendences et défis des politiques culturelles. Cas nationaux en perspective*, edited by D. Saint-Pierre and C. Aude. Québec: Presses de l'Université Laval.

Dubois, V. 2013. "Cultural Policy Regimes in Western Europe." In *International Encyclopedia of the Social & Behavioral Sciences*, ed. J. D. Wright, 2 ed. (2015), London: Elsevier.

Engberg, J. 2005. *Magten og kulturen. Dansk kulturpolitikk 1750–1900 I-III*. Copenhagen: Gads Forlag.

EU(European Union). 2016. *Culture Statistics*. 2016 ed. Eurostat.

Filer, R. K. 1989. "The Economic Condition of Artists in America." In *Cultural Economics 88: An American Perspective*, eds. D. V. Shaw, W. S. Hendon, and V. L. Owen, 63–76. Akron, OH: Association for Cultural Economics.
Fleming, T. 2015. *Cultural and Creative Spillovers in Europe: Report on a Preliminary Evidence Review*. Tom Fleming Creative Consultancy. Cambridge: Arts Council England.
Florida, R. 2002. *The Rise of the Creative Class: And How It's Transforming Work, Leisure, Community and Everyday Life*. New York: Basic Books.
Florida, R. 2017. *The New Urban Crisis. How Our Cities are Increasing Inequality, Deepening Segregation, and Failing the Middle Class — And What We Can Do about It*. New York: Basic Civitas Books.
Girard, A. 1973. *Kulturpolitik. Teori og praksis*. Copenhagen: Danish National Commission for UNES.
Gray, C. 2017. "Local Government and the Arts Revisited." *Local Government Studies* 43 (3): 315–322. doi:10.1080/03003930.2016.1269758.
Hansen, T., and F. Kjellberg. 1980. "Kommunale utgifter i Norge: Autonomi og sentral kontroll i lokalforvaltningen." In *Den kommunale virksomhet. Planlegging, finansiering og budsjettering*, edited by F. Kjellberg. Oslo: Universitetsforlaget.
Heian, M. T., K. Løyland, and B. Kleppe. 2015. *Kunstnerundersøkelsen 2013. Kunstnernes Inntekter*. Bø: Telemarksforsking.
Heian, M. T., K. Løyland, and P. Mangset. 2008. *Kunstnernes aktivitet, arbeids- og inntektsforhold, 2006*. Bø: Telemarksforsking.
Heikkinen, M. 2000. "Artist Policy in Finland and Norway: A Comparison of Two Schemes of Direct Support for Artists." *The International Journal of Cultural Policy* 7 (2): 299–318. doi:10.1080/10286630009358148.
Heikkinen, M. 2003. *The Nordic Modell for Supporting Artists. Public Support for Artists in Denmark, Finland, Norway and Sweden*. Research Reports of the Arts Council of Finland No. 26.
Henningsen, E. 2015. "Kulturpolitikkens Sedimentering - Kulturløftet Som Kulturpolitisk Vekstperiode." *Nordisk kulturpolitisk Tidsskrift* 01/2015: 28–40.
Henningsen, E., L. Håkonsen, and K. Løyland. 2015. "From Institutions to Events – Structural Change in Norwegian Local Cultural Policy." *The International Journal of Cultural Policy* 23/3: 352–371.
Hjorth-Andersen, C. 2013. *Hvad koster kulturen?* Copenhagen: Jurist- og Økonomforbundets forlag.
Höpel, T. 2011. "La politique culturelle en Allemagne au XXe siècle." In *Pour une histoire des politiques culturelles dans le monde – 1945–2011*, ed. P. Poirrier, 17–48. Paris: La Documentation Française.
Huntington, S. 1993. "The Clash of Civilizations?" *Foreign Affairs* 72 (3): 22–49. doi:10.2307/20045621.
- Jarness, V. 2013. "Class, Status, Closure. The Petropolis and Cultural Life." PhD dissertation in sociology, Bergen: UiB.
- Jonvik, M. 2015. "Forskjellar mellom folk." PhD diss., Stavanger: UiS, Faculty of Social Sciences.
Karhunen, P. 1998. "Labour Market Situation of Graduated Artists." In *Economics of Artists and Arts Policy*, eds. M. Heikkinen and T. Koskinen, 147–163. Helsinki: Arts Council of Finland.
Kjus, Y. 2018. *Live and Recorded: Music Experience in the Digital Millennium*. Palgrave. ISBN 978-3-319-70368-8.
Lee, H.-K. 2016. "Politics of the 'Creative Industries' Discourse and Its Variants." *The International Journal of Cultural Policy* 22 (3): 438–455. doi:10.1080/10286632.2014.991783.
Looseley, D. L. 1995. *The Politics of Fun. Cultural Policy and Debate in Contemporary France*. Oxford: Berg Publishers.
Mangset, P. 1992. *Kulturliv og forvaltning. Innføring i kulturpolitikk*. Oslo: Universitetsforlaget.
Mangset, P. 2003. "Norsk kulturråd. Armlengdesprinsipp under Press." In *Kunstråd. Kulturpolitisk forskning og debat 3*, edited by C. Rørdam Larsen. Århus: Kulturpolitisk forskningscenter.
Mangset, P. 2006. *Kulturpolitikk i Vest-Europa. Utviklingen av statlig kulturpolitikk i et utvalg vesteuropeiske land i etterkrigstida* [Cultural policy in Western Europe. National cultural policies in selected Western European Countries]. Unfinished manuscript
Mangset, P. 2009. "The Arm's Length Principle and the Art Funding System. A Comparative Approach." In *(2009): What about Cultural Policy? Interdisciplinary Perspectives on Culture and Politics*, edited by M. Pyykkönnen, N. Simanainen, and S. Sokka. Helsinki: Minerva Kustannus.
Mangset, P. 2012. "La politique culturelle en Norvège." In *(2011): Pour une histoire des politiques culturelles dans le monde – 1945–2011*, edited by P. Poirrier. Paris: La Documentation Française.
Mangset, P. 2013. *En armlengdes avstand eller statens forlengede arm? Armlengdesprinsippet i norsk og internasjonal kulturpolitikk*. Bø: Telemarksforsking.
Mangset, P., A. Kangas, D. Skot-Hansen, and G. Vestheim. 2008. "Editors Introduction: Nordic Cultural Policy." *The International Journal of Cultural Policy* 14(1). February 2008, Special issue: Nordic Cultural Policy. doi:10.1080/10286630701856435.
Mangset, P., L. Håkonsen, and H. Stavrum. 2017. "Festivalboom eller kulturpolitisk ønskedrøm? Om festivalisering og kommunal kulturøkonomi." In *Nordisk Kulturpolitisk Tidsskrift, Högskolan i Borås, Sweden, 20/1-2*, 71–78.
Mangset, P., M. T. Heian, B. Kleppe, and K. Løyland. 2018. "Why are Artists Getting Poorer? about the Reproduction of Low Income among Artists." *The International Journal of Cultural Policy*, 24 (4): 539-558.
Mangset, P., and O. M. Hylland. 2017. *Kulturpolitikk. Organisering, legitimering og praksis*. Bø/Oslo: Universitetsforlaget.
Martin, L. 2011. "La politique culturelle de la France depuis 1945." In *Pour une histoire des politiques culturelles dans le monde – 1945–2011*, ed. P. Poirrier, 241–264. Paris: La Documentation Française.

Menger, P.-M. 2006. "Artistic Labor Markets: Contingent Work, Excess Supply and Occupational Risk Management." In *Handbook of the Economics of Art and Culture*, eds. V. A. Ginsburgh and D. Throsby. Vol. 1. Amsterdam: Elsevier.
Moulin, R. 1992. *L'artiste, l'institution et le marché*. Paris: Flammarion.
Myerscough, J. 1988. *The Economic Importance of the Arts in Britain*. London: Policy Studies Institute.
NOU 2013:4. 2013. *Kulturutredningen 2014*. Oslo: Norwegian Government Security and Service Organisation (G.S.S.O).
Passeron, J. C. 2003. "Consommation et réception de la culture: La démocratisation des publics." In *Le(S) public(S) de la culture*, eds. O. Donnat and P. Tolila. Vol. 1((book).). Paris: Presses de Sciences Po.
Peacock, A. 1991. *Economics, Cultural Values and Cultural Policies*. Journal of Cultural Economics. 15(2): 9-20
Peterson, R. A. 1992. "Understanding Audience Segmentation: From Elite and Mass to Omnivore and Univore." *Poetics* 21 (1992): 243–258. doi:10.1016/0304-422X(92)90008-Q.
Puffelen, F. V. 1996. "Abuses of Conventional Impact Studies in the Arts." *The European Journal of Cultural Policy* 2 (2): 241–254
Quinn, B. 2010. "Arts Festivals, Urban Tourism and Cultural Policy." *Journal of Policy Research in Tourism, Leisure & Events* 2 (3): 264–279. doi:10.1080/19407963.2010.512207.
Ronström, O. 2014. "Festivals et festivalisations." *Cahiers d'ethnomusicologie* 27/2014: 1–19.
- Rosenlund, L. 2000. "Social Structures and Change. Applying Pierre Bourdieu's Approach and Analytic Framework". PhD dissertation, UiB/working papers, UiS.
Skarpenes, O. 2007. "Den "legitime kulturens" moralske forankring." *Tidsskrift for samfunnsforsking* 48 (4): 531–563.
Solhjell, D. 2005. "Når fikk Norge en kulturpolitikk? Et debattinnlegg mot den konvensjonelle visdom." *Nordisk kulturpolitisk tidsskrift*, Högskolan i Borås, Sweden (2/2005).
Throsby, D. 1992. "Artists as Workers." In *Cultural Economics*, eds. R. Towse and A. Khakee, 201–208. Heidelberg: Springer-Verlag.
Throsby, D., and A. Zednick. 2011. "Multiple Job-Holding and Artistic Careers: Some Empirical Evidence." *Cultural Trends* 20 (1): March 2011, 9–24. doi:10.1080/09548963.2011.540809.
Tjora, A, et al. 2013. *Festival! Mellom rølp, kultur og næring*. Oslo: Cappelen.
Urfalino, P. 1996. "L'invention de la politique culturelle." In *Comité d'histoire du ministère de la Culture*. Paris: La Documentation Française. Ministère de la Culture.
Vaage, O. F. 2017. *Norsk kulturbarometer 2016*. Oslo: Statistics Norway.
Vestby, G. M. 2012. *Fylkeskommunens rolle i kulturpolitikken*. Oslo: NIBR, paper 2012: 112.
Vestheim, G. 1995. *Kulturpolitikk i det moderne noreg*. Oslo: Det Norske Samlaget.
Vestheim, G. 2008. "All Kulturpolitikk er Instrumentell." In *KulturSverige 2009. Problemanalys och statistik*, eds. S. Beckman and S. Månsson, 56–63. Linköping: Swedish Cultural Policy Research Observatory.
Wassall, G. H., and N. O. Alper. 1992. "Towards a Unified Theory of the Determinants of the Earnings of Artists." In *Cultural Economics*, eds. R. Towse and A. Khakee, 187–200. Heidelberg: Springer-Verlag.
Weber, M. 1967 [1930]. *The Protestant Ethic and the Spirit of Capitalism*. London: Unwin University Books.
Weber, M. 1971. *Makt og byråkrati. (Selection of Texts)*. Oslo: Gyldendal.
Zimmer, A., and S. Toepler. 1996. "Cultural Policies and the Welfare State: The Cases of Sweden, Germany, and the United States." *The Journal of Arts Management, Law and Society* 26/3: 167–194. doi:10.1080/10632921.1996.9942961.

# Index

*Note*: Figures and tables are shown in *italics* and **bold** type respectively, and footnotes by "n" and the note number after the page number e.g., 33n11 refers to note number 11 on page 33.

For Product Safety Concerns and Information please contact our EU representative GPSR@taylorandfrancis.com Taylor & Francis Verlag GmbH, Kaufingerstraße 24, 80331 München, Germany

**Batch number: 10753375**

Printed by Printforce, the Netherlands